KV-605-615

re

WITHDRAWN

SOUTH DEVON TECH COLLEGE

ACC 44043 CLASS 371.5

DISRUPTIVE BEHAVIOUR:
A SOURCEBOOK FOR TEACHERS

Louis Cohen is Professor of Education and Head of the Department of Education at Loughborough University of Technology. He taught in primary and secondary schools in Britain and the USA and in Colleges of Education before taking up appointments at Bradford University and at Loughborough University of Technology. His publications include: *Educational Research Methods in Classrooms and Schools, Experiments in the Social Sciences* (with G. Brown and D. Cherrington), *Statistics for Education and Physical Education* (with M. Holliday), *Statistics for Social Scientists* (with M. Holliday), *Perspectives on Classrooms and Schools* (with L. Manion), *A Guide to Teaching Practice* (with L. Manion), *Multicultural Classrooms* (with L. Manion), *Linking Home and School* (with M. Craft and J. Raynor), *Educational Research and Development in Britain, 1970–1980* (with J.B. Thomas and L. Manion) and *Multicultural Education: a Sourcebook for Teachers* (with A. Cohen).

Alan Cohen is Lecturer in Education at Durham University. He, too, taught in primary and secondary schools in Britain and the USA and in Colleges of Education before taking up his appointment in the School of Education at Durham. His publications include: *Readings in the History of Educational Thought* (with N. Garner), *A Student's Guide to Teaching Practice* (with N. Garner), *Primary Education: a Sourcebook for Teachers* (with L. Cohen) and *Special Educational Needs in the Ordinary School: a Sourcebook for Teachers* (with L. Cohen).

DISRUPTIVE BEHAVIOUR: A SOURCEBOOK FOR TEACHERS

Edited by
LOUIS COHEN
Loughborough University of Technology
and
ALAN COHEN
University of Durham

Harper & Row, Publishers
London

Cambridge San Francisco
Mexico City São Paulo
New York Singapore
Philadelphia Sydney

Copyright © 1987. Editorial and selection material © Louis Cohen and
Alan Cohen. Individual chapters © as credited.

All rights reserved

First published 1987

Harper and Row Ltd
28 Tavistock Street
London WC2E 7PN

No part of this book may be reproduced in any manner whatsoever
without written permission except in the case of brief quotations
embodied in critical articles or reviews.

British Library Cataloguing in Publication Data
Disruptive behaviour: a sourcebook for
    teachers.
    1. Problem children —— Education ——
    Great Britain
    I. Cohen, Louis   II. Cohen, Alan
    371.8'1'0941   LC4803.G7

ISBN 0–06–318365–X

Printed and bound by Butler & Tanner Ltd, Frome and London

CONTENTS

Section 3
COPING WITH DISRUPTIVE BEHAVIOUR

INTRODUCTION

Increasing concern had been expressed during the past decade or so about the extent and frequency of disruptive behaviour in secondary schools and its growing incidence among younger pupils in junior and infant classrooms. Newspapers (CCCS, 1981), television (Belson, 1978) and, not least, teachers' unions (Comber and Whitefield, 1979; AMMA, 1985), appear to confirm a widely held view that disruptive behaviour in school is a serious and growing problem.

Some commentators (Lawrence, Steed and Young, 1984) go so far as to suggest that the interest taken by teachers' unions may well have been influential in focusing the attention of the press and media on problems of contemporary schooling. Violence against teachers, they observe, became newsworthy and television documentaries on secondary schools, none of them complimentary about comprehensive education, attracted wide audiences. Thus it was that 'concern over . . . drugs, football hooliganism, violence, student disaffection and mugging all became linked with what was happening in schools'.

Whatever the force of such an explanation, disruptive behaviour in school continues to evoke widespread disquiet and to attract frequent publicity. All the more strange therefore that hard evidence about the nature and the extent of disruption is very difficult to come by. Instant 'cures', of course, are readily at hand. As Brookman (1984) observes:

> Unlike the deaf, the blind, the physically and mentally handicapped, disruptive pupils are generally perceived as the authors of their own misfortune. In short, 'there's nothing wrong with them that a clip across the ear wouldn't cure'.

The purpose of this sourcebook is threefold:
1. to explore the concept of disruptive behaviour
2. to review attempts to identify its nature and understand its origins
3. to suggest to hard-pressed teachers ways of coping with disruption.

QUESTION OF DEFINITION

Disruption is not *behaviour* but *behaviour in context* (Frude and Gault, 1984). The same physical act may constitute a disruption in one context and not in another. But surely, it may be objected, most teachers have a fairly clear idea of what counts as disruption and are able to identify individuals who are disruptive. The trouble is that teachers have *different* ideas about what constitutes disruptive behaviour and identify *different* pupils! (Galloway *et al.*, 1982). How then does one recognize a disruptive act and how does one obtain reliable information on the frequency of disruptive acts if schools collect different kinds of data dependent on the particular definitions of disruption that they adopt?

It was just such an issue that the Scottish Education Department (1977) faced in its survey of truancy and indiscipline in schools.

> 'The problems of trying to determine what should constitute a record-able offence', it concluded, ' . . . were too problematical to make the exercise worthwhile.'

Essentially, there are two related issues. First, most children behave differently depending on their teacher and the school in which they are currently enrolled, and many misbehave only with certain teachers. Secondly, teachers vary considerably in the degree to which they are able and willing to tolerate different forms of pupil behaviour. 'Deviance', Galloway *et al.* (1982) remind us, 'like beauty, lies in the eye of the beholder'.

Coulby and Harper (1985) carry the argument a step further and assert boldly that there is no such thing as a disruptive pupil. Disruption, they contend, is a word better applied to *forms of behaviour* or *situations* than to pupils. If a situation is perceived as disruptive then it is a temporary state of affairs and one that involves two or more participants; if a particular form of behaviour is perceived as disruptive then this is something that can be changed or redirected into other more appropriate behaviour. If we perceive a pupil to be disruptive, Coulby and Harper argue, this is somehow to do with his/her personality or nature and we are more likely to regard this as permanent or, at least, difficult to change. Once a category of 'disruptive' exists, then it is easy for particular pupils to be stigmatized.

UNDERSTANDING DISRUPTIVE BEHAVIOUR

Personal and family pathology

There is a body of research that seeks to account for disorderly and disruptive behaviour in terms of the pathology of particular individuals and/or the pernicious effects of their familial circumstances. The literature contains studies where associations between aggressive, disruptive conduct, on the one hand, and intellectual and temperamental characteristics, on the other, are explored. Relations between individual pathologies and personal attributes are either considered separately or in conjunction with such factors as the emotional and financial impoverishment of homes, the conditions of early child rearing and the climate of parent–child interactions.

The individual

Evidence suggests that certain pupils are extremely disruptive in class and that, temperamentally, they are impulsive, unpredictable and unmalleable (Rutter, 1975). Moreover, highly aggressive and unruly behaviour in childhood often continues during adolescence and early manhood as evidenced by police convictions for criminal offences (Farrington, 1978; Olweus, 1980a,b; West, 1982). Research also suggests that disruptive behaviour may be associated with neurological impairment (Graham and Rutter, 1968; Galloway *et al.*, 1982). The issues of disruptive behaviour and educational subnormality in respect of children of West Indian origin have caused considerable controversy. Such children have been, and most likely continue to be, over-represented in schools for the educationally subnormal (Tomlinson, 1982). Two main conclusions have been drawn (Taylor, 1981) from research into behaviour disorders and deviance among children of West Indian origin (Bagley, 1972, 1975; Rutter *et al.*, 1974, 1975). First, West Indian children show many more antisocial disorders than do non-immigrant children who tend to manifest more neurotic emotional behaviours. This, according to Taylor (1981), suggests that the disorders may be more in the nature of immediate responses or reactions to certain specific situations. Second, and educationally more significant, is the relatively high rate of behavioural disturbance West Indian children reportedly exhibit in school situations.

Despite the fact that explanations of disruption couched in terms of individual pathology are currently out of favour, it is well to bear in mind that for some children persistent disruptive behaviour across a range of classroom and school situations is associated with identifiable personality characteristics (Fontana, 1985).

The family

A recent comprehensive review (Rutter, 1985) charts the associations between children's behavioural disorders and family circumstances. Disruptive pupils bring to the classroom the deleterious effects of their home backgrounds. These are frequently cold harsh environments, scarred by marital disharmony, inconsistent and unpredictable child-rearing practices, overcrowding and financial problems.

Although there is now a fair measure of consensus about the nature of family pathologies associated with disruptive behaviour in school, there is a danger in categorizing all pupils who present behaviour problems as the product of abnormal home conditions. As Tattum (1982) observes, the distinction between *conduct-disorder* children and other children is not clear-cut. The differences are situational, relative and a matter of degree. Rutter (1985), too, cautions that, although family influence effects are sizeable, they vary markedly across individuals and contexts. Moreover, they are transactional rather than undirectional in nature.

Disruption: interactionist approach

Studies of pupils and teachers in school settings are now firmly established in the British literature, although only recently has attention focused on the evolutionary nature of teacher–pupil interactions as they relate to disruptive behaviour (Ball, 1984; Pollard, 1984; Beynon, 1985). Underpinning interactionist studies is the view that disruptive behaviour is not simply an action engaged in by an individual; rather it is a process of interaction between active participants (Tattum, 1982). The principal participants in such interactions are pupils and teachers.

Pupils

Research on pupils' expectations and perceptions of school and schooling has a venerable history. The literature reveals a variety of research techniques ranging from paper and pencil questionnaires about the 'good' teacher (Hollis, 1935) to ethogenic methods seeking out the 'rules' underlying pupils' misbehaviour (Rosser and Harré, 1976). Woods' (1979) ethnographic study of one secondary school reaffirms the findings of previous investigations: that pupils expect teachers to be firm but not too strict, to make them work, to avoid picking on individuals or having pets and, above all, to apply rules equitably and consistently. Tattum's (1982) study of the motives of disruptive pupils shows them justifying their misbehaviour within a framework of school regulations and procedures and laying blame squarely on teachers who pick on them, treat them with disrespect and apply school rules inconsistently.

The view that the social structure of classroom peer groups may help account for disruptive behaviour informs several studies. Whereas Willis (1977) and Pollard (1980) find support for this assertion, Furlong (1976) draws attention to transient patterns of pupil interaction and contends that individuals construct their own actions rather than respond to the dictates of clique norms. Meyenn's (1980) study of girls' peer groups points to the distinctive pro- and anti-school orientations of different groups and their varying identification with the teenage culture beyond the bounds of the school.

Teachers

Research on pupils' perceptions of teachers is matched by equally numerous studies of teachers' perceptions of their pupils. But, whereas early investigations simply identify 'good' pupil characteristics (Hallworth, 1962) or extraneous influences on teachers' perceptions (MacIntyre, Morrison and Sutherland, 1966), later research attempts to elucidate the processes involved in impression formation and type casting as they relate to teachers' ideologies and classroom practices (Sharp and Green, 1975; King, 1979).

Educational researchers such as Hargreaves, Hester and Mellor (1975) have used the theoretical insights of labelling theory (Becker, 1963; Matza, 1964; Lemert, 1972) to unravel the complex processes that translate teacher-labelled pupils into deviants. Naylor's (1986) small-scale study suggests a number of ways in which teachers invoke self-fulfilling prophecies in their treatments of pupils on the basis of gender, ethnicity and ambitiousness. Older pupils show that they are very adept at picking up messages concerning their teachers' negative expectations of them. An important observation by Rogers (1982) on self-fulfilling prophecies is that, more often than not, teachers' perceptions of their pupils develop as ways of coping with the situations in which they are required to work. Teachers do not set out deliberately to bring about negative effects in their pupils. Those effects are best understood as the unintended consequences of teachers' attempts to deal with the realities of their working lives.

Disruptive schools

Increasingly, research evidence points to the effect that the organization of a school has on the conduct of its pupils. Its philosophy, its climate, its system of rewards and punishments, its counselling and pastoral care arrangements, the attitudes and actions of its staff toward children's academic, social and emotional needs bear directly on pupil behaviour.

The provocative title of a recent book (Lawrence, Steed and Young, 1984; *Disruptive Children – Disruptive Schools?*) attests to the explanatory power of school variables in accounting for pupil disaffection and disruption.

Early studies of pupil misbehaviour in school (Hargreaves, 1967; Lacey, 1970) sought to explain its source in a polarization of school culture arising out of the organizational structure of the school itself. Later research (Willis, 1977; Corrigan, 1979) draws on a wider framework of socio-economic forces in accounting for the origins of disaffected pupil groups. Woods' (1984) particular interest is in the complex ways that differences in social-class origin produce different educational experiences in school. His study of subject choice in a secondary school identifies the institutional channelling that shapes the destinies of different groups of children. Subject choice is a myth, Woods concludes. Despite meritocratic overtones, most pupils 'know' their place by the third year in school; they have internalized teacher definitions of success and failure and their application to themselves with the usual labels ('thick', 'dibby', 'lazy', 'pest'). Schostak's (1983) colourful account of Slumptown Secondary School strikes a similar note. Schools are primarily agents of social control where pupils are rendered impotent to control their destinies or develop independence and individuality. Schools actually create deviance. Power's and colleagues (1967, 1972) study of London secondary schools provided the impetus for several subsequent projects to do with the effects of schooling on children's behaviour. Power *et al.* argued that substantial variations in boys' delinquency rates (0.7 – 17 per cent) reflected variations in the effects of the schools they attended. Rutter (1973), too, showed wide disparities in behavioural-deviance rates in London primary schools. Rutter and colleagues' (1979) later study of twelve London comprehensive schools set itself two tasks: to discover whether or not the sample schools had differential effects on their pupils and, if so, to account for those differences. Despite strong criticisms about the methodology (Goldstein, 1980; Hargreaves, 1980), Rutter's (1985) identification of within-school influences on school outcome has received wide publicity. Reynolds and Sullivan (1981) provide a timely reminder of work that remains to be done on school effects on pupil behaviour. First, more research is needed on the effects of different kinds of schools, for example 'progressive' secondary schools, to determine whether the important 'school factors' so far unearthed apply also in other educational settings. Secondly, we need to find out whether schools have different effects on different groups of pupils, ethnic minorities for example. Thirdly, we need to discover the relative strength of school and home factors in determining educational outcomes. And most important of all, Reynolds and Sullivan conclude, we need to investigate the precise mechanics by which schools mediate their effects and, crucially, the key factors that generate the differences.

Analysis of critical incidents

In contrast to studies that explore schools as institutions to tease out associations between their organizational arrangements and the incidence of disruptive behaviour, there is a body of research that focuses on classroom interaction and on the actual events that occur during the course of disruptive episodes. By tracing the aetiology of disruptive sequences, it is hoped that teachers may be helped to acquire more effective management strategies in dealing with unwanted classroom behaviour (Parry-Jones and Gay, 1980; Clarke *et al.*, 1981). Several studies draw on the concept of the 'stream of behaviour' (Dickson, 1963) and, more recently, on Forgas' (1979) analysis of social episodes by means of structuralist-sequencing techniques. The literature reveals several ways in which researchers have compiled information about incidents of classroom disruption. Teachers' accounts are used by Comber and Whitefield (1979), children's reports form the basis of the analysis of Marsh, Rosser and Harré (1978), whereas Galloway *et al.* (1982) and Lawrence, Steed and Young (1984) both make use of pupil and teacher interviews in obtaining their data. In this last study, Lawrence and her associates employed detailed questionnaires to ascertain the exact nature of the incident, its seriousness in behavioural terms, the age, sex and form of the pupil(s) involved, the characteristics of the staff member reporting the disruptive act and the role of the senior school staff. From a close examination of thirteen incidents, the researchers distil a number of commonalities and offer some advice to teachers and administrators. The value of detailed analyses of critical incidents lies in the generalizations that can be made about those sorts of pupil–teacher interactions in those sorts of classroom situations that tend to be associated with a high risk of disruption (Kounin, Friesen and Norton, 1966; Hargreaves, Hester and Mellor, 1975; Rabinowitz, 1981).

Social, Political and Economic Considerations

Our earlier reference to Woods' (1984) explanation of school subject choice as a means of shaping pupils' life chances and to Schostak's (1983) description of schools as agents of social control leads us to a brief consideration of the role of the school in the wider socio/politico/economic context.

It is argued (Bash, Coulby and Jones, 1985) that schooling is a process by which the vast majority of children are trained for and accept (however unwillingly) their future position in the lower rankings of the urban and national social order. For many teachers, the crisis in contemporary education is the issue of social order and the disruptive behaviour of urban, working-class, secondary-school pupils is a constant threat to those whose manifest responsibility is to maintain social order. Social control is exercised in a subtle and pervasive way in schools. It is not enshrined merely in the rules and regulations that govern pupil behaviour; rather, it is built into the very structure of the educational process. The curriculum and the way it is organized is an important instrument of control. Even where schools profess a 'progressive' ideology, the subtle operation of social control can be observed in which pupils' identities are redefined and restructured according to a social hierarchy (Sharp and Green, 1975).

In summary, dominant groups within the economy, it is argued, have affected and continue to affect the organization and curricula of schools in sustaining and reproducing the social relations of work. That many young people perceive education as something that is imposed, and not as something in which they participate willingly, is demonstrated by their resistance to institutional control and their allegiance to expressive and delinquent subcultures (Willis, 1977; Corrigan, 1979; White and Brockington, 1983).

Coping with disruptive behaviour

The problem of coping with classroom disruption has provoked much written comment ranging from facile tips-for-harassed teachers to serious applications of psychological insights to the task of eliminating or modifying unwanted behaviour.

We employ Fontana's (1985) typology in discussing three broad orientations to the problem of classroom disruption. The *behavioural* approach concentrates on what people actually do and on the context and the consequences of their actions rather than what goes on inside their heads. For teachers, behaviourism can yield a range of useful readily applied strategies for obtaining class control. The *cognitive* approach, on the other hand, focuses attention on the child's inner world of thoughts, motives, memories and emotions. As such, it has at least as much to contribute to strategies of classroom control as the behavioural. Fontana's third strategy is *management techniques*. Essentially, these involve ways of structuring the day-to-day organization of the classroom so as to provide a satisfactory learning environment where problems of class control are kept to a minimum.

Wheldall and Merrett (1984) provide a good example of the behavioural approach in a book designed to help teachers improve their classroom performance. Denscombe's (1985) text is based more broadly in its orientation; so too, the contribution of Coulby and Harper (1985). Classroom management strategies are of central concern in books by Corrie, Haystead and Zaklukiewicz (1982) and Laslett and Smith (1984). A useful all-round guide for teachers is provided by Saunders (1979).

RATIONALE OF THE SOURCEBOOK

The 'shape' of this brief review of the literature on disruptive behaviour presages the selection of readings and extracts that constitute the sourcebook as a whole. It consists of three sections which deal, respectively, with *defining*, *understanding*, and *coping with* disruptive behaviour.

In Section 1, two readings are allotted to an examination of the problems of defining disruptive behaviour and the difficulties that arise when the criteria that are employed differ from authority to authority and from study to study.

Section 2 is composed of eight readings, two of which are intended to illustrate the viewpoint that individual and family pathologies can account for the incidence and the persistence of acts of disruption among certain pupils. The emphasis in Section 2 is on interaction. The selection of readings shows that the term interaction is used in the broadest sense to include not only the ongoing relations of pupils and teachers in the day-to-day work of the classroom and the variety of factors that constitute the organizational climate of the school, but also the functions that school policies and procedures serve in the wider society.

In Section 3 we are concerned with several strategies that have been suggested as ways of coping with disruption. The selection of readings is intended to reflect three current perspectives: the *behavioural*, with its concern to identify and eliminate unwanted behaviours; the *cognitive*, with its attempts to understand the personal motivational forces that present themselves as disruptive behaviour; the *managerial*, with its pragmatic prescriptions for procedures in classrooms and schools.

REFERENCES

Assistant Masters and Mistresses Association (1985) *The Reception Class Today*. Report of a survey carried out by AMMAs Primary and Preparatory Education Committee, AMMA, London.

Bagley, C. (1972) Deviant behaviour in English and West Indian children, *Research in Education*, Vol. 8, pp. 47–55.

Bagley, C. (1975) The background of deviance in black children in London, in G.K. Verma and C. Bagley (eds.) *Race and Education Across Cultures*, Heinemann, London.

Ball, S.J. (1984) *Comprehensive Schooling: a Reader*, Falmer Press, London.

Bash, L., Coulby, D. and Jones, C. (1985) *Urban Schooling: Theory and Practice*, Holt, Rinehart & Winston, Eastbourne.

Becker, H. (1963) *Outsiders: Studies in the Sociology of Deviance*, Free Press, New York.

Belson, W.A. (1978) *Television Violence and the Adolescent Boy*, Saxon House, Farnborough.

Beynon, J. (1985) *Initial Encounters in the Secondary School: Sussing, Typing and Coping*, Falmer Press, London.

Brookman, F. (1984) Disruptive children, *Modus*, Vol. 2, No. 7, pp. 232–3.

Centre for Contemporary Cultural Studies (1981) *Unpopular Education: Schooling and Social Democracy in England since 1944*, Hutchinson, London.

Clarke, D.D., Parry-Jones, W. L., Gay, B.M. and Smith, C.M.B. (1981) Disruptive incidents in secondary school classrooms: a sequence analysis approach, *Oxford Review of Education*, Vol. 7, No. 2, pp. 111–17.

Comber, L.C. and Whitefield, R.C. (1979) *Action on Indiscipline: a Practical Guide for Teachers*, NAS/UWT, in association with the Department of Educational Inquiry, University of Aston.

Corrie, M., Haystead, J. and Zaklukiewicz, S. (1982) *Classroom Management Strategies*, Hodder and Stoughton, London, for the Scottish Council for Research in Education.

Corrigan, P. (1979) *Schooling the Smash Street Kids*, MacMillan, London.

Coulby, D. and Harper, T. (1985) *Preventing Classroom Disruption: Policy, Practice and Evaluation in Urban Schools*, Croom Helm, London.

Denscombe, M. (1985) *Classroom Control: a Sociological Perspective*, Allen & Unwin, London.

Dickman, H.R. (1963) The perception of behavioural units, in R.C. Barker (ed.) *The Stream of Behaviour*, Appleton, New York.

Farrington, D. (1978) The family backgrounds of aggressive youths, in L.A. Hersov and M. Berger (eds.) *Aggression and Anti-social Behaviour in Childhood and Adolescence*, Pergamon, Oxford.

Fontana, D. (1985) *Classroom Control*, British Psychological Society and Methuen, London.

Forgas, J.P. (1979) *Social Episodes: the Study of Interaction Routines*, Academic Press, London.

Frude, N. and Gault, H. (1984) *Disruptive Behaviour in Schools*, Wiley, Chichester.

Furlong, V. (1976) Interaction sets in the classroom: towards a study of pupil knowledge, in M. Stubbs and S. Delamont (eds.) *Explorations in Classroom Observation*, Wiley, Chichester.

Galloway, D., Ball, T., Blomfield, D. and Seyd, R. (1982) *Schools and Disruptive Pupils*, Longman, London.

Goldstein, H. (1980) Fifteen thousand hours: a review of the statistical procedures, *Journal of Child Psychology and Psychiatry*, Vol. 21, pp. 364–6.

Graham, P. and Rutter, M. (1968) Organic brain dysfunction and child psychiatric disorder, *British Medical Journal*, Vol. iii, pp. 695–700.

Hallworth, H.J. (1962) A teacher's perceptions of his pupils, *Educational Review*, Vol. 14, pp. 124–33.

Hargreaves, D.H. (1967) *Social Relations in a Secondary School*, Routledge & Kegan Paul, London.

Hargreaves, D.H. (1980) Review of *Fifteen Thousand Hours*, *British Journal of Sociology of Education*, pp. 211–16.

Hargreaves, D.H., Hester, S.K. and Mellor, F.J. (1975) *Deviance in Classrooms*, Routledge & Kegan Paul, London.

Hollis, A.W. (1935) The personal relationship in teaching. Unpublished M.A. thesis, University of Birmingham.

Kounin, J.S., Friesen, W.V. and Norton, E. (1966) Managing emotionally disturbed children in regular classrooms, *Journal of Educational Psychology*, Vol. 57, pp. 1–13.

Lacey, C. (1970) *Hightown Grammar: the School as a Social System*, Manchester University Press.

Laslett, R. and Smith, C. (1984) *Effective Classroom Management*, Croom Helm, London.

Lawrence, J., Steed, D. and Young, P. (1984) *Disruptive Children – Disruptive Schools?*, Croom Helm, London.

Lemert, E.M. (1972) *Human Deviance: Social Problems and Social Control*, Prentice Hall, Englewood Cliffs, New Jersey.

MacIntyre, D., Morrison, A. and Sutherland, J. (1966) Social and educational variables relating to teachers' assessments of primary school pupils, *British Journal of Educational Psychology*, Vol. 36, pp. 272–9.

Marsh, P., Rosser, E. and Harré, R. (1978) *The Rules of Disorder*, Routledge & Kegan Paul, London.

Matza, D. (1964) *Delinquency and Drift*, Wiley, New York.

Meyenn, R.J. (1980) School girls' peer groups, in P. Woods (ed.) *Pupil Strategies: Explorations in the Sociology of the School*, Croom Helm, London.

Naylor, P. (1986) Some pupils' constructs of their teachers' fairness towards them. Unpublished M.A. dissertation, Loughborough University of Technology.

Olweus, D. (1980a) Familial and temperamental determinants of aggressive behaviour in adolescent boys: a causal analysis, *Developmental Psychology*, Vol. 16, No. 6, pp. 644–60.

Olweus, D. (1980b)The consistency issue in personality psychology revisited — with special reference to aggression, *British Journal of Social and Clinical Psychology*, Vol. 19, pp. 377–90.

Parry-Jones, W. L. and Gay, B.M. (1980) The anatomy of disruption: a preliminary consideration of interaction sequences within disruptive incidents, *Oxford Review of Education*, Vol. 6, No. 3, pp. 213–20.

Pollard, A. (1980) Teacher interests and changing situations of survival threat in primary school classrooms, in P. Woods (ed.) *Pupil Strategies: Explorations in the Sociology of the School*, Croom Helm, London.

Pollard, A. (1984) *The Social World of the Primary School*, Rinehart & Winston, Eastbourne.

Power, M.J. *et al.* (1967) Delinquent schools?, *New Society*, 19 October.

Power, M.J. *et al.* (1972) Neighbourhood, school and juveniles before the Courts, *British Journal of Criminology*, Vol. 12, pp. 111–32.

Rabinowitz, A. (1981) The range of solutions: a critical analysis, in B. Gillham (ed.) *Problem Behaviour in the Secondary School*, Croom Helm, London.

Reynolds, D. and Sullivan, M. (1981) The effects of school: a radical faith revisited, in B. Gillham (ed.) *Problem Behaviour in the Secondary School*, Croom Helm, London.

Rogers, C. (1982) *A Social Psychology of Schooling*, Routledge & Kegan Paul, London.

Rosser, E. and Harré, R. (1976) The meaning of trouble, in M. Hammersley and P. Woods (eds.) *The Process of Schooling: a Sociological Reader*, Routledge & Kegan Paul, London.

Rutter, M. (1973) Why are London children so disturbed?, *Proceedings of the Royal Society of Medicine*, Vol. 66, pp. 1221–25.

Rutter, M. (1975) *Helping Troubled Children*, Penguin, Harmondsworth.

Rutter, M. (1980) *Changing Youth in a Changing World*, Nuffield Provincial Hospitals Trust, London.

Rutter, M. (1981) *Maternal Deprivation Reassessed*, Penguin, Harmondsworth.

Rutter, M. (1985) Family and school influences on behavioural development, *Journal of Child Psychology and Psychiatry*, Vol. 26, No. 3, pp. 349–68.

Rutter, M., Yule, W., Berger, M., Yule, B., Morton, J. and Bagley, C. (1974) Children of West Indian immigrants — 1: rates of behavioural deviance and of psychiatric disorder, *Journal of Child Psychology and Psychiatry*, Vol. 15, No. 4, pp. 241–62.

Rutter, M., Maughan, B., Mortimore, P. and Oustin, J. (1979) *Fifteen Thousand Hours: Secondary Schools and their Effects on Children*, Open Books, London.

Rutter, M., Yule, B., Morton, J. and Bagley, C. (1975) Children of West Indian Immigrants — 3: home circumstances and family patterns, *Journal of Child Psychology and Psychiatry*, Vol. 16, No. 2, pp. 105–24.

Saunders, M. (1979) *Class control and Behavioural Problems*, McGraw-Hill, London.

Scottish Education Department (1977) *Truancy and Indiscipline in Schools in Scotland (the Pack Report)*, HMSO, London.

Schostak, J.F. (1983) *Maladjusted Schooling: Deviance, Social Control and Individuality in Secondary Schooling*, Falmer Press, Lewes.

Sharp, R. and Green, A. (1975) *Education and Social Control*, Routledge & Kegan Paul, London.

Tattum, D.P. (1982) *Disruptive Pupils in Schools and Units*, Wiley, Chichester.

Taylor, M.J. (1981) *Caught Between: a Review of Research of Pupils of West Indian Origin*, NFER-Nelson, Windsor.

Tomlinson, S. (1982) *A Sociology of Special Education*, Routledge & Kegan Paul, London.

Upton, G. and Gobell, A. (1980) *Behaviour Problems in the Comprehensive School*, Faculty of Education, University College Cardiff.

West, D.J. (1982) *Delinquency*, Heinemann, London.

Wheldall, K. and Merrett, F. (1984) *Positive Teaching: the Behavioural Approach*, Allen & Unwin, London.

White, R. and Brockington, D. (1983) *Tales Out of School: Consumers' Views of British Education*, Routledge & Kegan Paul, London.

Willis, P. (1977) *Learning to Labour*, Saxon House, Farnborough.

Woods, P. (1979) *The Divided School*, Routledge & Kegan Paul, London.

Woods, P. (1984) The myth of subject choice, in M. Hammersley and P. Woods (eds.) *Life in School: the Sociology of Pupil Culture*, Open University Press, Milton Keynes.

DEFINING DISRUPTIVE BEHAVIOUR

INTRODUCTION

The problems of defining disruptive behaviour are the primary focus of the first two readings. They reveal a confusion in conceptualization and terminology. Maladjusted, deviant, delinquent, troublesome, difficult, naughty, are but a few of the descriptions that are commonly applied to disaffected pupils. More recently, the distinction drawn between *problem children* and *children with problems* offers the hope that attention is beginning to turn more toward the nature of the experiences that pupils react against rather than to particular pathologies in the pupils themselves. *Inter alia*, Reading 1 differentiates between delinquency and disruption. The former is identifiable and measurable in terms of legal infractions. The latter is difficult to define and measure, not least because teachers identify different behaviour and different children as disruptive. The author of Reading 2 explores the extended concept of 'special educational needs' as promulgated in the Warnock Report (1978) and encoded in the 1981 Education Act. He concludes that the classifications commonly employed by educational administrators and teachers bear no relation to the needs of the children concerned.

One of the suggestions for further study addresses the same distinction drawn between problem children and children with problems, the initial focus moving from *disturbed* or *disturbing* to wider issues to do with the exclusion of disruptive pupils. Another argues that the category ESN-M is a social construction that can only be understood within a broad politico/economic context. Other suggested readings are directed to a consideration of the recent and rapid growth in the provision of special units for disruptive children and to the arguments for and against retaining them within ordinary schools.

Reading 1
DEFINING AND UNDERSTANDING
DISRUPTION
J. Lawrence, D. Steed and P. Young

As far as the incidence of disruptive behaviour in the schools of this country is concerned, information so far gathered and published is very incomplete and often uncertain. That the problem is extensive is indicated by the opening statement of the paper for guidance published by a mainly rural Local Education Authority (LEA), Devon County Council, in 1975. 'Expressions of disquiet from several quarters indicate that the kind of misbehaviour within schools which receives publicity in other parts of the country is not unknown in some schools in Devon'. Unfortunately, from the point of view of the collation of statistics, the criteria used to define the problem of disruption vary from study to study. Thus the largely rural county reported on by McNamara (1975) focused on 'problem children', including 'difficult children', 'children with problems' and 'primary school children who might become problem children', under this heading. Not only do the criteria used vary from study to study, but the methods used to gather data are often such that they are very incomplete. Sometimes headteachers only are asked to supply information and though they may know of most 'spectacular' incidents, others may not be reported to them by assistant staff who are anxious to conceal difficulties or do not wish the pupil to be reported onwards for punishment. In the most extensive survey, reported on by Lowenstein (1975), it was made very clear that the data, particularly those from secondary schools, were very incomplete; in secondary schools large numbers of teachers are involved, and many will be too busy to supply data, and the press of events will make the accurate recall of incidents hazardous.

We have no published statistics at all for the number of difficult schools in the country, though the Department of Education and Science (DES) (1981) must know most of them, nor have we any knowledge of the number of difficult classes at any one time. There are, however, criteria that could be used to assess the difficulty of schools, such as the rates of truancy, suspension and exclusion from the school, and the various indices of social disadvantage. However, some twilight-area schools are not difficult, and statistics such as the number of suspensions or referrals

J. Lawrence, D. Steed and P. Young (1984) Defining and understanding disruption, in *Disruptive Children – Disruptive Schools*? Croom Helm, London.

for special educational treatment can be very misleading as some schools contain or conceal their problems. Inspection (thorough) and careful review of data are needed if we are to get at the truth about our difficult schools. Careful researches shed light on the dimensions and nature of the problem.

Analytical research into the factors which predispose to disruptive behaviour and trigger it off is clearly of the utmost importance. Side by side with this we need to develop simple techniques which will help schools to analyse their own particular situation and to modify it if they wish, using the tools and resources which are at their disposal. Over and above the help which these techniques can give, the very fact of the analysis, the very taking-up of a research stance, can be of benefit to a school and to its teachers. All too often disruptive behaviour is dealt with in an atmosphere of aggression, and acrimony, rather than one of rationality. Of course, anger can be useful, but all too often in incidents of disruption it becomes destructive, rather than constructive. To use an analytical approach, and to use planned techniques in coping with disruptive behaviour, may also reduce the feeling of impotence which teachers sometimes have, the feeling that they have 'tried everything', have come to the end of the road and that the end is failure or degradation, or the total rejection of the child in a form of exclusion. There will almost inevitably be failure at times, particularly in this area, where criminologists also fail. But the failure can be less frequent if we utilize our resources and realize, indeed, how extensive they are. It is this belief that underpins this book. The difficulties involved in the attempt to study disruption in schools are similar to those involved in the study of deviancy in society at large. Deviancy is complex in origins and usually defies solution. There are many perspectives from which it can be viewed.

The concepts used in the area of disruption in schools are themselves interesting. Sometimes the talk is about 'disruptive children', around whom there is already a body of literature. The distinction is made now between the 'disruptive child' and the 'maladjusted child', the latter often seen as being unwell rather than culpable and suffering from a psychiatrically diagnosable disorder. However, it is accepted that the line is blurred between the two 'types' of child, so that, for example, a disruptive child may be temporarily prone to maladjusted behaviours and many so-called 'disruptive' children would be categorized as maladjusted if they underwent the necessary procedures.

As a term, 'the disruptive child' has the advantage of being more specific than descriptions such as 'naughty', 'troublesome', less clinical than 'maladjusted' and less criminological than 'delinquent'. There is at least some suspicion that the term has originated in the recent concern about the increase in violence in schools coupled with the frequently expressed desire to reassert the authority of the teacher.

In more recent years a distinction has been drawn between 'problem children' and 'children with problems', both of whom are likely to be 'disruptive children'. This seems more promising in that it does not attempt to prejudge the nature of the problems which children experience and does not rule out the possibility that these problems may have more to do with the nature of the experience against which the child reacts than with any inherent defect in the child itself. School for many children is a problem. So is learning. So is relating to some teachers, meeting their requirements, getting to grips with their 'understanding' of the pupil/ teacher relation. There is some evidence to suggest that some children find 'relating to teachers' more problematic than others and need more help in adjusting to the demands made on them. There is also evidence to suggest that this facet of schooling is not all one-sided: teachers also have their problems; they find it easier to relate to some children than others. If one accepts that, to explain the difficulties people experience in interacting with others around them, one needs to take into account both sides of the interaction, then a social–psychological perspective may be useful.

'As well as 'the disruptive child', who presents a severe and persistent non-conformity, there is a general category labelled 'disruptive behaviour'. This may refer to the occasional or persistent behaviour of individuals, groups or whole classes and, very rarely, to the behaviour typical of large numbers of children in a 'difficult' school. The behaviour of the 'disruptive child' may be disruptive at certain moments, but children who are not 'disruptive children' may also exhibit 'disruptive behaviour' more or less frequently. These distinctions are obvious but important.

Recent research has served to remind us of the importance of school differences. Any school environment is a highly complex phenomenon. Innumerable factors may affect pupil behaviour: time of the day, weather conditions, children who are absent so that the nature of work groups is changed, the moods of individual teachers and pupils, the system of rules employed in the school, buildings, timetable, grouping procedures, quality of teaching skill, continuity of curriculum and so on. The list of pertinent factors is enormous. A great deal of research still needs to be done in this area. Within LEAs and schools there is now a greater willingness to admit to having problems but this is still a sensitive area because questions of teacher competence are involved.

If disruptive behaviour prevents teachers or schools from functioning normally we have to look constantly at what is considered normal. For example, it may well be considered desirable that children should move about the school in an orderly way: it becomes potentially disruptive when some children push and shove. This is as true of schools as of institutions or factories or underground railway systems where idiosyncracies of behaviour are seen as potentially dangerous and disruptive of smooth order and therefore a fit subject for external control. As J.S. Mill remarked in a different context, freedom to 'do one's own thing' stops short of shouting 'Fire!' in a crowded theatre. This is not to argue that children should not be expected to move quietly and in an orderly way. If movement in relation to others, whether in a small or large group, is expressive of attitudes, then we need to create conditions in which desirable attitudes can be learned.

Prosaic organizational matters then assume considerable importance and simple behavioural injunctions become more than matters of preferred etiquette. Holding open a door for others is not just a middle-class example of manners, it is both an organizational and attitudinal imperative.

Unlike delinquency there is no easy way to study and measure disruption. Disruption implies a context and an activity – one always disrupts something and the use of the term implies a frustration of the intentions of one partner in the interaction. Thus, unlike delinquency that is measurable in terms of infractions of the legal requirements, there is no 'it' which one can identify easily and label in disruption. Its value as a term lies precisely in that it gives access to understanding the underlying and implicit norms and values which are inherent in situations. To ask about disruption is to explore different notions of order and regularity. To use Mary Douglas' analogy, to identify dirt is also to explore the concept of orderliness; dirt is matter which is out of place (Douglas, 1966). This is a valuable notion because it reminds us that there are not necessary or intrinsic qualities which one could itemize and measure across a variety of contexts; the appropriateness of the use of the term is largely dependent on the context of its use. To talk about disruption in schools is then to highlight behaviours which are perceived as appropriate in this context. Given this qualification, it would still seem possible to identify types of behaviour to which the terms apply. The problem, however, is compounded because of the lack of consensus which allows scope for individual interpretive activity and because it is arguable that schools themselves are divided on what might be considered appropriate.

So to describe something as threatening is at the same time to make a statement of preference for a form of order which is threatened. In schools such labelling and identification are clearly associated with the teacher's power to assert the legitimacy of his/her perferred sense of order.

In an educational system that is increasingly defined in terms of cultural diversity, of cultural heterogeneity rather than cultural homogeneity, there is clearly a wide area of discretion in invoking rules. Culturally different behaviours, whether ethnic or class or religious in origin, may be perceived and reacted to differently (DES, 1981). The question of when and why teachers invoke rules of disorder to apply to such behaviours, which at other times and other places may be found acceptable and even laudable, is a major concern of our research.

Disruption in school is behaviour out of place; the conditions for identifying it are a set of ordered relations and a contravention of that order. Disruption is a by-product of systematic ordering and classification, involving rejection of inappropriate elements. Thus like the notion of 'dirt', disruption is a compendium term which includes all the rejected elements of ordered systems. Behaviour is not disruptive *per se*; there are times when we positively encourage children to be talkative, boisterous or extrovert. Behaviour only becomes disruptive at certain times and in certain places; it is disruptive to wander about in a French lesson but not in drama, in the corridors at certain hours but not in the craft room; it is disruptive to keep silent in English discussion but not in Mathematics. What is seen as disruption by A may be welcomed as creativity by B and for both the same behaviour may change its significance depending on time of the day or week. In each case what is identified as disruption is a response to a situation. Nor does the existence of explicit statements of school rules give any clear indication of whether, when or by whom they will be applied. For behaviour to be defined as disruptive it first has to be identified and then acted on. There seems to be no easy way of categorizing the precipitating circumstances although, in many, the element of teacher stress seems important. Descriptive studies reveal an unending series of circumstances in which the teacher's patience will be exhausted and it is difficult to move from the specific to the general. Time of day, time of year (especially when examinations make heavy demands on teachers' time), poor health, overwork, domestic upset, previous experience, age, sex, and class all may contribute to explanations of why particular forms of behaviour in individuals are sometimes allowed, sometimes stigmatized. These factors may combine and contribute to the teacher's stress. This in turn may communicate itself to pupils and bring about further disruptive behaviour; a clear example of the self-fulfilling prophecy.

For a child to become disruptive, then, it is necessary to look both at the behaviour engaged in (sometimes tolerated, sometimes punished) and at the perceptions and response of the teacher who reacts to it. Like deviance, disruption is also what people define as such. Its identification and punishment serve to highlight the moral purpose of the school and to reassert the legitimacy of its sense of order. If, as Durkheim (1956) has suggested, the scaffold serves a dramaturgical function in asserting and marking out the parameters of order by punishing those who transgress its boundaries, then the school disruptive may serve the same function in signifying the boundaries of acceptable behaviour in the school.

A recognition of the importance of the element of labelling in school disruption, on the part of the person who reacts, serves as a reminder that disruption is normal wherever there is an underlying sense of order. Concern for the level of disruption then is an indication of the precariousness of the underlying order. The danger is that threats to order will be seen only as external and located in the pathological responses of children rather than as integral to the purposes and organization of the institution. Children who disrupt may be immediately metamorphosed into 'disruptive', 'maladjusted' or 'problem' children where these in fact only constitute a very small percentage of the perceived problem. Children so identified and labelled may then experience the subtle shifts in attitude and expectation of their teachers and a closing of options. In relation to identifying mental illness, Erickson (1965) describes this process as a 'betrayal funnel'. Persistent disruption and failure to respond to schools' established norms of acceptable behaviour or work may then lead to the retrospective reconstruction of individual biographies to confirm the emergent identity of the disruptive; past histories are scanned for confirmation of the present emergent identity so that it becomes apparent that the child was a disruptive all along. The danger here is of what Matza (1969) describes as a 'drift' from a primary form of deviance, which in itself may have little importance or persistence, through a process of public and institutional response and labelling (what he terms 'signification') into a stage of secondary deviance where the child subtly takes on the identity of deviant and becomes more like what he is cast as. Unless the chain is broken early, so that the child is enabled to establish satisfactory links with the institutional aims of the school, the danger is that the child will then become more like his label. Then the increased salience of the peer group to compensate for the withdrawal of school approval as a source of strength and identity, may actually serve to minimize the disruptive child's opportunity to respond positively. Given a bad name a child may discover pleasure in his new identity. The vicious circle is complete and the school has inadvertently compounded the process of becoming disruptive which all its measures were initially designed to prevent.

Schools and teachers differ in how they define disruption, where they perceive it and how they respond. Lateness, for example, has as its measure an optimal level of punctuality; deference is a socially learned attribute which at one extreme may be perceived as a form of sycophancy or 'creeping' and on the other as insolence. Whether or not pupils and teachers coincide on what is expected will often be fortuitous and uncertain and will depend on the whole range of personality factors, contingent situational variables and, more importantly, on the willingness of both sides to sustain the social definition of the situation and activity engaged in.

Some observations from the Goldsmiths Project will perhaps make this point more clearly. In this school, systems of control appeared to come into operation when boys were excluded from a lesson and sent to the hall where their names were entered in a book by the deputy head. The presumption was that teachers would not exclude pupils for trivial or non-serious reasons. At this point their exclusion was treated as a serious matter and could lead to automatic punishment: in the first instance detention and being brought to the attention of the head of year.

What was also apparent, however, was that this system could have unintended consequences. Designed to control and minimize disruption, it could also serve to amplify and transfer it from a level of personal conflict in the classroom between teacher and pupil to the level of institutional conflict, in which the outstanding issue became the acceptance of the authority of the school. Thus there seemed to be a 'fast' route which, starting at the level of exclusion from class, led by rapid stages, through failure to turn up twice for detention, to an escalation of seriousness and consequences: decision to cane, a boy's refusal to accept the cane, then suspension. To the extent that staff recognized this pattern, it was possible that such a system heightened rather than diminished the stressfulness of the classroom. Staff, who on conscientious grounds, refused to use the exclusion strategy, may well have been in the position of having no alternative but to cope as best they could on their own in the classroom. Similarly, if staff excluded children only for very serious disruptive behaviour, it may be that there was no way in which they could receive even temporary respite from problems which, although not 'very serious' in themselves, were nevertheless serious to the teacher in that they disrupted the flow of the lesson, interfered with the pattern of work and involved considerable stress. In this category came disruption from constant talking, lateness, interruptions, failure to settle, etc. In addition, the system appeared to close the door on the exclusion of particular children for short periods of 'cooling off' without this leading to punishment and the risk of an escalation of consequences. If, as appears to be the case, there is in any school a sizeable minority of children who have behaviour problems, it could be argued that any school system which operates to a considerable extent within a context of punishment, is not best equipped to deal with the issue.

In this research, the number of incidents and the number of boys involved suggested a disruption that was fairly widespread, though in a pyramid reflecting the broad banding system of the school. The 'A' band was rarely disrupted. There was some reason to question whether the system of control and staff support adopted here was functional. What was initially intended as a device for enabling teachers temporarily to exclude disruptive children risked, under the weight of institutional use, becoming rigid and fraught with dangers. Such a procedure could magnify rather than diminish the problem and feed back into the system an expectation of disruption through the impression created by large numbers of boys receiving the cane or being suspended.

The effect of disruption on teachers should not be minimized; at its lowest level, it is the peculiar occupational hazard of any teaching encounter where the participants may not share the same interests and may operate with differing perceptions of their role. All teachers are aware of the difference between their intentions for learning, however well conceived, and the actual learning that takes place. Disruption of plans is a frustrating business and this is accompanied by an inevitable degree of strain and stress where the disruption takes unpredictable, less conventional and more overt forms. To understand and cope with the problems this creates for learning requires teachers who are mature, secure in their teaching skills, understanding of their subject and of its value and capable of distancing themselves sufficiently to see beyond the immediate situation to underlying problems, which may well lie outside the classroom.

Disruption is now, as it has always been, a special problem for young and inexperienced teachers. It is also a problem for teachers of all ages coming into a new school until they 'learn the ropes' and establish themselves with the children as a person to be trusted. It remains a problem to those who lack flexibility or who are either unwilling or unable to accept the conflicting nature of demands made on them. It is because education is always such a risky business that it is full of conflict and stress.

Many teachers are understandably reluctant to acknowledge that the reasons for pupil misbehaviour may be found as often in their teaching as in the pupil's inability or failure to learn. Having problems of classroom control is not easy to admit to. Teachers are expected to cope. Senior staff may express irritation at the number of behavioural problems referred to them which they consider should have been dealt with in the classroom. An increase in the number of exclusions may produce pressure on staff to operate selective procedures; they may become more tolerant and settle for lower expectations by lowering their demands on children to avoid conflict. In this way it might be possible for the level of disruption in a school or classroom to increase without this being perceived as a problem within the school system. More insidiously, there is the temptation to blame pupils and to attribute disruptiveness to their personal characteristics: as a defence mechanism against the strains and stresses arising from seemingly intractable problems. Writing about the reactions of personnel in industry undergoing rapid change, Burns and Stalker (1961) noted 'the tendency of people, when faced by problems in human organisation of an intractable nature, to find relief in attributing difficulties to the wrong headedness, stupidity and delinquency of the other with whom they had to deal or more widely to the irreconcilable differences in attitude and codes of rational conduct'.

Galloway *et al.* (1982) provide a useful account of exclusion and suspension in schools which lends strong corroborative support to the findings of other research on the important effects of school differences on attainment and behaviour. They claim that a pupil's chances may be influenced at least as much and probably more by which school he/she happens to attend, as by any stress in the family or any constitutional factors in the pupil him/herself. Their detailed study of Sheffield pupils suspended from school includes a careful account of ten special groups set up to deal with them. They make the important point that these groups seemed to concentrate on the pupil more than the context in which the problem has presented. Galloway *et al.* emphasize the potential of such groups to offer a cooling-off period during which staff and teachers can look at the stresses in school or home which have precipitated the child's problem and at the means of overcoming them. They conclude that the problem of disruptive behaviour is most readily solved by prevention, that special groups cannot reasonably be seen as a solution to the problems which disruptive pupils cause in schools, that effective pastoral care must embrace all aspects of a pupil's welfare in school if it is to make an impact on the level of disruptive behaviour and that all pupils should feel that the school values their achievement. Like ourselves, Galloway *et*

al. believe that tackling the problem through the school's policy organization and ethos is by no means wishful thinking. A similar point is made
by Ford, Mongon and Whelan (1982). They express concern at the
growing popularity of disruptive units, at the disproportionate increase in
the number of pupils identified as maladjusted or educationally subnormal and the concentration of interest on certain types of violent and
extravagant behaviour to the relative neglect of behaviours which may
be less threatening to teachers but which indicate deep-seated needs.
Regularities in the patterning of problem behaviour in schools (it is
experienced more with boys than girls, more in county than voluntary
schools, more with older than younger pupils, more with lower-working-
class and ethnic than with middle-class pupils) suggest that explanations
and remedies are more likely to be found in the system of schooling than
in the psychologies of individual children. They express dissatisfaction
and impatience with what they see as a medical model attempting to
explain away problems in terms of individual pathology which are essentially either social, economic or institutional. Reliance on such explanations serves to direct us to remedial approaches when we should be more
concerned with preventative work.

A book on disruptive units (Tattum, 1982) incorporates a study of
pupils' expressed motives for the behaviour as a way of perceiving and
analysing secondary schools as a step toward understanding the disruptive
pupil. It critically examines the setting up of the special units as an
innovatory measure which creates problems of identification, selection
and the reintegration of pupils back into schools. The pupils' study
comprises data from unstructured interviews with twenty-nine secondary-
school pupils in a detached disruptive unit which leads to the categorization of pupils' declared motives or explanation of their behaviour into
five types:
1. it was the teacher's fault
2. being treated with disrespect
3. inconsistency of rule application
4. we were only messing
5. it's the fault of the school system.

Acknowledgement of the increased reliance on systems theory to
explore the complicated ecologies of schools is a feature of Gillham's
(1982) collection of essays which brings together some of the writings of
the foremost researchers into school difference in this country. It is this
rethinking of the problem within a 'systems' framework, rather than
anything contained in the individual contributions, which makes this book
something of a landmark. The title of the final chapter expresses well

the dilemma, 'Institutional change or individual change?'. A 'systems' approach does not imply that all behaviour problems will disappear as a result of manipulation of institutional processes but it does suggest a missing element from an adequate psychology of individuals: the investigation of other intersecting systems whether individual or institutional.

REFERENCES

Burns, T. and Stalker, G.M. (1961) *The Management of Innovation*, Tavistock Publications, London.

Department of Education and Science (1981) *West Indian Children in Our Schools* (The Rampton Report), HMSO, London.

Douglas, M. (1966) *Purity and Danger*, Routledge & Kegan Paul, London.

Durkheim, E. (1956) *Education and Sociology*, Glencoe, IL.

Erickson, E. (1965) *Childhood and Society*, Penguin, Hogarth.

Ford, J., Mongon, D. and Whelan, M. (1982) *Special Education and Social Control: Invisible Disasters*, Routledge & Kegan Paul, London.

Galloway, D., Ball, T., Blomfield, D. and Seyd, R. (1982) *Schools and Disruptive Pupils*, Longman, London.

Gillham, B. (ed.) (1982) *Problem Behaviour in the Secondary School: a Systems Approach*, Croom Helm, London.

Lowenstein, L.F. (1975) *Violent and Disruptive Behaviour in Schools*, NAS.

McNamara, D. (1975) *The Distribution and Incidence of Problem Children in an English County*, British Association for the Advancement of Science Paper, No. 251.

Matza, D. (1969) *Becoming Deviant*, Prentice Hall, Englewood Cliffs, New Jersey.

Tattum, D. (1982) *Disruptive Pupils in Schools and Units*, Wiley, Chicester.

TOPICS FOR DISCUSSION

1. In what ways might 'the very taking-up of a research stance' (p. 16) toward disruptive behaviour be of benefit to a school and to its teachers?
2. On what grounds do the authors assert that *delinquency* is easier to study than *disruption*?
3. Is it really possible to define *disruption* if, as the authors allege, 'schools and teachers differ in how they define disruption, where they perceive it and how they respond'?

SUGGESTIONS FOR FURTHER READING

1. Barton, L. and Meighan, R. (eds.) (1979) in *Schools, Pupils and Deviance*, Nafferton Books, Driffield. pp. 7–16, Schools, pupils and deviance.

In this short paper the meaning of deviance is analysed. The concept is discussed in the following ways: (a) deviance is referenced against cultures; (b) deviance is referenced against alternatives within a culture; (c) deviance is referenced against different interpretations within the teaching profession; (d) deviance is referenced against layers of meaning within schools; (e) deviance is frequently descriptive and evaluative simultaneously; (f) positive deviance is overlooked, negative deviance is highlighted; (g) psychological and sociological explanations of deviance are explained briefly.

2. Galloway, D., Ball, T., Blomfield, D. and Seyd, R. (1982) Introduction: who are the disruptive pupils?, pp. 9–16, in *Schools and Disruptive Pupils*, Longman, London.

The authors discuss the problem of definition in light of the different ideas that teachers have about what constitutes disruptive behaviour. Essentially, they suggest, there are two issues. One is that many pupils behave in different ways, dependent on their teacher and the school they are attending. Thus, experienced teachers can frequently recall pupils with a hair-raising record of misbehaviour who present no further problems after a change of school and, in similar vein, many pupils who are disruptive only with certain teachers. The second issue is related to this and centres on the teacher's tolerance level for different forms of pupil behaviour. Deviance, like beauty, the authors contend, lies in the eye of the beholder.

3. Tattum, D.P. (1982) Definitions of disruptive behaviour, pp. 44–50, in *Disturbed or disturbing?*, pp. 10–20, and *Disruptive Pupils in Schools and Units*, Wiley, Chichester.

Tattum's title to the first section (pp. 10–20) is no mere rhetorical device. Rather it is intended to focus attention on the complexity of defining disruptive behaviour. 'Disturbed or disturbing' addresses the same distinction that Lawrence, Steed and Young (1977) draw between 'problem children' and 'children with problems'. In this first section British research is reviewed and statistics from Teacher Union, Headteacher Association and Governmental surveys are included. In the second part of the report (pp. 44–50) the problem of definition is pursued in greater depth and examples of definitions of disruptive pupil behaviour and the wide interpretation given to the concept are discussed. Relevant sections of the Plowden (1967) and Warnock (1978) Reports are quoted. The extract ends with a perceptive treatment of a central question to do with the exclusion of disruptive pupils: *cui bono?*, i.e. who benefits?

REFERENCE

Lawrence, J., Steed, D. and Young, P. (1977) *Disruptive Behaviour in a Secondary School*, An Education Studies Monograph, Goldsmiths' College, London.

Reading 2
SPURIOUS CATEGORIES
D. Galloway
INTRODUCTION

Criticisms may be levelled against the extended concept of special educational needs proposed by the Warnock Report and enshrined in the

1981 Education Act. These criticisms may apply with greatest force to the implication that children have special needs when teachers find their behaviour difficult. There may, indeed, be clear evidence that children's behaviour at school depends largely on the school and its teachers, leading to the conclusion that whether children show evidence, through their behaviour, of having special educational needs may depend mainly on the school rather than on factors in the children themselves or their families. It, nevertheless, remains the case that teachers in many schools do find the behaviour of a substantial minority of their pupils disturbing. The popularity of screening instruments such as Rutter's (1967) Behaviour Questionnaire or Stott's (1971) Bristol Social Adjustment Guides may depend less on their diagnostic usefulness than on their successfully identifying behavioural problems which are relatively prevalent, yet constitute real and legitimate sources of concern to teachers.

In this chapter we look briefly at some problems of definition, concluding that the categories most widely used by teachers and educational administrators are of little or no value in understanding the needs of the pupils concerned. The tone of the chapter is somewhat negative. This is unavoidable in discussing the red herrings that constitute the most frequent responses to behaviour problems. There is no cause, however, for despondency. Evidence accumulated over the last decade shows that many behaviour problems can be prevented and that teachers can play an essential part in catering for those whose problems do still indicate that they require special attention.

Spurious categories
Disturbed or disturbing

When teachers or psychologists say that a child is disturbed they are making a value judgement about the child's behaviour. When they say that they find the behaviour disturbing, they are describing their own reaction. There is no objective quality in a child's behaviour which justifies a conclusion that a child is disturbed. To say so would be to infer an unspecified mental state from observed behaviour. This is acceptable, even necessary, when there is general agreement about the nature of the mental state. For example, we can conclude from someone's behaviour that he is happy or unhappy. No such consensus exists with respect to the quasi-medical concept of disturbance. Teachers, psychologists and psychiatrists use the term in different ways, with little idea what others

D. Galloway (1985) Spurious categories, in *Schools, Pupils and Special Educational Needs*, Croom Helm, London.

mean by it, and frequently with only a hazy idea of what they mean by it themselves. The case of ten-year-old Joanne illustrates the argument.

Joanne had always been regarded as one of the class's slower pupils, but toward the middle of her penultimate junior-school year her teacher started to complain to the headteacher that her work was deteriorating still further. At the same time the teacher was becoming increasingly irritated by Joanne's behaviour, which she described as 'sulky', 'insolent' and 'couldn't care less'. Having taught the class herself in the teacher's absence the head recognized the descriptions. Unlike her colleague, though, she did not regard them as evidence of disturbance. She knew that Joanne was finding much of the work difficult. In addition, her parents were academically ambitious and put considerable pressure on her to do better. The head was on the point of yielding to the class teacher's insistence that Joanne be referred to the school's psychologist when the teacher was taken ill, and was away for two months. The young supply teacher who took over the class had no complaints and no worries about Joanne's behaviour. Indeed he described her as one of the livelier members of the class, responsive to praise and encouragement. When the head looked at Joanne's work, it became clear that she had achieved more in the last two months than in the whole of the rest of the year.

Neither teachers nor psychologists will find anything surprising in this account. It does, however, indicate the logical and practical difficulties in saying that a child, or a child's behaviour, is disturbed. All that Joanne's class teacher could legitimately say was that *she* found her behaviour disturbing. The headteacher witnessed similar behaviour and did not find it disturbing. The young supply teacher elicited a different and much more constructive pattern of behaviour from Joanne, so the question whether she was disturbed or disturbing did not arise.

When teachers say that they find a child's behaviour disturbing, they are implying that the child is the focus of their concern, while acknowledging the significance of their own response to the child. The distinction between saying that children are disturbed and saying that they are disturbing is therefore not merely semantic. It brings us back to the question of responsibility. As a teacher, if I say a child is disturbing I am accepting that the problem lies as much in my responses as in the behaviour itself. Hence, I retain some sense of responsibility for dealing with it. If I say that the child is disturbed I imply that the problem is someone else's, since as a teacher I am trained to teach and not to deal with 'disturbed' children.

Maladjusted or Disruptive?
The Warnock Report made no use of the term disturbed. Although the committee recommended the abolition of the old categories of handicaps they retained the term maladjusted on the grounds that behaviour can meaningfully be considered only in relation to the circumstances in which it occurs. As Joanne's case indicates, this is true. Yet the objections to the term maladjusted are at least as strong as to the term disturbed. LEAs have special schools for maladjusted pupils. Thus if pupils are maladjusted they may be seen as someone else's responsibility.

Warnock's retention of the term maladjusted is not explicitly reflected in the 1981 Education Act but, since the number of special schools for maladjusted pupils and centres for disruptive ones shows no signs of decreasing, this is a somewhat peripheral point. More important is the spurious distinction, rapidly becoming enshrined in DES folklore, between maladjusted and disruptive. In the 1970s centres and units for disruptive pupils gradually increased in popularity. An Her Majesty's Inspectorate of Schools (HMI) 1978 survey showed that 72 per cent of ninety-six LEAs surveyed had established units by 1976. The number has increased since then. By 1983 more than 6,000 pupils were in so-called disruptive units (Newell, 1983), nearly as many as were in schools for the maladjusted. LEAs generally have been adamant that the units catered for disruptive, and not maladjusted, pupils. In our work in Sheffield we regarded this as a cynical argument:

> Education officers gradually realized that it was usually cheaper and always administratively easier to open special centres for disruptive adolescents rather than expand the special school system . . . units were faced with fewer staffing constraints in the form of recommendations on pupil:teacher ratios in special schools (DES, 1973). They could be more flexible in their admission and discharge procedures. Pupils would always remain on the roll of their original school, to which it was theoretically hoped they would return. Having established these units LEAs found themselves forced to deny that they catered for maladjusted children, since maladjusted children must — under the 1944 Act — be educated in special schools or classes for the maladjusted. (Galloway *et al.*, 1982, p. 60)

It is not at all clear how far the 1981 Act has changed the situation. Pupils cannot normally be transferred to special schools on the grounds of maladjustment without the 'protection' of a statement based on a formal assessment. On the other hand, the DES (1983) has advised that formal procedures are not required when ordinary schools provide special educational provision from their own resources in the form of additional tuition and remedial provision or, in normal circumstances, where the child attends a reading centre or unit for disruptive pupils (paragraph 15).

The DES guidelines are extraordinary for at least two reasons. First, the majority of centres for disruptive pupils are 'terminal' in the sense that few pupils are expected to return to the mainstream. Secondly, *all* pupils sent to units for the disruptive could equally well have been described as maladjusted if it could have served any useful administrative purpose. Their behaviour, according to teachers, is at least as disturbing as that of maladjusted pupils. The same applies to their family backgrounds. Whether a child is labelled disruptive or maladjusted has nothing to do with educational, psychological or medical assessment. It depends solely on the type of provision available locally.

Pupils not categories

The muddle which, in different ways, both Warnock and the DES got themselves into over the usefulness of terms like maladjusted and disruptive should not be allowed to obscure three points. First, pupils' behaviour at school is strongly influenced by their experiences at school. The evidence shows that schools vary widely in their 'production' of pupils with behavioural problems and that these differences are not attributable to catchment-area factors. Secondly, pupils who present behaviour problems are regarded in terms of Warnock's report and of the 1981 Act as having special educational need. Since, however, their needs may to a large extent have arisen from their experiences at school it seems logical that responses should be based on analysis of the school's contribution as well as of the pupil. Thirdly, Warnock's insistence on the extended concept of special needs is both legitimate and useful to the extent that it acknowledges that teachers are disturbed by the behaviour of a substantial minority of their pupils.

A further point, implicit in the discussion so far, is that there are no satisfactory criteria for distinguishing between groups of pupils who disturb, nor for distinguishing between those whose needs can be met in an ordinary school and those requiring separate special education. In the great majority of cases children are referred to special schools for the maladjusted or centres for the disruptive when teachers and education psychologists decide that the ordinary school cannot or should not be expected to contain them any longer. Their decision may be influenced by pressure from the pupil's class teacher or by the view that the child needs to be removed for the benefit of other pupils. The decision is rationalized though, as being in the child's best interests. We should therefore consider briefly whether there is in fact much evidence for the view that pupils benefit from transfer to separate provision.

Case against separate provision

On commonsense grounds it might seem surprising if pupils improved after transfer to special schools or centres. All teachers and all parents know that children learn from each other. One wonders what they are supposed to learn when placed in a separate school or class with a lot of other pupils presenting similarly severe behaviour problems. In this connection it is irrelevant whether the special provision is a class operated as part of the school's special education network or a separate school or centre serving the whole LEA.

The limited available evidence on the progress of pupils in special schools for maladjusted or delinquent pupils is reviewed elsewhere (Galloway and Goodwin, 1979). The evidence does *not* suggest that these schools are frequently successful in returning pupils to the mainstream nor that placement results in any long-term improvement in the pupil's behaviour. The most plausible conclusion is that the behaviour of pupils, like that of adults, changes according to the circumstances. In other words, disturbing behaviour must be investigated and tackled in the context in which it occurs. Seen in this light, the failure of attempts to tackle the problem out of context is predictable (Clarke and Cornish, 1978). Even when the aim of special centres for disruptive pupils is successful entry to employment, rather than return to school, there is little evidence that this is frequently achieved (e.g. Galloway and Barrett, 1984).

The evidence, then, does not suggest that pupils' special needs are served well by removal from ordinary schools. In one sense, the debate is of peripheral importance. However extensive an LEAs provision for maladjusted or disruptive pupils may be, separate schools or centres will never cater for more than a tiny minority of the pupils whose teachers find aspects of their behaviour disturbing or troublesome. We return therefore to the school environment.

REFERENCES

Clarke, R.V.G. and Cornish, D.B. (1978) The effectiveness of residential treatment for delinquents, in L. Hersov, M. Berger and D. Schaffer (eds.) *Aggression and Anti-social Behaviour in Childhood and Adolescence*, Pergamon, Oxford.

Department of Education and Science (1973) *Children with Specific Reading Difficulties: Report of the Advisory Committee on Handicapped Children*, HMSO, London.

Department of Education and Science (1983) *Assessments and Statements of Special Educational Needs*, Circular 1/83, DES, London.

Galloway, D. and Barrett, C. (1984) Off-site centres for disruptive secondary school pupils in New Zealand, *Educational Research*, Vol. 26, pp. 106–10.

Galloway, D. and Goodwin, C. (1979) *Educating Slow-learning and Maladjusted Children: Integration or Segregation?* Longman, London.

Galloway, D., Ball, T., Blomfield, D. and Seyd, T. (1982) *Schools and Disruptive Pupils*, Longman, London.

Her Majesty's Inspectorate of Schools (1978) *Behavioural Units*, DES, London.

Newell, P. (1983) *ACE Special Education Handbook*, Advisory Centre for Education, London.

Rutter, M. (1967) A children's behaviour questionnaire for completion by teachers: preliminary findings, *Journal of Child Psychology and Psychiatry*, Vol. 8, pp. 1–11.

Stott, D.H. (1971) *The Bristol Social Adjustment Guides*, University of London Press.

TOPICS FOR DISCUSSION

1. On what grounds does the author assert that, 'there is no objective quality in a child's behaviour which justifies a conclusion that a child is disturbed' (p. 27)?
2. Why does the author refer to the distinction between the terms maladjusted and disturbed as spurious?
3. What is Galloway's major objection to separate provision for children presenting severe behaviour problems?

SUGGESTIONS FOR FURTHER READING

1. Barton, L. and Tomlinson, S. (1981) The social construction of the ESN-M child, pp. 194–211, in *Special Education: Policies, Practices and Social Issues*, Harper & Row, London.

The argument in this paper that the category ESN-M is socially constructed by the decisions and the beliefs of professional people may equally be applied to the classification of disruptive behaviour. The authors contend that the development of categories must be understood within a wider historical, social and political context. This applies particularly to those non-normative categories of ESN-M, children with learning difficulties, disruptive children, and maladjusted children and obtains whether these categories are statutory or merely descriptive.

2. Galloway, D.M. and Goodwin, C. (1979) *Educating Slow-learning and Maladjusted Children: Integration or Segregation?*, Longman, London, pp. 140–50.

This conclusions chapter to the book contains a summary of arguments for and against ordinary schools and special schools. It provides a useful outline of the respective strengths and limitations of teaching children with problems in ordinary schools. The authors conclude that political controversy should cease its focus on the sterile dichotomy between special and ordinary schools and turn its attention to the resources and the facilities that are required to meet children's needs in their neighbourhood schools.

3. Tattum, D.P. (1982) Disruptive behaviour; problems of control or change?, pp. 272–308, in *Disruptive Pupils in Schools and Units*, Wiley, Chichester.

Inter alia, the author is concerned with the rapid growth of special units for children with behaviour problems. Candidates, he asserts, can always be found to fill available places. Tattum reviews the official statistics and cites Warnock's observation that 20 per cent of the school population will need some form of special education at some time in their school career. Given a label by which to classify a 'new' category of pupil, will schools proceed to identify their incidence in the school population in even greater numbers?

UNDERSTANDING DISRUPTIVE BEHAVIOUR

INTRODUCTION

The selection of readings in Section 2 focuses on interaction in a variety of settings that includes homes, schools and sectors of the education system as they relate to the wider world of work, occupational mobility and life chances. In addition, there is concern in the choice of readings to illustrate ways in which curriculum planning and innovation may serve to include, within the academic and social goals of the school, the needs of many pupils who currently are disheartened and disaffected with what is on offer.

In the first extract (Reading 3) children whose aggressiveness is manifested as early as the nursery-school years are discussed. They are disruptive and difficult to manage; so much so that headteachers may be tempted to direct such pupils so as to contain them rather than try to understand the root cause of their difficulties. Reading 4 is an account of social, psychological and educational characteristics of primary- and secondary-school pupils suspended from school for conduct disorders by one northern LEA. Suggestions for further reading include references to longitudinal studies of aggressive children, their family backgrounds and the patterns of child-rearing practices prevailing in their homes. Together, in the first two extracts and support materials, the use that has been made of personal and familial pathologies in the explanation of disruptive behaviour in school is reviewed.

The central theme of Reading 5 is that schools are organized predominantly to perpetuate social inequality. The reading contains graphic accounts of violent acts described by their perpetrators and is supported by references to further studies of disruption and violence by Corrigan (1979), Werthman (1977) and Furlong (1985). Teachers' attitudes and behaviour toward West Indian and Asian children is the focus of Reading 6. It is complemented in Reading 7 by an outline of Tomlinson's research and her insistence that the over-representation of pupils of West Indian origin in ESN-M schools ('the stigmatized part of the education system'), ensures that blacks remain in low socio-economic status positions in the wider society.

In Reading 8 Hargreaves asserts that secondary schools inflict loss of dignity on many pupils through their curricula and organizational procedures and thereby sow the seeds of discontent and rebellion. The impact of relevant curricula and imaginative teaching in the amelioration of disaffection is discussed in suggested readings from the Brunel University study group (Bird *et al.*, 1980) and the DES Document, *Better Schools* (1985). Galloway's concern (Reading 9) is with the quality of pastoral-care provision as it relates to rates of disruptive behaviour in schools. An important aspect of such care, he shows, is that it includes teachers themselves when they encounter disciplinary problems.

Finally, Reading 10 presents sections of the Hargreaves Report (*Improving Secondary Schools*, 1984) that contains suggestions for curriculum and organizational changes in ILEA secondary schools. In particular, the reasons for and against a common curriculum in fourth and fifth years are presented, together with arguments that relate such initiatives to potential improvements in pupils' disaffection and disruption rates.

REFERENCES

Bird, C., Chessum, R., Furlong, V. J. and Johnson, D. (1980) *Disaffected Pupils: a Report to the DES by the Educational Studies Unit, Brunel University*, Brunel University, Uxbridge.

Corrigan, P. (1979) *Schooling the Smash Street Kids*, Macmillan, London

Department of Education and Science (1985) *Better Schools*, HMSO, London.

Furlong, V. J. (1985) *The Deviant Pupil: Sociological Perspectives*, Open University Press, Milton Keynes.

Werthman, C. (1977) Delinquents in school, in B.R. Cosin (ed.) *School and Society*, Routledge & Kegan Paul, London.

Reading 3
GROWING UP IN THE PLAYGROUND: A SOCIAL DEVELOPMENT OF CHILDREN
A. Sluckin

THE FUNCTION OF AGGRESSION IN THE PRE-SCHOOL AND PRIMARY-SCHOOL YEARS
M. Manning and A. Sluckin

Much of our knowledge about individual children's goals and strategies in social interaction comes from two impressive observational studies. (Manning, Heron and Marshall, 1978) One is by my colleague, Margaret Manning, in Edinburgh, and the other comes from Hubert Montagner (1978) and his team in Besançon, France.

There are as many individual styles as there are children. How many we choose to lump together and call a group depend on the particular aims of the research. Hubert Montagner wanted to 'discover the manner in which communication develops at a time when language has not yet appeared'. He filmed children aged between seven and thirty-six-months in a crèche and three six-year-olds in a nursery school and comments about how their interaction styles endure through to the primary school. The investigation by Manning *et al.* centred on a narrower theme: is it possible to classify three-to-five-year-olds according to their dominant style of hostility and, if so, do the groups share other characteristics? She observed seventeen children over their last year and a half at nursery school and watched them again four years later in their primary-school playgrounds when they were eight years old.

Despite their rather different goals, both Montagner and Manning and colleagues independently identify ways of interacting that are remarkably similar. We start by looking at the behaviour profiles that Montagner noted.

MONTAGNER'S STYLES OF INTERACTING

Leaders

As their name suggests, the leaders are the best-adjusted children. In the crèche Montagner describes them as being friendly and appeasing, in

A. Sluckin (1981) *Growing up in the Playground: a Social Development of Children*, Routledge and Kegan Paul, London, pp. 76–81; M. Manning and A. Sluckin (1984) The function of aggression in the pre-school and primary-school years, in N. Frude and H. Gault (eds.) *Disruptive Behaviour in Schools*, Wiley, Chichester, reproduced with permission.

ways that are appropriate to the situation. For instance, they often greet their friends at the door when they arrive in the morning and rush to console them should they burst into tears or be about to cry. All this causes others to approach, and imitate them, and frequently they are offered objects.

Their attractive manner even extends to conflicts, when rather than seize objects, threaten or fight they are similarly friendly, and in this way manage to avoid further aggression. When the leaders are themselves threatening, they express it most often through a sequence of non-ambiguous gestures, which are neither preceded nor accompanied by aggression. Indeed, they usually wait for a reply to their threat before hitting out. But generally a leader would only be as aggressive as was strictly necessary to obtain the desired goal, the victim usually turning away, standing aside or abandoning the object without complaint. They show much the same pattern at nursery school. There are frequent friendly and appeasing acts but their threats are now shorter and less distinct. These are often reduced to pushing out the chest, raising the arms, furrowing the forehead, all accompanied by what Montagner coyly refers to as 'naughty words'.

The leaders are the ones who organize activities in the classroom and playground, create new games, play with objects in an original way and are used by the teachers to organize others. All in all, they can be considered to be the best adapted to the changing rhythms of life and to interchanges with others. They move easily between home and school, have many diverse ways of communicating and are easily understood both by children and by adults. Sixty-five per cent of Montagner's leaders showed the same style of communication at the crèche, the nursery school and the primary school. In only 15 per cent of cases did leaders at three years old become more fluctuating or more aggressive in their behaviour at four years. These changes coincided with modification in the family environment between the third and fourth year.

It is worth mentioning in passing a group of children who resemble leaders in being friendly and rarely aggressive, but who are not so successful in competitive situations. Compared with the leaders in nursery school, these ones are twice as often displaced from a location, and similarly unsuccessful in obtaining a desired object. They are less attractive than leaders, being followed and imitated by fewer children but, because they are nevertheless friendly, they do not become isolated.

Dominant-aggressive

Some children in the crèche frequently are aggressive both in free play as well as in competitive situations. Their aggression seems to be spontaneous and not as a response to any threat. Sometimes the aggression alternates with isolation and, the greater the frequency of the aggression, so the duration of the isolation increases. These children are not at all responsive to their peers. For instance, when they make a threat they do not wait for the victim's reply, but pass straight to aggression, and they rarely initiate any friendly overtures. Even when they are friendly, their sequences are often interrupted without any clear reason. 'In other words, dominant-aggressive children, perceived by their peers as turbulent and aggressive can, at any moment, express a succession of disordered gestures and gratuitous violence.'

At nursery school the profiles of these children remain basically the same, though the frequency of their aggression diminishes considerably between three and five years old. However, they are still very brusque and disorganized in their movements and disrupt others' activities frequently. It is not surprising that teachers come to label them as naughty. Although other children often avoid their presence, they are at times followed and imitated, especially during noisy games, such as 'cops and robbers' or 'cowboys', which often take place in the playground. Their well-developed gestures and very noticeable activities are potentially very inviting but, should any conflict arise, then their aggressive side quickly shows itself. This causes them to be abandoned and rejected by others, which in turn brings further aggression and isolation. They show the same style at primary school, though Montagner suggests that the presence of teachers in the playground leads them to simulate aggression with pretend blows rather than resort to real fighting. Their aggression shows itself in starting scraps by interrupting or disorganizing games and they are sometimes so violent as to cause injury. Even more than in nursery school, they can give the illusion of being leaders, but in reality they are not the leaders they claim to be. They do not have the same power to draw away others and are abandoned by many of their followers. With their reputation for naughtiness, they tend to use aggression and isolation as ways of replying to adults who, not surprisingly, threaten and reject them.

Lastly, Montagner noticed some children who fluctuate, either daily or weekly, between being a leader and being dominant-aggressive. He notes that they usually stay fluctuating up to three years old and then either become more unstable and tend toward the style of dominant-aggressive or stabilize toward the profile of a leader. The way it goes, he claims, depends on the nature of any changes within the family.

Dominated children

Certain children only rarely assert themselves in competitive situations. However, within this dominated group, there are still differences in behaviour profiles. I have already mentioned the dominated ones who resemble leaders and Montagner points to three other styles: dominated-aggressive, timid-dominated and totally withdrawn children.

Dominated-aggressive

These children are rather like the dominant-aggressive ones. Their behaviour is not organized into sequences and teachers watch out for them being isolated and aggressive. They change little between three and eight years old, though the frequency of their friendly exchanges tends to increase, while their aggression diminishes. Their hostility still arises for no obvious reason and alternates with long periods of isolation, often between fifteen and thirty minutes.

Timid-dominated

Some children in the crèche are particularly fearful and withdraw from their peers at the slightest provocation. However, after a prolonged period of isolation they often go in for bouts of very violent aggression, comparable in its nastiness with dominant-aggressive children. Despite the fact that they offer and appease like leaders, they still suffer the most hostility. In addition, these children constantly solicit the teachers' attention and are thus very demanding. They are much the same at four and five years old, though their fear, withdrawal and flight are now both less marked and less frequent. If they are at all jostled, threatened, upset or attacked, they nearly always burst into tears and just as before they can suddenly come out of their isolation and be extremely aggressive. These children find it very difficult to accept any new structures, like, for instance, changing school. They take two to three months to settle in but, once accepted into a group, they too can give the illusion of being leaders. When a conflict or competition develops or they are attacked or repulsed, then they quickly take on their true profile.

Withdrawn

Montagner has little to say about the few children who are totally withdrawn in the crèche. At four or five years old some are still like that; they seem without any goal, lean against a tree or wall, or just curl up on the ground. Should others try to interact with them, they fail to reply and isolate themselves even further. Even when they are older, they can spend the whole of the playtime without ever being seen to give or receive any solicitation.

MANNING'S STYLES OF HOSTILITY

Specific specialists

These children mainly practise what Manning has called specific hostility; manipulative hostility aimed at settling a dispute about property, precedence, roles or rules, etc. They use hostility only in situations which frustrate or annoy them, as a tool to get their own way, and the victim is often incidental. Most of them show little aggression and very little violence. They are outgoing, sell-assertive and friendly and often become popular leaders of the nursery class.

Harassment specialists or teasers

Other children specialize in harassment; unprovoked, 'out-of-the-blue' teasing. These ones are among the most hostile and violent children in the nursery. They are less friendly and less popular and often wander from table to table in the classroom disrupting activities. At times these children are imitated and followed, but they get very angry when opposed, and this leads to them being rejected and abandoned by their peers.

Manning *et al.* noticed two types of teasers. Some show a lot of initiative and are good at attracting other children to them. However, their games rarely last long because they fail to allow the other participants any scope. These children resemble Montagner's dominant-aggressive group. Other teasers are more like his dominated-aggressive ones; they tend to be withdrawn and for long periods do not interact at all. They do not appear to enjoy their isolation; these are not children who are happily absorbed in a task.

Manning *et al.* suggest that these various characteristics of teasers can best be understood if we see them as intent on proving to the world and to themselves that they can be someone, that they can do things of importance that have an effect on people. The outgoing ones, in particular, want to be the boss, to dictate the rules and to say how things should be. They like to be the leader and so play games in which they can exercise their power over others, such as Batman, Tarzan, witches or ghosts. The more withdrawn ones just seem to bear a 'grudge' against other children. Although some specific specialists share the aspirations of the outgoing teasers, with them it is tempered by the desire to be liked, to co-operate and to be friendly. 'To my mind teasers in general are so abnormally "hung-up" with a need to assert themselves that more normal attitudes go by the board.'

Games specialists

Manning *et al.* identified a third group of children who are normally friendly, but who go in for bouts of very violent aggression during games. These ones also spend a lot of time seeking the teacher's attention, demanding help, complaining when in difficulties and tending to make a great fuss when hurt. Their approaches to other children are also strange, sometimes teasing and often displaying or boasting. Although normally little trouble, these children have periods of wild excitement, usually in a game of some sort, when they appear to become 'out-of-control', and almost invariably manage to hurt someone. One four-year-old, for instance, found that when he was a robber, there was one little girl who was particularly frightened by his frequent invasions of the Wendy House. She always cowered into a corner and screamed. Soon he took to singling her out and became even more frightening and intimidating on each successive robbery. Eventually, she had to be rescued by a teacher.

These children, obviously, need to be the centre of attraction. They find that the easiest ways of attracting attention are to tease, to display as a monster, to splash water and so on. They do not seem to notice that they are actually hurting their friends. Manning *et al.* suggest that because they give so much of their thought to attracting others to them, they less often do things which would in fact make them interesting and enable them to achieve their goal.

The extent to which the observations of Montagner and Manning *et al.* complement each other is remarkable. Manning's specific specialists are equivalent to a combination of Montagner's leaders and the ones he saw who are dominated but, nevertheless, resemble leaders. Manning's teasers are a combination of Montagner's dominant- and dominated-aggressive children, and her games specialists resemble Montagner's timid-dominated group. A point by point comparison reveals no major points of disagreement.

IMPLICATIONS FOR MANAGEMENT IN NURSERY SCHOOLS

Aggressive children in nursery schools are difficult to manage. They tend to disrupt the peace of the nursery, to intimidate the other children and to promote fights in which other children may be hurt. Often, too, in nurseries containing even a few very aggressive children, good, co-operative, fantasy games cannot develop or flourish for long. Demanding children are irritating rather than disturbing, yet the teachers are worried that they do not fit in and their revengeful, teasing behaviour is often resented.

Hence teachers often try to contain and divert difficult children for the sake of the others, rather than attempt to understand their difficulties. Aggressive children, becoming too noisy and wild, are often diverted to quieter games, and sometimes this is successful if it leads to friendly contact with the teacher. But, frequently, such children become defiant and do not co-operate. Sometimes, however, there is an eager response that still fails because perhaps the teacher does not help enough. It is apparent that all these children do have a strong desire to play and be friendly but their other needs interfere with their ability to do so. Moreover, their past behaviour and their reputations have often antagonized other children. On one occasion a teacher suggested to a boy, who was teasing others in the Wendy House by throwing objects over the wall, that he go in and play a friendly game with them. Surprisingly, he responded eagerly and she led him into the Wendy House. But then she left; she did not stay to see that a game did get going. The boy stayed awkwardly at the sink, the others did not speak to him; later when they left, he followed them, still eager to play but they ignored him. Sometimes these children need to be helped to play in a friendly way.

Other examples of instructing in successful tactics also appear successful. Teachers will show a boy that another is more likely to play with him if he tries to persuade him rather than try to drag him into a game. With a girl who complains that no-one will play with her they will suggest how she could start to play in a way that would attract the attention and interest of the other children.

These suggestions may well be useful, but more important is the realization that these children could perhaps do well enough on their own if they felt differently about the situations; if other aims did not intrude. The same criticism may be made of behaviour modification which alters children's tactics (usually through rewards of attention and praise) but without modifying attitudes. Hence the teaching is likely to be short lived and situation bound, although sometimes the friendly outcomes of the new tactics lead to more lasting effects.

However, if teachers understand what it is that the child is trying to do, what are its aims and what is the point of the difficult and aggressive behaviour, then they might modify, at least to some extent, their grievances. They can also help them to meet some of their needs in ways likely to lead to friendly, rather than hostile, response. Thus an aggressive child, given tasks to help, teach and take care of other children or to help the teacher in nursery tasks, will gain kudos and admiration in ways he has never thought of. In one nursery the teacher asked a boy who hit some of the younger children habitually to look after the newcomers and to 'show them the ropes'. As a result his behaviour (at least as regards violent hostility) improved considerably. On another occasion the effect of two different teachers' treatment of the same boy was observed. The boy had made a large and dangerous sword with which he was threatening other children. The teacher reprimanded him repeatedly and, finally, removed the sword. Soon the boy was teasing other children and further reprimands increased this behaviour. Another teacher (the next day, with the same sword) admired the sword, called others to admire it too, and suggested useful things which might be done with the sword. The boy was enthusiastic and co-operative and soon was seen to be helping another to knock down a wall with the sword.

Similarly, an appreciation of the fact that the irritating and demanding child really wants to demonstrate that he is lovable may lead teachers to forego their natural and understandable behaviour in trying to make the child stop hanging around the cookery class and to become more independent. Alternatively, if they show spontaneous offers of interest, help and attention (not on demand), and help the child to make him/herself more interesting, the child will begin to feel more assured and will pester less.

Sometimes well-adjusted children, whose natural approach is friendly and approving, are more adept at coping with teasing, hostile children than are the teachers. One such boy was approached by another who had spent some time 'biting' others with a toy crocodile with very sharp teeth. Instead of showing fear and distress, he admired the crocodile and then suggested that it could pick up objects off the floor in its teeth. Soon a good game was going. Similarly, Rosalind, pestered by a boy who continuously knocked down her tower expressed pleasure and changed her game to a 'knocking down towers' game in which the teaser joined with pleasure. In all these cases the friendly approach evoked pleasure in the aggressive boy and his teasing did not reappear during that session. Finally, an example comes from a teacher's treatment, also of harassment. John was teasing Emma by interfering with and destroying her puzzle. The teacher watched for a while. She did not reprimand or demand an apology (which would probably have brought about a defiant confrontation) but, when the behaviour persisted, she approached the victim and sympathized, ignoring the aggressor. She started to help Emma reconstruct her puzzle. John watched, then offered a piece to help. The teacher professed delight, praised John's efforts and soon left the two doing the puzzle together. Again friendly treatment, ignoring and failing to react to the hostile malicious behaviour, can lead to friendly responses and perhaps an increasing appreciation of the pleasures of co-operative behaviour.

Children of three to five years old are still malleable and it is still possible to change their attitudes, and hence their tactics, unless they have become frustrated and disturbed seriously. Many seem to have some grievance and believe the world is against them. They express this in hostile aggression and in the desperate pursuit of needs in which they feel frustrated. Attempts to accommodate these needs, together with the persistent maintenance of a friendly, understanding approach rather than confrontation and disapproval, can often have surprising results. It requires sensitivity on the part of the teacher but, above all, it requires an appreciation of why the child is aggressive and of what he or she is trying to do.

REFERENCES

Manning, M., Heron, J. and Marshall, T. (1978) Styles of hostility and social interactions at nursery, at school and at home. An extended study of children, in L.A. Hersov, M. Berger and D. Shaffer (eds.) *Aggression and Anti-social Behaviour in Childhood and Adolescence*, Monograph of the Journal of Child Psychology and Psychiatry, Vol. 1, Oxford.

Montagner , H. (1978) *L'Enfant et la Communication*, Pernoud/Stock, Paris.

TOPICS FOR DISCUSSION

1. What evidence is adduced for the assertion that it is possible to characterize certain children as aggressive and hostile from as young as three years of age?
2 What is meant by the assertion that (aggressive) children 'could perhaps do well enough on their own if they felt differently about the situations'? (p.44).
3 What implicit explanations of young children's aggression are contained in the extract?

SUGGESTIONS FOR FURTHER READING

1. Olweus, D. (1980) Familial and temperamental determinants of aggressive behaviour in adolescent boys : a causal analysis, *Developmental Psychology*, Vol. 16, No. 6, pp. 644–60.

In this somewhat technical paper factors are identified in the personalities and the home backgrounds of two representative groups of thirteen- and sixteen-year-old boys that relate to their habitual levels of aggressive behaviour as rated by their peers. Four factors were found to contribute in an additive way to the development of an aggressive reaction pattern. They were (a) mother's negativism, (b) mother's permissiveness for aggression, (c) father's use of power-assertive methods and (d) boy's temperament. Of the four associated factors the first two were found to have the greatest causal impact; that is to say the degree to which the mother's basic attitude to the boy during his first four or five years of life was characterized as hostile, rejecting, cold and indifferent and the degree to which the mother was lax and permissive of the child's aggressive behaviour during those early years.

2. Farrington, D.P. (1978) The family backgrounds of aggressive youths, pp. 73–93, in L.A.Hersov, M. Berger and D. Shaffer (eds.) *Aggression and Anti-Social Behaviour in Childhood and Adolescence*, Pergamon Press, Oxford.

This report is part of the Cambridge Study in Delinquent Development, a prospective longitudinal survey of a sample of 411 males who were 22 years of age at the time of writing and who had first been contacted at the age of 8 years when they were in primary schools in a densely populated part of working-class London. Farrington attempts to relate measures of aggressiveness (derived from teachers' questionnaire ratings) to background factors in the pupils' lives. Thus he argues that low income and large-size family significantly predict whether a boy will become violent. The report contains a section on the backgrounds of aggressive boys which tends to confirm American studies that show aggression to be related to cold, harsh, disharmonious family environments.

3. Hoghughi, M. (1983) Schools and Delinquents, Ch. 7, pp. 127–42, in *The Delinquent:Directions for Social Control*, Burnett Books, London.

Hoghughi focuses on teachers and the educational system, viewing them as formal agents of social control predominantly concerned with 'preserving certain standards, enhancing children's potential towards the achievement and curbing yet other forms of behaviour, thought and feeling which are deemed unacceptable' (p.127). The author examines the evidence which points to the influence of the school in facilitating or impeding delinquency, tracing the complexity of influences (genetic endowment, basic intellectual potential and style, fundamentals of personality structure and degree of socialization) which the young child *brings with him* to school. A central argument that Hoghughi develops here is that, although teachers demonstrate ability to identify and predict troublesome and later delinquent behaviour, they seem to do little to either enable the parents to do a better job or, indeed, to take over the wider socialization of the child and adapt their educational methods to the needs of such children. The futility of simply exhorting parents to be 'interested' in their children is highlighted by the fact that a large number of the families of delinquents are so 'beset with problems that they are now more preoccupied with their own survival than the niceties of their children's social development' (p. 128). In short, poor parental interest is not 'the cause' of the child's school difficulties: rather, children from such homes frequently make demands on the time, patience and competence of teachers which cannot be met adequately.

The author charts the progress of the future delinquent child through the primary-school years, probably retarded scholastically in the basic subjects despite some variable attempts at remedial help and socially with a reputation for troublesome and wayward behaviour, cheekiness, bullying and the like. Thus, the writer affirms, the child's difficulties become part of the aura he bears, rather than reflections on the inadequacies of the school. Hoghughi identifies how the child's problems are compounded by the secondary-school environment: larger, more formal and impersonal, less homely and helpful, more alienating and easier to get lost in, demanding much greater self-direction, profoundly more influenced by peer-group relations.

A consideration of how schools might be improved for the unattached socially handicapped youngster who makes up the large bulk of the persistent delinquent population is taken up in the last section of the chapter. Hoghughi's suggestions centre round the importance of the school being seen *explicitly* not only as a place for scholastic education but as *the* prime place for social training and for the inculcation of the knowledge and values necessary for effective parenthood and citizenship.

Reading 4

A STUDY OF PUPILS SUSPENDED FROM SCHOOL

D. Galloway

INTRODUCTION

The ultimate disciplinary sanction available to headteachers is to suspend a pupil indefinitely from attendance at school. The less severe sanction of temporary exclusion involves sending the pupil home pending discussions with parents and an assurance that the school's rules and regulations will be respected. In cases of suspension the LEA has to decide what alternative education can be offered. In view of the immense amount of time which educational psychologists and administrators spend on pupils who have been suspended or excluded from school, it is surprising that there have been few systematic studies of the subject.

Information about suspended pupils is limited. York, Heron and Wolff (1972) reported a mean age in their Edinburgh sample of twelve years (range five to fifteen years). In contrast, Galloway (1980) found that 70 per cent of all the pupils concerned were in their last two years of compulsory education. The Edinburgh pupils were described as 'extra-

D. Galloway (1982) A study of pupils suspended from school, *British Journal of Educational Psychology*, Vol. 52, pp. 205–12.

ordinarily delinquent and aggressive', with a primary psychiatric diagnosis of 'conduct' or 'mixed' disorder in the majority of cases. In contrast, Longworth-Dames (1977) obtained no significant differences when he used Cattell's (1975) High School Personality Inventory to compare the personality characteristics of a small sample of suspended secondary-school pupils with 'normal' control pupils. The suspended pupils did, however, obtain significantly higher scores on the Bristol Social Adjustment Guide (Stott, 1963). Longworth-Dames suggested that the suspended pupils might be 'behaving in a very socially precise way to maintain their images in their subculture'. This sociological view contrasts with the evidence on child and family psychopathology in the Edinburgh study.

There is evidence that suspended pupils are unevenly distributed between schools, at least in some LEAs. Grunsell (1979) found that five of fourteen secondary schools in 'Baxbridge' accounted for 60 per cent of all suspensions. Galloway (1976, 1980) also noted major differences between schools, and reported a tendency toward high suspension rates in schools which on secondary reorganization had incorporated a selective school, though this was by no means an invariable relationship. He also found no significant relationship between suspension rates and structural variables, such as size, or intake variables, such as social class.

The principal aim of the present study was to investigate the psychological, social and educational characteristics of pupils suspended from Sheffield schools. Subsidiary aims were: (1)to obtain information on the events leading up to suspension; (2)to comment on the pupils' future educational needs; (3)to determine whether these needs could be met within existing resources.

METHODS

The sample consisted of pupils who: (1)had been formally suspended; (2)had been temporarily excluded, but were still out of school, with no immediate prospect of return, four weeks after their exclusion. Altogether fifty-eight pupils met the conditions of suspension or long-term exclusion. The pupils, their parents and their headteachers were interviewed. In addition, information about known delinquency was obtained from police records.

Response rate

The parents of six pupils declined to be interviewed. The parents of a further six were not interviewed as their children were in residential care at the time of their suspension or were placed in care very shortly afterwards. One child's suspension did not come to light until after the study was completed. This meant that the parents of forty-five pupils were interviewed. Including children in care, fifty-one pupils were available for interview, but four of these could not be contacted or declined to take part in the study. Information was obtained from the headteacher in the case of fifty-three pupils.

TABLE 4.1 Age and Sex of Pupils Suspended from School

Age range (years)	Boys	Girls	Total
Primary schools (5–11)	4	0	4
Middle schools year 4 and secondary schools year 1 (12–13)	1	0	1
Secondary schools year 2 (12–13)	1	2	3
Secondary schools year 3 (13–14)	6	6	12
Secondary schools year 4 (14–15)	5	4	9
Secondary schools year 5 (15–16)	24	4	28
Total	41	16	57

TABLE 4.2   Number of Pupils Suspended from Secondary Schools

No. of pupils suspended	No. of schools	Total no. of pupils
12	1	12
5	1	5
4	1	4
3	2	6
2	5	10
1	14	14
0	15	0
Total	39	51

Age, sex and school

The pupils' age and sex are shown in Table 4.1. It is seen that the twelve-month period was characterized by an extremely large rise in the number of boys suspended in their final year of compulsory education. Only 14 per cent were attending primary schools or their first year in a secondary school. One of the secondary-age pupils was suspended from a special school. This meant that fifty-one were attending a comprehensive school before suspension. Table 4.2 shows that five of the LEAs thirty-nine secondary schools suspended twenty-seven of the fifty-one comprehensive school pupils in the sample (53 per cent).

TABLE 4.3   Families of Pupils Suspended from School

Family	% of pupils ($n = 45$)
One or both parents dead	7
Parents separated/divorced	40
$\geq$ four children in family	38
Neither parent employed	22
Parents had received social security or similar benefit within last twelve months	42

TABLE 4.4   Medical History of Pupils Suspended from School as Reported by Parents

History	% of pupils ($n = 45$)
History of chronic illness	16
$\geq$ one sibling with history of chronic illness	24
History of serious illness or accident	69
$\geq$ one sibling has history of serious illness or accident	40
Illness or accident possibly associated with subsequent neuropathology	27

Interviews with parents
Family background
Although 51 per cent lived in pre-war council accommodation, suspended pupils were not confined to the most disadvantaged areas of the city. Thirty per cent of parents owned their own house. It was noted, however, that 34 per cent of the parents interviewed had been at their current address for less than one year. Details of family structure are shown in Table 4.3. The mean number of children per family, including the target pupil, was 3.5. There were no only children, but 20 per cent were the oldest in their family, and a further 20 per cent the youngest.

Medical history
Most of the children were reported to be in good health at the time of the interview. Nevertheless, data from medical histories in Table 4.4 show

that 69 per cent had a history of serious accidents or illnesses. This was not true of their siblings. 'Serious' was defined arbitrarily, as having required in-patient treatment. Chronic illness was defined as any illness which caused discomfort several times in the course of the year and which required medical attention. Examples were bronchitis or asthma. An important minority of the pupils had experienced illnesses or accidents with the possibility of subsequent neuropathology. Examples were head injuries following road traffic accidents, and meningitis with associated convulsions.

Poor health was a frequent characteristic of the pupils' parents: of the parents interviewed, 49 per cent of the mothers and 24 per cent of the fathers had a history of chronic illness. Evidence of psychiatric disorder was obtained from a health questionnaire (Rutter, Tizard and Whitmore, 1970) and from parents' reports at interview. The health questionnaire was completed by thirty-six mothers, but by only fifteen fathers. A high score on this questionnaire is known to be a fairly reliable predictor of psychiatric disorder. The number of parents who scored above criterion on the health questionnaire was combined with the number who did not score above criterion but reported psychiatric symptoms, mainly depression, for which they had received medical treatment. It was thus possible to calculate how many parents showed evidence of psychiatric ill health. The results are shown in Table 4.5.

TABLE 4.5   Evidence of Psychiatric Ill-health in Parents*

Parents	%of parents
Mothers ($n = 42$)	48
Fathers ($n = 32$)	22

*Score ≥ 7 on health questionnaire, and/or psychiatric symptoms and medical treatment reported at interview

Involvement with social-work agencies and police

Schools were not alone in their concern about the suspended pupils. Social-work agencies outside the LEA had statutory or voluntary responsibility for 49 per cent of them. This involvement pre-dated their suspension. Twenty-four per cent of the pupils had been in care at some time in their lives, but only 18 per cent had one or more siblings who had been in care. If we include the pupils whose parents were not interviewed because they were already in care, 30 per cent of the original sample of fifty-seven pupils had been, or were currently, in care.

Police records showed that 66 per cent of the boys and 87 per cent of the girls were known to have committed offences. At the time of interview, 34 per cent of the boys but only 13 per cent (i.e. two) of the girls were currently, or had been in the past, the subject of a supervision order.

Social and educational adjustment

Truancy, defined as absence without parental knowledge or consent, was reported by the parents of 78 per cent of the pupils. According to parents, only 11 per cent expressed concern at home about their educational progress, but parents of 50 per cent of pupils commented that their children were bored at school and 48 per cent mentioned extreme dislike of one particular subject. The most frequently mentioned subject was physical education (PE) (18 per cent), followed by maths (9 per cent), religious education and science (7 per cent each).

It was clear from parents' comments in the interviews that by no means all the children presented problems at home as well as at school. This impression was supported when parents completed the Rutter (A2) Behaviour Questionnaire (Rutter, Tizard and Whitmore, 1970). This parents' questionnaire was developed as a screening device to identify children showing signs of 'psychiatric disorder'. It distinguishes 'conduct', 'neurotic' and 'mixed' disorders. Details are given in Table 4.6.

Interviews with pupils

Intelligence and reading ability

Except when independent information was available, a brief psychometric assessment was carried out, by using the vocabulary and similarities subtests from the WISC–R (Wechsler, 1974). Schonell's Graded Word Reading Test (Schonell and Goodacre, 1974) was also administered. The results suggested that the pupils studied might experience considerable scholastic difficulties at school (Table 4.7). Ten pupils obtained an IQ below 70; the highest was 109.

Pupils' perceptions of school

This part of the interview was semi-structured, and covered a wide range of pupils' social and educational experiences at school. The pupils were by no means undiscriminating in their attitudes toward teachers: 85 per cent expressed liking for at least some of their teachers. With 32 per cent, however, there was evidence in the interview of a major clash with one particular teacher. An interesting point which emerged from accounts of the incident which led to their suspension was that many pupils claimed it had escalated from something relatively minor. A confrontation between a pupil and his or her subject teacher could develop into a confrontation with the year tutor, deputy head and, ultimately, with the headteacher. At interview, 51 per cent of pupils claimed to feel pleased, or at least indifferent, about their suspension. The implication was that these pupils saw suspension as legitimizing their removal from an unsatisfactory situation.

Interviews with teachers

The interview was with the head and/or with his or her nominee who knew the pupil.

Attendance and behaviour at previous school

Two-thirds of the pupils had entered the school from which they were suspended as an ordinary transfer from infant to junior school or primary to secondary school. Only 11 per cent were known to have had a poor attendance record at their previous schools and 21 per cent a record of unsatisfactory behaviour. Several teachers did, however, make the point that these results would be underestimates due to incomplete record keeping at other schools.

Behaviour at school from which suspended

Almost all the pupils (92 per cent) had been in trouble at school before their suspension and 46 per cent were specifically mentioned as having an undesirable influence on other pupils. Teachers believed that only 64 per cent had truanted regularly: a lower proportion than reported by parents. Before the event that precipitated suspension, 72 per cent of the boys and 39 per cent of the girls had received corporal punishment. A minority of 28 per cent of pupils had presented problems only with male teachers or only with female teachers.

TABLE 4.6   Pupils at Risk of 'Psychiatric Disorder' on Basis of Parents' Responses on Rutter (A2) Behaviour Questionnaire

Disorder	% of pupils suspended from school ($n = 42$)
Neurotic	17
Conduct	26
Mixed	2
Total scoring above criterion	45

Teachers' estimates of intelligence and attainments

Most of the teachers interviewed were able to make an informal assessment of the pupil's intelligence and educational attainments. The results are shown in Table 4.8. They should be compared with the results of psychometric assessment in Table 4.7.

TABLE 4.7 Intelligence of Pupils Suspended from School and Prevalence of Reading Backwardness

% of pupils with RA $\geq$ 3 years below CA ($n = 46$)	67
% of pupils with RA $\geq$ 2 years below CA ($n = 46$)	76
Mean verbal scale IQ ($n = 47$)	82
% of pupils with verbal scale IQ $\leq$ 70	21.3
71–85	38.3
86–100	34.0
101–110	6.4

TABLE 4.8 Teachers' Estimates of Intelligence and Attainments

	% of suspended pupils in each category ($n = 49$)				
	Excellent	Above average	Average	Below average	Very poor
Intelligence	0	10	53	35	2
Educational attainments	0	4	20	51	25

TABLE 4.9 Subsequent Education of Pupils Suspended from School

	Outcome	No. of pupils ($n = 57$)
Fifth-year secondary-school pupils	Education no longer compulsory, because pupil reached school leaving age	23
	Home tuition	2
	Transfer to another school	2
	Return to school from which suspended	1
All other age-groups	Transfer to another ordinary school	7
	Return to school from which suspended	4
	Transfer to special school	10
	Transfer to special centre	5
	Over school leaving age, or placed in custodial care	2
	Not known	1

Subsequent education

The subsequent education of the sample pupils is shown in Table 4.9. With only five exceptions, the fifth-year secondary-school pupils remained out of school until they reached the legal school-leaving age. The mean period without formal education for the fifth-year pupils was ten weeks. For the remainder it was eight weeks. The suspending schools provided only four pupils with work to complete while they were out of school.

DISCUSSION

In Sheffield, suspension occurs far more frequently from secondary schools than from primary schools. It is not clear that this is because deviant behaviour of the 'conduct disorder' type becomes more frequent in adolescence (Rutter *et al.*, 1976). A more likely explanation lies in the greater availability of special school places for younger pupils. Severely disruptive primary-school children are often transferred to a special school for maladjusted pupils before suspension becomes necessary. This becomes increasingly difficult to arrange as pupils get older.

Family circumstances of suspended pupils were frequently stressful, and in at least two respects they appeared more vulnerable than their siblings. They were more likely to have suffered a serious illness or accident, sometimes with the possibility of subsequent neuropathology, and they were more likely to have been in care. The evidence does not justify any statement about cause and effect. It is possible that both the medical history and reception into care could have been associated with the same factors, constitutional or environmental, that led to disciplinary breakdown at school. On the other hand, the medical history and disruption of family life through reception into care could have caused increased vulnerability to disruptive behaviour at school.

At school they were also vulnerable by reason of their generally low intelligence and severe backwardness in reading. It was clear that many of them would have great difficulty in following the ordinary curriculum without special help. Such help was not always available. Some schools, for example, concentrated remedial teaching provision in the first three year groups, and made no special provision for older pupils. On the whole, headteachers recognized the pupils' educational backwardness, but not their low intelligence. The possibility that these pupils' disruptive behaviour might have reflected frustration, or apathy, at failure to cope with the school's curriculum was not always acknowledged.

Yet evidence about the pupils and their families must be assessed alongside the fact that 53 per cent of the secondary-age pupils come from four of the LEAs thirty-nine secondary schools. Elsewhere it is shown that high suspension rates are not associated with any easily identified set of catchment-area variables (Galloway, 1976, 1980; Galloway, Martin and Wilcox, 1982). It appears, for example, that neither social class nor the prevalence of socio-economic disadvantage are reliable predictors of suspension rates in Sheffield. Four of the five secondary schools with three or more pupils in the present study had incorporated a selective school when secondary schools were reorganized into a selective system. This was also true, however, of two schools with exceptionally low exclusion and suspension rates. A further study (Galloway *et al.*, 1982) identifies some of the internal characteristics of schools with exceptionally high and exceptionally low exclusion or suspension rates.

On the present evidence, pupils 'at risk' of suspension have educational, and possibly constitutional, problems which would cause concern at any school. Nevertheless, it appears that these problems only lead to suspension in a small minority of schools. Knowledge of policy in other secondary schools in the LEA suggested that schools with high exclusion and suspension rates sometimes resorted to this sanction for disciplinary offences which other schools would have dealt with internally. However, the evidence does not permit firm conclusions.

Most forms of clinical treatment have a poor prognosis with children and adolescents who display disruptive 'acting out' behaviour. It is suggested that both advisory and treatment services should focus on the social mores and educational curriculum of the school as well as on the individual pupil. This view receives indirect support from recent interest in the school's influence over its pupils' behaviour and attainments (Rutter *et al.*, 1979).

REFERENCES

Cattell, R.B. (1975) *Handbook for the Jr.–Sr. High School Personality Question-naire*, Institute for Personality and Ability Testing, Champaign, Illinois.

Galloway, D. (1976) Size of school, socio-economic hardship, suspension rates and persistent unauthorised absence from school, *British Journal of Education and Psychology*, Vol. 46, pp. 40–7.

Galloway, D. (1980) Exclusion and suspension from school, *Trends in Education 1980/2*, pp. 33–38.

Galloway, D., Martin, R. and Wilcox, B. (1982) Persistent absence from school: the predictive power of school and community variables, *Educational Research*, Vol. 24, No. 3, pp. 188–96.

Galloway, D., Ball, C., Blomfield, D. and Seyd, R. (1982) *Schools and Disruptive Pupils*, Longman, London.

Grunsell, R. (1979) Suspensions and the sin-bin boom, *Where*, pp. 307–309.

Longworth-Dames, S. M. (1977) The relationship of personality and behaviour to school exclusion, *Educational Review*, Vol. 29, pp. 163–77

Rutter, M., Tizard, J. and Whitmore, K. (1970) *Education, Health and Behaviour*, Longman, London.

Rutter, M., Graham, P., Chadwick, O. F. D. and Yule, W. (1976) Adolescent turmoil: fact for fiction, *Journal of Child Psychology and Psychiatry*, Vol. 17, pp. 35–56.

Rutter, M., Maughan, B., Mortimore, P. and Ouston, J. (1979) *Fifteen Thousand Hours: Secondary Schools and their Effects on Children*, Open Books, London.

Schonell, F.J. and Goodacre, E. (1974) *The Psychology and Teaching of Reading* (5th edn), Oliver and Boyd, Edinburgh.

Stott, D.H. (1963) *The Social Adjustment of Children* (2nd edn), University of London Press.

Wechsler, D. (1974) *Wechsler Intelligence Test for Children: Revised Manual*, Psychological Corporation, New York.

York, R., Heron, J.M. and Wolff, S. (1972) Exclusion from school, *Journal of Child Psychology and Psychiatry*, Vol. 13, pp. 259–66.

TOPICS FOR DISCUSSION

1. Discuss the implications of the finding that only 11 per cent of the suspended pupils were known to have had poor attendance records at their primary schools.

2. What can be deduced from the finding that 53 per cent of the suspended pupils came from four out the LEAs thirty-nine comprehensive schools?

3. Looking at Tables 4.7 and 4.8 (p. 55), how can one account for the fact that teachers assessed more accurately the educational attainment of suspended pupils than their intelligence?

SUGGESTIONS FOR FURTHER READING

1. Croll, P. and Moses, D. (1985) *One in Five: the Assessment and Incidence of Special Educational Needs*, Routledge & Kegan Paul, London, pp. 135–46.

This section of the study is concerned with an analysis of learning and behaviour problems of some fifty-three primary-school children. *Inter alia*, the authors report that many children with learning difficulties also have behavioural problems. They distinguish between pupils with behaviour problems which present as classroom indiscipline and those whose behaviour problems do not disrupt procedures and organizations. Table 10.3 (p. 140) is worthy of careful examination; differentiation between types of classroom behaviour and classification of pupils by learning and/or behavioural difficulties can be seen. A group of children who surprise their teachers by an unexpectedly high performance on tests of non-verbal reasoning despite exhibiting behaviour patterns typical of slow learners is identified in the final subsection of the reading (pp. 144–6).

2. Reid, K. (1985) *Truancy and School Absenteeism*, Hodder & Stoughton, London, pp. 64–7.

This is the most up-to-date account of truancy and school absenteeism currently available. There is little specific research into the relationship between absenteeism and school behaviour. *Inter alia*, Reid reports his own study conducted in secondary schools in South Wales which shows higher incidences of antisocial behaviour and disobedience in school among truants and absentees. He explores the theory that disruptive behaviour is related to truancy and persistent school absenteeism, citing evidence from interview data gathered in the south Wales study. The extract ends with some useful advice to practitioners who have to deal with disruptive pupils.

3. Chazan, M., Laing, A. F., Jones, J., Harper, G. C. and Bolton, J. (1983) Recognizing behaviour difficulties, in *Helping Young Children with Behavioural Difficulties: a Handbook*, pp. 8–15, Croom Helm, London.

The extract is a part of a text designed to help nursery-school teachers and others responsible for looking after groups of young children to deal constructively with any behaviour problems that they may encounter during the course of their day-to-day work. Guidance is provided on (a) identification of children who are especially in need of help, (b) finding out about the nature of the child's difficulties and (c) planning and initiating measures that are likely to lead to the better adjustment of the child in the group or classroom. In the extract the following questions are raised: What behaviour should be expected of children of this age? Which children are likely to need special attention because of their behaviour? This latter section deals with shy/withdrawn children, immature/dependent children, restless/overactive children and aggressive antisocial/destructive children.

Reading 5
THE VIOLENT SOLUTION
J. F. Schostak

In 1981 the nationwide street disturbances came as a 'surprise' to many, but such violence has a long history. Many, including senior government ministers, saw the root causes of the violence as a breakdown of traditional morality and, particularly, of traditional forms of school discipline. Almost incredibly, in the spring of 1982 a so-called 'riot' occurred in a primary school, St Saviours in Toxteth, where reportedly, the teachers lost control of the pupils. However, such eruptions by their infrequency may disguise rather than reveal the endemic and pervasive nature of violence in our society. Unlike deviance, violence has official, legalized and, indeed, heavily government-funded forms (organized violence in the form of military aims and actions). Similarly, from a research point of view at least, violence in schools cannot be defined

J. F. Schostak (1983) The violent solution, in *Maladjusted Schooling: Deviance, Social Control and Individuality in Secondary Schooling*, Falmer Press, London.

exclusively in terms of 'pupil violence'. Thus in February 1982 the European Court of Human Rights ruled that Britain was wrong to allow corporal punishment in schools if it is against the parents' wishes. On the other hand, there are pupil assaults against teachers which teacher unions are now monitoring. For example, the Leeds branch of the 'National Association of Schoolmasters/Union of Women Teachers, reports 73 recorded assaults on staff by pupils during the school year 1981–2, and 178 recorded incidents of abusive behaviour toward staff by pupils'. Schools are under pressure.

Schools are organized predominantly to perpetuate inequality. The extensive system of examinations separates winners from losers; the state and independent schools separate the upper and lower classes. Research has shown how social-class bias, sex bias and racial discrimination are endemic in the school system. Schools are not organized to bring change. In a democratic society they are not even organized to give pupils the experience of democratic control over their lives.

The comprehensive system was an innovation that did not seriously make fundamental changes to education. All the old evils of streaming, covertly or overtly, continued to exist; social mixing was minimal; the success of such schools progressively depended on the extent to which they could send one or two of their pupils to Oxbridge and others to universities who would not otherwise have had a chance under the tripartite system of secondary modern, grammar school and technical school. But this cannot be a serious criterion of success for the thousands who did not reach such heights.

When headmasters do seriously try to bring about change they become political targets. If such headmasters also are inept or brash politically they are likely to be ousted from their schools, as seems to have been the case with Risinghill and Tyndale. The American experience of innovators also seems to be primarily negative. Teachers who try to bring about less authoritarian styles of teaching, unless they are very skilful, appear to fall foul of the traditional expectations of both pupils and colleagues of what a teacher ought to be. Sharpe and Green (1975) have also argued that progressive techniques introduced into primary schools are shaped by the economic power structures outside the school. It would seem that significant change is unlikely, and if it occurs is rare. On this theme Jules Henry (1971) has written:

A bureaucracy is a hierarchically organized institution whose purpose is to carry out certain limited functions. Thus a school system, the army, a university, the government, all are bureaucracies. It is common knowledge, however, that bureaucracies have three functions, rather than one. Although the first is ostensibly to carry out the tasks for which they were established, the definition of roles and the routinization of procedures in bureaucracies brings it about that an important function of the organization becomes that of preventing anything within it from changing. Even small change might make it necessary for the entire organization to change because each part is so interlocked with every other, that to alter any procedure in a bureaucracy without changing the rest is often like trying to increase the height of one wall of a house without modifying its entire configuration. A third function of a bureaucracy is to perpetuate itself, to prevent itself from disappearing. Given the functions of preventing internal change and struggling to survive, bureaucracies tend to devote much of their time to activities that will prevent change.

As Henry points out, all are vulnerable within the large bureaucracy which is overlooked and supervised by bureaucrats in other bureaucracies. Those who deviate from the expected are likely to be punished in some way, whether they be headmaster, teachers or pupils.

Is it not possible that through the violent assertion of individual will, constructive change may take place? Is it not possible that individuals may co-operate violently to end inequality? If change is desired and felt to be necessary, and if change is not brought about by the authorities willingly, then force becomes a compelling and rational solution. It would seem that a strong argument can and in the past has been made to justify political violence. To right injustices, violence may be necessary if the injustices are maintained wantomly and through force entrenched in the institutions of a society. However, much violence does not have such a nature and may be entirely negative in its personal and social effects.

Interpretation of violent acts

Political action forms a context for interpretation of individual actions. Individual actions may be interpreted as novel, conformist or deviant and criminally deviant according to whether they further or militate against the prevailing order. In a violent situation the individuals take sides. An action may be interpreted as being for a 'proper reason' or 'for the hell of it'. During the 1981 'riots' some black boys said:

Ray   Some kids just like goin' for the fightin'.
Frankie   Yeah.
Ray   That's all they like.
Alex   They're just usin' it as an excuse to go out an' fight an' loot.

J.F.S.   Mm.
Alex   But some people are fightin' for a proper reason.
Ray   Yeah.

The proper reason, it was felt, included the fight against alleged police harassment, unemployment, poor living conditions, lack of money and opportunity to acquire the better things of life and a decent quality of life. But whether those who fight are 'fighting for a proper reason' or are fighters and looters, the effect is the same:

> *Dave*   You got to fink there's a great atmosphere there to burn, fight, loot, 'cos they've seen it 'appen before an' all it takes is one person to kick something an' make a sound an' that's it. They all start. [He continues on the same theme later] I mean youngsters nowadays ... nineteen year olds. They're easy to wind up, aren't they, you can really wind someone up so easy. An' all it takes is a lot of little kids to go an' say 'Go on smash that'. Or 'You're frightened' or something, an' they do it. I mean all the little kids jump in there an' get all the stuff don't they? [And finally] I mean it's a natural mutual feeling now, isn't it, if you can nick something, nick it without gettin' caught. It's quite natural.

Dave has begun to analyse his experiences of the 'riots' in which he has participated. He takes a view very different from Alex who considered there were 'proper' and by implication 'improper' reasons for fighting in the streets at that time. Dave is more interested in the thrill. The 'great atmosphere'.

Dave is a natural leader, a big lad of fifteen years who has been 'expelled' from three secondary schools, with time spent in a detention centre before coming to Slumptown Comprehensive. He likes his new school because 'you know where you are'. He likes its emphasis on strong discipline. According to Dave 'One machine gun up the end of the road would've stopped all riots everywhere.' He is enthusiastic about the violent solution to end violence. He did not like his previous schools because teachers were too soft. According to Dave, if the teachers and the police are hard they will keep him under control and so he will not get into any more trouble; at least, for most of the time.

Dave, in his interpretations of violent acts, does not typically use a political frame of reference. His frame of reference is 'a great atmosphere' that enables one person to 'wind up' another. The whole atmosphere leads to a 'natural mutual feeling' which makes stealing seem natural. The atmosphere is permeated with feelings of excitement. To lead an exciting life adds to one's reputation and fuels the imagination.

Eddy, for example, now a sixth former told me of the time when he was against his school and was 'soccer hooligan'. He loved the excitement that football gave. Wherever the team went, Eddy would go, and he went to 'hit out at the opposite number'. He describes meeting 'a lad from Chelsea who 'ad half of his left hand missin'. And his bald head, he was a black wasn't he, a coloured fellow, and he's got lines running all over across the back of this and he said it was bricks and bottles broke 'is head open.' He described the awe which he felt for this lad at the time, he 'looked up to him'. To have such scars was 'a very great honour'. Why? 'To me then it seemed like scars of experience. He had more experience . . . had more experience. I mean . . . meet after the pub, it'd all be pretty excitin'. Everyone was after a bit of excitement then. And I thought I'd like to 'ave the excitement and the scars to prove I 'ad, I'd led an excitin' life.'

Eddy has 'calmed down a bit now.' It was his uncle, now in his twenties, who introduced Eddy to all the football but he too has calmed down. He has married. As Thrasher (1927) has noted, the gang is largely an adolescent phenomenon and marriage its greatest threat. But Eddy does not appear to be merely emulating his uncle. He is also reflecting 'I think I can feel what he feels. Feel a lot better. I feel wiser. Calmed down in school. And like you were saying about the system either beat it or use it and there's no way you're gonna beat it. It's not us who made the system but we need it to get through things together. And that's why I feel a lot better for that. And that's why I'm back in the sixth form now, to get on a bit better.' He's hoping to 'squeeze into an apprenticeship'. He is not academically successful but now wants to try to get what he can out of the system. Eddy is, at least for the time being, trying on the attitude of the 'clever' pupils, the 'ones who wanna work'. He realizes that the 'system' can be used to get what he wants. However, he realizes also that the chances of getting an apprenticeship are slim. What if he fails? His answer is that he'd 'like to be one of the bosses'. He has the possibility of joining a family business. It would seem, like the prodigal son, he is returning to the fold. Eddy has taken on a different frame of reference which he now uses to reinterpret his previous experiences as a soccer hooligan. This alternative frame of reference provides him with feelings of 'calmness' since there is less conflict with the dominant 'system' as he now aspires to be a 'boss' within that system. From the point of view of this alternative frame which embraces the school-approved social roles, system of production and career structures, his previous violent self at best seems immature, at worst appears like madness. From the point of view of the school-approved frame of reference, one sixth-form girl described her daily experience 'It's got worse since we've been here. I live in a really rough part now ... It's terrible, the gangs there every night. We can't sleep. They, they're always tryin' to let our dogs out ... They, they set fire to rabbits an' everythin'. They've stolen my brother's rabbit, I don't know how many times but he finds it ... There's nothing you can do about them.' There was a sense of hopelessness in her voice. She had no comprehension of the acts of those around her.

It is not easy for one person using one frame of reference to communicate with another person using an alternative frame of reference. Moreover, it is difficult for each to see that frequently they draw on a common fund of cultural images. We will see this to be so if we move now to the dramatic context which allows different people to interpret and enact cultural images in different ways.

Dramatic context for interpretation and enactment of violent episodes

If we start from Toch's view of violence being at least a two-man game, 'the fight' may be analysed as an example of a violent social drama. The fight can be seen to have the function of creating a dramatic unity out of previously unrelated individuals. It may produce in its wake a new social order or reinforce existing social orders.

Taylor is a principal character in many fights. He has a hatred of school, truants frequently, walking in and out of school when he feels like it:

Taylor [Teachers] make me feel terrible like, make me feel stupid 'cos they're callin' me all names.
J.F.S. Yeah.
Taylor An' all the class start callin' out then.
J.F.S. So the other kids do it too? As soon as the teacher does it ....
Taylor Soon as the teacher says it.
J.F.S. Yeah.
Taylor It's them that start it.
J.F.S. Yeah ... Why do you think the teacher does it?
Taylor I don't know ... it's just that they don't like me and I don't like them.

Taylor, after the interview, asked to hear the tape recording I had made. He repeated frequently, 'I sound just like a little girl.' He was small, slender and had a high-pitched squeaky voice. In many interviews I heard explanations as to why a particular pupil was violent attributed to 'he thinks he's big'. It seems to me there is a need or a desire to grow big, or seem big in the eyes of the other, that is, to grow in stature. Willis (1977) has written on the role of masculine violence in the social world of 'the lads' that:

> It should be noted that despite its destructiveness, antisocial nature and apparent irrationality violence is not completely random, or in any sense the absolute overthrow of social order. Even when directed at outside groups (and thereby, of course, helping to define an 'in-group') one of the most important aspects of violence is precisely its social meaning within 'the lads' own culture. It marks the last move in, and final validation of, the informal status system. It regulates a kind of 'honour' — displaced, distorted or whatever. The fight is the moment when you are fully tested in the alternative culture.

The images of violence, however, that Taylor revels in are not alternative to 'straight' culture but are embedded in and nurtured by whatever may be meant by British, European, Western or world culture. These are the images of the hero, the righteous war (as in the case of the recent Falklands 'war'), the right of the state to enforce its laws and the images of the relatively powerful taking from the relatively powerless. In his day-to-day life Taylor reproduces the forms of violence on which a violent society thrives.

One of the deputy heads talked of Taylor's fighting prowess and the role fighting plays in his social relations:

> He had five fights in the week we're away (at the school's outward bounds centre). Not always because he was ... uh ... arguing with somebody but he would interfere when two other people were arguing and decide which side he was on and then resolve the argument between the two others by fighting the one whose side he wasn't on. An' ... he got really vicious actually ... and we had to drag him off on one occasion and sit him in the bus for ten minutes and calm him down ... For example, he arrived a day late ... he didn't come the day we went. Uh, somebody drove him up the second day ... and within an hour of arriving he had fought every boy in the group ... except one who refused to fight and ran off home. You know, I mean, it was absolutely incredible. He just had to demonstrate he was cock of the group. And havin' arrived late it was the only way he could do it 'cos they'd already set up their pecking order.

Through his fighting Taylor appears to find stature within a group.

Walking home with some pupils I noticed Taylor's name written in large letters sprawling across the entire side of a house. The pupils with me assured me it was the Taylor I knew. Taylor, they said, is famous. To be famous in a community is to grow big in the eyes of the street. During the 1981 street disturbances Taylor was one of the first to know what was happening and where it was rumoured to happen next. He came into school excited. He was playing a central part in the impact of the riots on the school's fantasy life. He was called in to see a deputy head and questioned concerning the likelihood of coming riots. The school passed on whatever information it received from any source to the police. Taylor believed there would be a major riot, he believed eventually that soldiers would be needed to patrol the streets. The lads would be taking over, imposing a new social order. The streets would become 'no-go' areas for the police, only the army with tanks would be able to cope. The street boys would grow big in the eyes of the public.

Taylor drew on the images of armed conflict currently available in our culture, taking the logic of playground fighting into the streets as a way of imposing a desired social order. And one night, there was the 'fight'. This was recounted by an adult, Harry.

Harry's father saw the barricades being put up by 'yobboes' in his road. He said. 'I'm not having this.' Harry, his brothers and his father began to dismantle the barricade. Some neighbours helped. 'The women were marvellous — they really belittled the yobboes. One of the yobboes yelled out as a reason for his actions, "I've got no fuckin' job." One woman replied, "If you 'ad a fuckin' job you'd faint."' The yobboes cleared off before the police came. Harry said, 'It's a law an' order thing here. People are very strong on it.'

On other nights in other areas the street disturbances were not so easily dampened. Darren Bailey was involved in one such incident, although it did not develop into a large disturbance; at most there were about 250 involved. For him the disturbances were not isolated incidents but extensions of everyday gang or 'mob' activities. The images he used in his descriptions were reminiscent of the cinematic love of 'car chases' and dramatic confrontations:

> on the first night, right, I was up there, right, an' there was about 30 people there right, you know ... There was this bizzie car [police car] which come burnin' round right, an' some bizzie fella come out lookin' dead 'ard right an' he was sayin' 'Come, let's move, come on. Start movin'.'
>
> No one'd move, right. Everyone was just standin' there for a laugh 'cos he was by 'imself. So 'e got back into his car, right. Then

everyone, you know, started shoutin' an' everythin'. Then the car starts goin' back an' as the car was goin' back someone just 'ad, 'ad a petrol bomb an' thrown it, an' it landed in front of 'im right. An' about five minutes later, right, seen about ... about two meaties, you know, couple of others, you know, couple of other cars come burnin' round the corner. An' they all jumped out, started leggin everyone, right, an' then that was it in the end, of the first night. An' everyone said 'Come on, we're gonna come back 'ere tomorrow. Everyone meet down 'ere.'

[On the second night there were] I'd say about 200 odd people there, 250 right, an' they were all there, right ... the bizzies provoked everyone, that's all I can say. [If] the bizzies weren't there, there wouldn't have been no so called little riot at all. Everythin' would be just all passed on. But the bizzies come down there, right, decided to make somethin' of it, you know, the local police tried to make somethin' of it. When they couldn't 'andle it, well they called other officers in from all over the place. They come down. Then loads of people started gatherin'. They 'eard all about it. Then you got all little crews [gangs] from all over the place, down Edgeplace, all up Topside – an' all of them, all of them comin' over in crews to 'ave a go with the bizzies, to get their own back at them.

The bizzies come down in the riot shields goin' 'Come on, come on', 'cos I 'eard them shoutin' see, 'Come on, get us', an' all this. They were not local bizzies. An' when I got dragged in I could tell from the accent. They didn't even know the way to the police station ... there was just loads of fightin' an' everythin' goin' on, loads of stone throwing' — couple of bizzies gettin' caned like, couple of kids gettin' caned by bizzies. Oh ... the bizzies were really givin' it to them, like they was givin' them plenty with all the sticks an' everythin' they 'ave.

Darren was charged by the police for his involvement in the riot. Darren's description is reminiscent of his earlier description of the first-year mobs fighting in the playground in order to determine the new leaders and new gangs. In his interpretation of the riot he stated specifically that 'it wasn't a riot through hatin' bizzies.' He felt it was an act of police provocation which attracted the 'crews' who came to ''ave a go with the bizzies to get their own back at them.' Rather than hatred, there were scores to settle. For some, however, it was simply entertainment, a thrill, like watching television. Some disappointed girls told me how dozens of primary-school and first-year secondary-school children sat waiting for a rumoured riot to happen. They would chase all over town hoping to see a riot.

The 1981 riots were over by the start of the autumn term. Perhaps little like them will happen again for several years. Or at least, the smaller more frequent disturbances will be overlooked. The 'riot' as a persistent structure of Slumptown street life is ignored. Thus we are perennially surprised when the big ones occur. However, we may note the structural similarities between Darren's description of a riot (large enough to merit attention from national newspapers) and fights between rival schools as described by these fourth-year girls:

Sally   Only old Town Boys and Slumptown Comp. turned up.
Ann   Was there um any of you there, Jilly Jones was there as well. An' there was loads of our first and second years waitin' by the gate too scared to go 'ome because there was a big gang of old Town Boys. We 'ad to take them 'ome.
Sally   Rumours goin' round, there was rumours, a coupla months goin' round — all our girls were goin' to get raped by old Town Boys wasn't there?
Ann   Yeah. That was supposed to be true 'cos I asked some of the lads at old Town Boys . . . .
Julie   Then there was supposed to be a battle over that wasn't there?
Ann   Yeah.
Julie   [acting ''ard'] Just knock them down, when yer 'ard with yer mates, don't yer? [laughter]
Julie   Think yer 'ard with the gang. [laughter]
Ann   They're all 'ard at old Town Boys though aren't they?
Julie   Course they're all 'ard, they'd 'av to be tough, you know what I mean, an' you'd 'av to be tough in that school.
Ann I know.

The fights are exciting and eagerly awaited by these girls. I ask the reason for the fighting:

Ann   They're just fightin', it's just fightin'.
Sally   That's just it, it's good though isn't it, sometimes [laughs]
J.F.S.   No I mean . . .
Liz   There's all police all the police round our school.
Julie   There's all the police an' everythin'.
Liz   Waitin' when they come . . .
J.F.S.   Well, is it because you can't stand each other or . . .
Chorus   No.
Julie   No it's not that 'cos all the girls are mates . . .
Sally   Mates of old Town Boys.
Julie   Old Town Boys an' 'alf the lads 'ere are mates. But we just fight.

J.F.S. What, just for fun?

Chorus Yeah, fun.

Julie But old Town Boys'll start it. They'll say, 'Oh, we'll get Slumptown Comp. somehow . . .

Liz I think It's 'cos they have no, 'cos there's not any girls, you know in the school.

Ann That's why they're so jealous because we've got all the girls.

Sally That's why they fight ours.

There is no particular feeling of hatred involved, the fights are exciting and when a fight is rumoured to occur people turn up. The police seem a natural accompaniment. Going to a fight is much like going to a dance. It is an ongoing drama with fun and occasional tragedy to add spice:

Ann I was walkin' down an' then, the next minute, Oh there was seventeen New Town Boys lads that jumped us. One lad an' 'e's got a bad 'eart, an' e took an 'eart attack when they were batterin' 'im. An' the school didn't do nothin' about it.

J.F.S. This school?

Ann Yeah.

Sally They didn't do nothin'.

Ann They said they were gonna, 'cos I was there an' Jilly Jones was there, they said they was gonna take us into old Town's to identify them. An' they said. 'Well, then we're gonna need police patrol' to watch us, to watch the school, 'cos we'd get done over. But eh, we'd get jumped an'that. We just lucky they didn't go any further with it.

Gang organization, and people held together by complicity in crime or criminal acts of violence, is said to lie at the foundation of our civilization. Along this line of reasoning there is 'fraternal organization' in rebellion against the 'father', that is, youth in rebellion and jostling for dominance against authority. The energy of youth when it is in rebellion, occasionally overflows the confines of adult social order, bringing to the street youthful concerns.

Classroom violence

No clear assessment of the generality and frequency can be given. Teacher unions are beginning to collect information on reported incidents of assault or abuse against teachers. The Society of Teachers Opposed to Physical Punishment (STOP) brings to the public notice caning as a form of legalized assault. However, there is a variety of forms of unofficial assault and abuse against pupils, of the scale of which we have no knowledge. However, it is reasonable to say that underlying classroom control is a climate of threat which in some, perhaps most, classrooms results in expressions of violence or abuse, the frequency of which will depend on the individuals concerned. Teacher assault and abuse, however, tend to be rationalized and concealed. For example, I entered the deputy head's office to find a boy, Duane, 'on the carpet'. Duane had insulted a teacher, Mr Wills, obscenely in front of the class. As I entered the deputy head was trying to convince Duane that it was in his interests to apologize. Duane refused. The deputy head modified the demand to Duane 'retracting' his statement rather than apologizing. Duane had been in trouble frequently and currently was in trouble with the law. Further trouble would mean he would lose any possibility of getting an apprenticeship. Duane refused to retract his statement. 'I don't want to suspend you', said the deputy. 'Do you understand the difference between an apology and retracting a statement?' 'Sir, no.' The deputy explained, using the example of politicians in the House of Commons, 'If one politician uses hotly insulting language the Speaker would ask to have the statement withdrawn. There is no apology. You reserve the right to think it but acknowledge it wrong to state your thoughts aloud.' Duane said he now understood the difference but continued to refuse to retract his statement. The deputy then tried to get Duane to see that he was 'soon going to be a man, and a man can think things but also act in a way so as not to be rude. Would you like it if someone behaved to you in the way that you did to Mr Wills?' 'Sir, no.' 'Will you retract your statement?' 'Sir, no.' In frustration the deputy decided to postpone his decision to suspend Duane to give the boy time to think it over.

When the boy had left the room I asked the deputy why he had not suspended Duane. 'If I suspend him there will be a governors meeting and Wills will be called in front of the panel. It's well known that Wills strikes out at the kids and Duane will accuse him of doing just that. It could ruin his career.' The deputy did not approve of Wills' behaviour but thought Wills was a sufficiently good teacher not to harm him for a boy who was bad clearly. However, Duane had been told previously that if he got into further trouble he would definitely be suspended. The threat did not work. Duane was in a powerful position to hurt the career of a valuable, if not entirely respected, teacher.

The deputy had tried to give Duane a lesson in polite political duplicity: think one thing yet say another. He next tried to place the incident in the frame of reference of 'becoming a man'. He tried to use threats: suspension and losing a desired apprenticeship. The solution that 'worked' and satisfied both parties was this: 'You want to be suspended, don't you?'

'Sir, yes.' 'Well, then, in that case I won't do it. I'll give you work and detentions instead.'

The deputy thought the solution to be illogical yet satisfactory. Neither party lost face in the eyes of the other. It was a childish solution but one which befitted the childishness of the dispute. The daily drama between Wills and his pupils involved confrontations, threats and counter-threats. The relation between Wills and Duane was one of open opposition, in short, they hated each other's guts. Duane could accept punishment because that was in the nature of the drama. He could not accept apologizing or 'retracting' his abusive statement because that did not serve in the construction of his own identity and his perception of the identity of Wills. It was not a part of the dramatic context of interpretation and thus could not make sense in his own eyes or the eyes of his mates. The dramatic context which Wills used to enforce discipline, while working with the great majority, set the conditions for rebellion and abusive behaviour by indentifying roles in the drama, strategies and conflictual incidents.

In the classroom there is generally a climate of command which, if broken by pupils, will lead to a number of threats being carried out. Such threats may be experienced by many pupils as a violation of their desired freedoms of expression and action and, as a violation of their sense of security, their self-image and their sense of community with others. In short, certain kinds of teacher action may be experienced as abusive behaviour. For example, in my questionnaire, completed by approximately half the third year, only 6 per cent of boys and 8 per cent of girls said that teachers never shouted at them; 60 per cent of boys and 43 per cent of girls considered teachers never called them names. About 58 per cent of girls and 44 per cent of boys said teacher at least sometimes frightened them. Shouting is a form of abuse. How may education (that is, critical reflection on experience) take place in such a climate of fear?

The violent solution may seem irrational, dark, chaotic. But it may be the only rational solution left to an individual who feels abused. The violent solution is a course of action framed within a violent society, fuelled by violent images and violations of individuality. Indeed, there are many contexts for the interpretation, some official, some unofficial, of a particular act. School may be seen as an incubator for violent images and violations of individuality, and, indeed, of a healing sense of community. Such an effect may not be intentional, but organizational, impersonal demands step between the intention and the effect, acting as a distorting filter. To change the effect, the conditions of schooling require rational, reflective and critical reform. There is now at least a century of empirical evidence, of theory and of practice which supports the necessity for further reforms which will allow teachers and pupils to work together in a learning environment uninhibited by a climate of command and compulsion, impersonal authority and violations of the dignity, sense of individuality and community of individuals who happen to play the roles of teachers and pupils.

REFERENCES

Henry, J. (1971) *Essays on Education*, Penguin, Harmondsworth.
Sharpe, R. and Green, A. (1975) *Education and Social Control: a Study in Progressive Primary Education*, Routledge & Kegan Paul, London.
Thrasher, F.M. (1927) *The Gang: a Study of 1313 Gangs in Chicago*, University of Chicago Press.
Willis, P. (1977) *Learning to Labour*, Saxon House, Farnborough.

TOPICS FOR DISCUSSION

1. Discuss the author's contention (p. 60) that schools are organized pre-dominantly to perpetuate inequality.
2. On what grounds does the author argue that Taylor's violence is embedded in and nurtured by 'British, European, Western or world culture'? (p. 65).
3. Examine the details of the confrontation between Mr Wills and the pupil, Duane, and the suggestion that the dramatic context which the teacher used to enforce discipline set the conditions for rebellion and abusive behaviour.

SUGGESTIONS FOR FURTHER READING

1. Tomlinson, S. (1984) Minority groups in English conurbations, pp. 18–32, in P. Williams (ed.) *Special Education in Minority Communities*, Open University Press, Milton Keynes.
   The author deals with the special needs of minority children via three case studies: Ayub, a six-year-old of Turkish–Cypriot parentage, Winston, a child of West Indian origin, suspended from school for disruptive behaviour, and Zahia, the daughter of Muslim Pakistani parents.

2. Werthman, C. (1984) Delinquents in schools: a test for the legitimacy of authority, pp. 211 – 24, in M. Hammersley and P. Woods (eds.) *Life in School: the Sociology of Pupil Culture*, Open University Press, Milton Keynes.
   Werthman's analysis of North American high-school students eschews explanations of their behaviour couched in terms of the organizational structure of the school or the students' membership of particular social-class groups. Rather, he points to the contextual variability in their behaviour and the rational appraisals that particular students make of the situations in which they find themselves. The major focus of the analysis is on the teacher's distribution of grades and the behaviour of students in relation to their perceptions of the fairness or otherwise of the teacher's assessments. Both academically successful and less successful

students resorted to classroom deviance in certain classrooms depending on their appraisal of the correctness of teachers' judgements of their work.

3. Furlong, J.(1984) Black resistance in the liberal comprehensive, pp. 212 – 36, in S. Delamont (ed.) *Readings on the Interaction in the Classroom*, Methuen, London.

This is a study of seven black British boys in a London comprehensive school who constitute a regular problem for the school because of their verbal and physical confrontations with teachers. From the outside, Furlong suggests, it looks as though these students are engaged in a constant war of attrition with the staff. The author's interviews with them leads him to describe the theme and the form of their *culture of resistance* which revolves centrally around their concern to establish a reputation as a man. Furlong indentifies the difference in the meaning of 'hardness' and 'masculinity' that separates these black working-class boys from their white contemporaries. 'Hardness', he contends, relates more closely to 'style' and 'maturity' and affects all the central aspects of their lives: their dress, music, girlfriends and relations with the school.

Reading 6
TEACHERS' EXPECTATIONS AND ATTITUDES
and TEACHERS' ATTITUDES TO BEHAVIOUR
M. J. Taylor
TEACHERS' ATTITUDES TO ASIAN PUPILS' BEHAVIOUR
M. J. Taylor and S. Hegarty

The study which made people aware that teacher expectation could be an important factor in their child's performance was that by Rosenthal and Jacobson (1968) who claimed to have shown that manipulated teacher expectancies could become self-fulfilling prophecies. In their experiment they handed teachers lists of children, chosen at random, whom they said would make much or little school progress during the year. It appeared that at the end of this year they found the IQ scores of the younger, but not of the older, pupils matched their predictions. When reported the

M.J. Taylor (1981) Teachers' expectations and attitudes, Teachers' attitudes to behaviour, in *Caught Between: a Review of Research into the Education of Pupils of West Indian Origin*, NFER–Nelson, Windsor; M. J. Taylor and S. Hegarty (1985) Teachers' attitudes to Asian pupils' behaviour, in *The Best of Both Worlds? A Review of Research into the Education of Pupils of South Asian Origin*, NFER–Nelson, Windsor.

study as a whole provoked severe criticism and most attempts at repli-
cation in the USA failed. However, a considerable amount of research
evidence in the UK, including English longitudinal studies of streaming,
tended to support the conclusion that the interaction between the teacher
and pupil, especially the teacher's expectations of a pupil, are important
determinants of achievement. On the other hand, studies of different
design have shown that most teachers are not swayed by test scores which
run counter to the child's actual performance at school. Other studies of
the relation between teacher expectation and teacher behaviour show
marked differences between teachers, some of whom respond positively
to high achievers and some to low achievers, yet others showing no
tendency in either direction. Further light is shed on a likely explanation
by a study (Seaver, 1973) which demonstrated that if a teacher has taught
two children from the same family and the older child had been a good
student his/her expectations may well be favourable for the younger child
also, although this was not found to apply when two different teachers
taught the children, thus suggesting that there is a teacher expectancy
effect. As the situation exists it is probably not possible to replicate
studies undertaken in the USA since teachers are now generally aware of
these findings. Overall it may be said that, although the evidence points
toward a real effect on the child's performance by the expectations of his
teacher, the influence may possibly not be as direct or determining as
some of these studies have been taken as showing.

In fact, the situation with respect to pupils of West Indian origin is
rather more complex than this brief review has suggested. For as well as
the possible effects of teacher expectation in particular school situations
there is also the question of teachers' general attitudes to ethnic minority
pupils. Although much is often made of this it is perhaps not particularly
surprising to find that there has been comparatively little research on such
a delicate issue. One major research, however, which involved a national
sample of 510 teachers, 171 primary and 339 secondary, in 25 schools with
18–84 per cent ethnic-minority-group pupils revealed that teachers held
considerable and important differences of opinion about the various
ethnic minority groups. However, there was a high degree of consensus of
opinion concerning the academic and social behaviour of pupils of West
Indian origin. More than two-thirds of teachers in the sample expressed
agreement or disagreement on three items, thereby indicating unfavourable opinions of West Indians, with only very small percentages express-
ing the opposite point of view. Moreover, teachers appeared to be more
willing to make generalizations about West Indian pupils as a group, and

on the basis of comments made on the questionnaire the researcher concluded that there appeared to be 'large scale stereotyping of "West Indian" pupils'. This was also indicated by informal replies by heads and teachers concerning the achievement and occupational potential of West Indians. Similarly, Tomlinson (1979) interviewed 30 heads in connection with ESN–M assessment and found that they were prone to respond at length about West Indian pupils, but not Asian pupils, and to have generalized views about them. Heads had strong feelings that the learning process was slower for West Indian pupils, that they lacked long-term concentration and that they would tend to under achieve and be remedial.

Thus it is not possible to consider teacher expectation toward ethnic-minority-group pupils in general. What is needed is much more specific evidence about what kind of attitudes teachers have in particular toward pupils of West Indian origin and to what extent these attitudes are manifested in their behaviour to such pupils in the classroom. This is an area in which it is most difficult to disentangle cause and effect, for which comes first, behaviour or attitude? Another issue which a broad consideration of teacher expectation tends to overlook is that teachers are not just a uniform group but each teacher is an individual and teaches in his or her own style. This is the kind of reasoning that has led some researchers to make claims that, although there were 75 per cent West Indian children in one Manchester junior school, there were no significant teacher expectation effects. Moreover, surely it is correct to observe that, though there have certainly been many misclassifications of West Indian children who were adjusted poorly to the school situation as ESN, there have also been successful black pupils, many of whom, no doubt, have in the general run of things done better than their teachers might have expected.

Two black writers who provide somewhat anecdotal and descriptive evidence on the issue of teacher expectation would be certain to argue otherwise. Coard (1971), himself a teacher of ESN pupils, claimed that most black pupils who were being diagnosed as ESN were assessed incorrectly by their teachers who held biased views toward such pupils. He suggested that the teachers were biased in three ways: culturally, in so far as they misunderstood the linguistic differences between them and their pupils; socially, in as much as they were middle class and held different values and beliefs associated with their class; thirdly, in so far as they failed to appreciate the temporary emotional disturbance which such pupils were undergoing as a result of removal from the Caribbean to the UK. He further claimed that the attitude of the teacher could also affect the performance of the black child not only by his low expectation but also by open prejudice and patronization which he maintained were a frequent feature of interactions between teachers and black pupils.

Another study by a black researcher that involved some observation in multiracial schools in London (Giles, 1977) also tended to support the view of Coard that stereotyping was both subtle and overt. Giles made contact with fifteen out of twenty-one infant and junior schools in nine divisions of the ILEA and eight out of thirteen secondary schools, selected for their sizeable percentages of West Indian pupils, and interviewed headteachers, some teachers and two groups of black pupils about their perceptions of life in their schools. Giles avowedly started from the premise that teachers' attitudes and perceptions are crucial in the education of black children. And yet he found that most headteachers felt that 'since the same quality of education was available to both black and white children from working-class backgrounds if would not be valid or fair to infer a relationship between the racial composition of disadvantaged schools and poor achievement and performance among West Indian pupils as a selected group.' In his somewhat superficial description of the case study schools Giles noted a tremendous variety in their social and cultural environments and also in the major features of the heads' and teachers' perceptions. However, he made little attempt to draw comparisons between schools or to highlight the genuine concern and confusion which most of the heads and teachers seemed to express. The research and its conclusions have been thoroughly criticized by Jeffcoate (1977) and Kirp (1977). The latter points out that Giles seemed to have approached the research presuming teachers held discriminatory attitudes and having a ready-made conclusion and set of policy recommendations to fit this presupposition. Whereas he actually found that, in general, heads and teachers did not see that black children had any particular problems over and above their socially disadvantaged white peers. Hence they did not treat them differently on account of their colour. On the other hand, Giles himself argued that pupils of West Indian origin had both a different class and cultural orientation. However, he conceded that they were possibly less co-operative and more disrespectful. But he also claimed that teachers saw 'a disproportionately bigger margin of underachievement among West Indian girls than among the white girls, due to social rather than cultural factors'. Teachers also often cited the problem which black pupils experienced in learning to handle freedom and choice in a relatively permissive school atmosphere whilst often living in repressive home environments. This was particularly noticeable in comparison with the children who came from the fairly lax discipline of white working-class homes, hence causing a problem for teachers who were trying to operate two standards at the same time to take account of pupils' differing needs. Even these few observations, would, however, tend to suggest that teachers were indeed recognizing differences between black and white pupils and attempting to treat them appropriately. Yet, in general, they did not feel able to support a programme designed to address the special needs of West Indian students that would ignore similar needs among the indigenous white pupils who were also disadvantaged socially. Giles acknowledged this in the opening chapter of his book and also realized that

> 'no one policy statement regarding the goals for multi-cultural education could serve the needs of Britain or London as a whole since characteristics of different cultural and racial minorities vary from authority to authority and even within schools in some authorities. This situation makes study of multi-cultural education and recommendations for effective programmes an extremely complex and questionable endeavour if it were to be undertaken as a basis for policy recommendations for Britain as a whole.'

Yet he nevertheless went on to do just that: in the form of a black-studies programme.

Despite some obvious deficiencies in the study by Giles, it is important for indirectly highlighting the genuine confusion among teachers as to how to treat pupils of West Indian and other ethnic minority groups in relation to similarly socially disadvantaged white pupils. Yet this confusion is not new. Testimonies to it have been produced both by groups of teachers and individual teachers who pointed to both the sensitivity and uncertainty with which many teachers approached the difficulties of organizing school life and teaching in schools with varied ethnic compositions. The confusion, expressed simply, seems to be as to whether a black pupil is to be assimilated into the school so that he is seen primarily as an individual sharing a common humanity, but having his own particular needs; or, whether he is to be seen as different, one black child among a group of black children with a different culture, and who requires different treatment by virtue of his membership of the black group. The issue seems to amount to whether differences are to be ignored or accepted and accommodated but treated largely as if they were absent, or, on the other hand, acknowledged and distinguished in such a way as to highlight them. Such confusions have not been helped by changes in the policy orientation of different governments or by general lack of professional rationale. As long ago as 1973 there was a need to identify and investigate the features of successful multiracial schools so that these could be publicized more widely as examples of good practice.

Overall, the evidence on teacher expectation and attitudes does not really permit firm conclusions as to whether teacher expectations for black children are a determining influence on their school life and performance. While it is most likely that some teachers do have negative perceptions of and attitudes toward (some) black pupils, it would appear also that many teachers are sensitively and actively concerned to evolve a consistent and fair policy toward the treatment of their black pupils both in respect to continuity of school organization from year to year and in their daily interaction with children of West Indian origin in their classrooms.

Teachers' attitudes to behaviour

To judge by teachers' reports black pupils would appear to be much more deviant than whites. As with teachers' attitudes to language, however, it is difficult to disentangle cause and effect. Does poor behaviour lead to lower expectation for achievement, for example, or does low expectation lead to poor behaviour?

In the ILEA Literacy Survey (Mabey, 1980, 1981) teachers rated West Indian pupils aged eight years, and their parents, negatively. They thought only 25 per cent of the West Indians compared with 50 per cent of the indigenous pupils had good relations with other pupils, teachers and attitudes to school work. Similarly, they felt that only half of the West Indian parents were interested in their children's schools and they thought that only 3 per cent of the West Indian children came from culturally stimulating homes. More specifically in relation to behaviour, a study that looked at aspects of school life in relation to pupils and teachers found a consensus of opinion relating to the academic and social behaviour of West Indian pupils. Seventy-five per cent of the 171 primary teachers and 78 per cent of the 339 secondary teachers disagreed with the statements 'West Indian pupils are usually better behaved than English pupils' and 'West Indian pupils tend to raise the academic standard of this school'. West Indian pupils were similarly regarded unfavourably in relation to the correction of their behaviour: 57 per cent of primary- and 72 per cent of secondary-school teachers agreed with the statement 'West Indian pupils resent being reprimanded more than English pupils do.'

One important study that investigated behavioural deviance of 2,043 ten-year-old children in London (Rutter *et al.*, 1974) provides information on teachers' attitudes toward West Indian pupils' behaviour. The Rutter Behaviour Questionnaire, a reliable measure in which teachers are asked to rate a child in relation to twenty-six descriptions of behaviour, was employed. Forty-nine per cent of West Indian boys were judged by their teachers to be 'behaviourally deviant' according to the norms of this measure compared with 25 per cent of the English boys. Just over a third of West Indian girls were seen by their teachers as 'deviant' compared with only 13 per cent of English girls. Thus, a total of 41 per cent of the 354 black children in the study were judged deviant compared with 19 per cent of the 1,689 white children, a highly significant difference. Both boys and girls of West Indian origin were more often rated as restless, squirming, unable to settle, destructive, quarrelsome, not liked by other children, irritable, disobedient, telling lies, stealing, unresponsive, resentful and often bullying. In addition, black girls, but not boys, were likely to be judged solitary, miserable and fearful. It is also of interest to note that migration appeared to influence teachers' ratings of children as 'deviant' since 83 per cent of the children inaccurately categorized by birthplace were perceived as deviant compared with 30 per cent of those accurately classified. The researchers suggested that although the Rutter scale is meant as a screening devise the teachers may be looking at black children in biased or over-dramatic terms. Yet in a follow-up study when a number of 'deviant' children where studied intensively the clinical interviews indicated some excess of acting-out behaviour in black children. Also to a large extent black and white parents' descriptions of their children's behaviour were very similar, but quite different from those given by their teachers. Moreover, it is of interest that a clinically based interview with teachers indicated a much lower prevalence of behavioural deviance in black children. It remained the case, however, that many more black children were behaviourally difficult and rebellious in the school situation than at home where they appeared, on their parents' evidence, to be as well adjusted as their white peers. Once again, it is difficult to know whether it is the school situation that is causing behavioural difficulties or whether the standards of behaviour that teachers expect are different from those which parents are prepared to tolerate, especially in the home. In view of the alleged authoritarianism in the West Indian home the position would seem particularly difficult to unravel.

Green (1972) describes an investigation into the attitudes of eighty-seven teachers from infant, junior and secondary schools in which there were large numbers of children from different ethnic groups, and found that the experiences reported most frequently in terms unfavourable to West Indian children involved discipline, sulking, social behaviour, aggressiveness and resentment, in that order. The friendliness of West Indian children was most frequently mentioned in favourable terms during the free-response interviews which were individually conducted. Such favourable statements were made most often by teachers who were rated on an independent measure as tender minded, radical and having naturalistic attitudes. The researcher also found that older more-experienced teachers who hold more senior posts of responsibility are more likely to be less racially tolerant.

In an ethnographical description of one fourth year in a multiracial school in the West Midlands Driver (1977) noted that, although the staff made particular efforts to respond to what they saw as the special educational needs of their ethnic-minority pupils, limits in their 'cultural competence' led teachers to take on authoritarian roles, especially when challenged, which was usually by boys of West Indian origin. The relative frequency of these events led such teachers to make critical judgements of West Indian boys whom they generally considered to be difficult. Driver found that there was a high intercorrelation on two rating scales for academic and social behaviour and that this was twice as high for the boys of West Indian origin. The researcher's interpretation was that teachers' assessments were therefore 'problematic' and he suggested that teachers' own difficulties and uncertainties in teaching in multi-ethnic classrooms focused on the West Indian pupils as a whole, and especially the boys in the fourth and fifth years.

In conclusion, it appears from research evidence that the attitudes of teachers, and hence probably their expectations, are likely to be of considerable influence on the performance of children of West Indian origin in schools. However, it should be remembered that many of the research studies reviewed here tap only crude measures of teachers' attitudes, sometimes on forced-choice questions which allow little variation in the pattern of response and no qualifications to be made. Yet teachers as a profession, as with other groups of workers, are a diverse group of people, with different personalities, attitudes and expectations. It is by no means to be assumed therefore that they are racialist when considered as a professional group. The reservations that many teachers seem to express on the implementation of a multicultural curriculum may well be for professional rather than racially biased reasons; no research yet appears to have assessed their reluctance in sufficient detail to say definitely. Moreover, several studies have pointed to the honest bewilderment and genuine concern and sensitivity which many teachers who have to deal daily with difficulties in teaching pupils of minority ethnic origin obviously feel. Doubtless, these are the teachers who are doing their best in this situation, often in the absence of practical guidelines. They are probably, too, the kind of teachers in whom many children of West

Indian origin confide, for as Pollak (1979) found, West Indian children are just as likely to talk to their teachers as to their mothers about their concerns. It seems reasonable to expect that all pupils will achieve more and do better when their teachers are approachable and available as the study by Rutter *et al.* (1979) indicates. Again, it may be that the quality of the school, the whole ethos of school life, the hidden as well as the overt curriculum are more important for their effect on performance than teachers' attitudes in particular. No research has yet been sufficiently detailed to give anything like an adequate account of these more intangible qualitative factors. However, one or two individual descriptions have told how certain individual multiracial schools have approached the education of pupils of ethnic minority origin by means of a close partnership and interaction between home and school.

Teachers' attitudes to Asian pupils' behaviour

It is accepted widely that teachers' expectations and attitudes can be a significant determinant of a child's achievement and may lead to differential treatment and teaching. Research undertaken in the 1960s in the USA and the UK showed that teachers' expectations and attitudes could become self-fulfilling. Teacher expectation was taken up eagerly as an explanation of low academic achievement among some pupils of West Indian origin by certain commentators in the early 1970s. Yet the same phenomenon has received relatively little attention with respect to pupils of Asian origin. Green's (1983) work, for example, shows how teachers' attitudes and teaching style, which may differ according to the ethnicity of pupils being taught, can affect the self-concept of Asian pupils. If it is assumed that pupils' self-concept level affects their motivation to learn, and hence perhaps their academic achievement, then Green's research demonstrates that teachers' attitudes to education and race and their teaching style can have a real effect. Other research has indicated that teachers' attitudes draw on stereotypes, especially perhaps with respect to ethnic minority pupils when teachers are ill-informed.

To what extent do such attitudes condition and affect behaviour and progress in the school? It is relevant therefore to examine evidence on teachers' attitudes to Asian pupils, especially their behaviour in school, and to see whether teachers perceive such pupils differentially from their white and West Indian peers. Some writers have maintained that other professionals, such as social workers, have stereotypical views of young Asians and it is important to know whether teachers hold stereotypical views and, if so, of what kind. Is the commonplace view, that Asian pupils exhibit a range of behaviour similar to that of white pupils, or, that they are, if anything, more quiescent in the classroom, borne out by research evidence? The research data are of two main types: those that draw on teachers' expressed attitudes derived from their observations of behaviour in the classroom; those that derive from more systematic measures of the personality and behaviour of pupils of Asian origin, either completed by teachers in the light of their experience of pupils, or undertaken by pupils of Asian origin themselves.

Evidence is reviewed chronologically within the context of Asian pupils' general adjustment to school, which may have been affected differentially by an experience of immigration or birth in the UK. Saint's (1963) study of newly arrived Punjabi pupils in Smethwick schools reported that, although pupils appeared to be well adjusted emotionally, neither boys nor girls participated actively in class work, largely due to their lack of English, but also to the different social orientation of the learning environment. The relatively few Punjabi girls then present in schools were reported by teachers to be shy, restrained and well mannered; many were gifted at embroidery. Similarly, teachers were enthusiastic about Punjabi boys' handicraft skills and mathematical facility, but there was evidence that they sometimes found the social context of learning stressful. On the other hand, McCrea (1964) reported some ebullience on the part of Asian pupils and also late attendance. In their description of Spring Grove, Burgin and Edson (1967) reported that, although newly arrived Asian pupils experienced some difficulties in adjusting socially to the life of the school, behavioural problems were rare and they were conscientious in their approach to school work.

This was corroborated by Dosanjh (1967) whose study was devoted to an assessment of the adjustment of Punjabi pupils to schooling in Nottingham and Derby. He saw hard work and conscientiousness as evidence of a predisposition toward adjustment. Dosanjh found that almost half the teachers thought that Punjabi children were well adjusted to school life, better, in fact, than West Indian pupils, although just over a third said that they experienced more difficulty in adjusting. The overwhelming majority of teachers considered the behaviour of Asian pupils to be much the same as that of English children. A few reported undue chattering, which Dosanjh attributed to frustration in the formal teaching situation and lack of English. Teachers observed that Punjabi children considered the school to be the place for study rather than play, possibly reflective of their earlier school experiences in the Punjab, and over 80 per cent of teachers considered that Punjabi pupils paid as much attention to their studies as English children and a further 14 per cent, especially in Nottingham, thought that they paid more attention to school work. As in Saint's study, teachers observed that Punjabi children were more interested in subjects such as arithmetic and handicrafts, which involved less use of English, although a quarter of the teachers in Nottingham claimed that Punjabi pupils showed greater concentration in the study of English. Over half of the teachers thought that the learning capacities of Punjabi children were the same as those of English children. On the whole, Punjabi children were considered to be quick at understanding and remembering facts, again perhaps reflective of their early education in the Punjab.

During a study of Indian Sikh children in Southhall, it was found that teachers perceived Indian children as more stable emotionally than English children. This was attributed to their relatively settled and secure home life. An investigation that involved forty-six teachers, from twenty primary and secondary schools, also noted the emotional stability of Asian pupils, which was again linked to perceived parental enthusiasm for education and secure home backgrounds. Yet, the teachers in both studies reported relatively poor social adjustment. This was also mentioned by fifty head teachers in secondary schools across the country with Punjabi pupils. Seventy per cent reported no behaviour problems and 18 per cent very few behaviour problems with Asian pupils, 7 per cent mentioning chattering in Punjabi children in lessons; a third reported the insularity of Indian pupils due to lack of confidence. Although 38 per cent considered the behaviour of Asian pupils to be the same as that of English pupils, 45 per cent claimed that it was better, although some were said to be more subdued and introverted.

Some more specific indications of perceived behavioural differences are reported for seventy-two Indian and Pakistani pupils aged eleven years in 1969. According to their teachers' ratings these Asian pupils were not thought any more likely than white pupils to be squirmy or fidgety, often running or jumping about or hardly ever still, or rebellious, though they were slightly more likely to be judged by their teachers as having some personality or character weakness and half as likely to be accorded these traits as West Indian pupils. Similarly, according to teachers' ratings, on the Bristol Social Adjustment Guide, Asian pupils were no more likely to have disturbed behaviour and less likely to have extremely disturbed behaviour than white pupils. They were no more withdrawn, depressed, hostile to adults (if anything, less), hostile to other children, restless or likely to behave inconsequentially. However, only 28 per cent of Asian pupils compared with 45 per cent of native pupils were considered to show no sign of 'unforthcomingness' and 30 per cent, three times as many as their native peers, and twice as many as their West Indian peers, were considered by their teachers to show marked signs of unforthcomingness. Indian and Pakistani pupils were said to be twice as likely as native pupils and more likely than West Indian pupils to display some miscellaneous symptoms (childish, bullied, truanting, destructive, etc.) which might link with slightly more frequent parental reports (in comparison with native but not West Indian pupils) of destruction of their own or others' belongings at home. However, according to Asian parents their children were less likely to worry or to be irritable or aggressive, and 69 per cent, compared with 48 per cent of native peers, were said to be always obedient at home. Although teachers generally have remarked on the passivity of pupils of Asian origin, some have observed a tendency to demand attention by young newly arrived Indian and Pakistani pupils and adolescents. It is only possible to speculate whether this might be a response to possible perceptions of a freer environment at school, compared with that at home or the possibility of greater personal attention, or whether the school ethos liberates latent individualism or competitive egocentricity.

In their survey of the organization of multiracial schools Townsend and Brittan (1972) reported that just over one-third of 114 primary-school headteachers, regardless of concentration of immigrant pupils in school, claimed a specific contribution by immigrant pupils to the life of their school, 46 headteachers commenting overwhelmingly favourably, especially on their sporting contributions and charitableness. Headteachers in 52 out of 98 secondary schools also claimed significant contributions by immigrant pupils, especially where they were present in concentration of more than 20 per cent in the school, which may be summed up in one headteacher's comment:

> We feel that the presence of Asian pupils in this school has added to the tone of the school. They have an eagerness to please and to work together with poise, natural courtesy and generosity seldom found in indigenous pupils.
>
> (Townsend and Brittan, 1972, p. 125)

In the follow-up survey of 510 teachers (171 primary and 339 secondary) from 25 multiracial schools, Brittan (1976) found that teachers held less stereotyped and uniform views of Asian pupils than of West Indian pupils. The greatest consensus of opinion was that Asian pupils did not resent being reprimanded more than English pupils (64 per cent of teachers). But while 42 per cent of teachers agreed or strongly agreed that Asian pupils usually were better behaved than English pupils, 27 per cent disagreed or strongly disagreed, and 28 per cent were neutral. Although more secondary than primary teachers were likely to agree that Asian pupils tended to raise the academic standard of their school, overall only 19 per cent of teachers felt this to be so, 32 per cent were neutral and the majority, 42 per cent, disagreed or strongly disagreed.

Bagley (1976) reported the findings of an observational study of the behaviour of 2,587 girls in a large number of junior and secondary schools in the London area, in which girls of Indian and Pakistani origin, including those from Kenya, were said to be the second best-behaved group of pupils after Japanese and Chinese girls, and slightly ahead of British girls, according to the norms of the English observer. Crishna (1975) noted teachers' claims that Asian adolescent girls in Southall and Bradford were well behaved, polite and more reserved, participated in classroom activities with enthusiasm and enjoyed school to the full.

As part of a study in Handsworth in 1976 Rex and Tomlinson (1979) conducted interviews with thirty headteachers of special schools. As in Brittan's research these headteachers were far less exercised about the behaviour of pupils of Asian origin than those of West Indian origin. They were much more concerned with Asian pupils' language difficulties and communication or with family and cultural differences. Tomlinson (1981) claimed also that Asian pupils are seen as less boisterous and disruptive or aggressive compared with West Indian pupils and more like white pupils in their general behaviour.

Furthermore, a small-scale study observed 10 teachers (8 indigenous and 2 Asian) in one junior and infant school in the West Midlands who taught 302 children in classes comprising 12 per cent indigenous, 55 per cent Asian and 32 per cent West Indian pupils and subsequently asked them to clarify and comment on events which had occurred in the classroom during the observation period. Teachers drew on three types of constructs: those that were fairly specific non-academic aspects of the child's behaviour such as impulsivity, hyperactivity, or aggressive, destructive and antisocial behaviour; academic behaviour and attitudes such as industry, responsibility, maturity and writing skills; those that centred around personality traits, such as task-orientated behaviour, hostility and extraversion or introversion. In both interactions and discussions teachers tended to see Asian pupils in the second category of behaviour constructs and West Indian pupils in terms of the first and third constructs. Moreover, there were comparatively few behavioural interactions between teachers and Asian pupils, who were positively stereotyped as industrious, responsible, keen to learn and having none of the behaviour problems associated with West Indian pupils, although they possibly lacked social awareness.

Short (1983) investigated the attitudes of sixty-five primary teachers (including three Asian teachers), in eleven multiracial first and middle schools in a London borough, who were asked to identify three boys and three girls in their classes of above average, average or below average intelligence and to assign relevant characteristics from a checklist of thirty-one. Asian girls were seen as significantly quieter, less talkative, less resentful of punishment and more self-controlled by their teachers than English girls who were regarded as significantly more sociable and as more likely to have a good sense of humour. Asian girls were thought also to have a more serious attitude to work. Fewer significant differences were perceived by teachers between the behaviour of Asian and English boys, although again the Asian boys were seen as better behaved, less likely to be attention seeking or resentful of punishment, aggressive or rude. Teachers also perceived Asian pupils' classroom behaviour and academic motivation more positively than that of West Indian pupils, especially girls, who were seen as more hardworking. Only in the case of Asian boys compared with West Indian boys was there a significant difference in perceived intelligence and scholastic attainment. By contrast, teachers saw West Indian pupils as better at sport than Asian pupils. Short points to the sex differences in teachers' perceptions as supporting dismissal of the charge of 'unintentional racism'. But, although the research approach lends itself to stereotyping it tends to support other evidence of teachers' attitudes to pupils of Asian origin, especially concerning their behaviour, which tends to be perceived positively, with the notable exception of social interaction.

Evidence from a few studies, undertaken mainly in the late 1970s, provides complementary data on clinical measures of behaviour and pupils' personality assessed in school. In a study in Leicester 52 Indian boys and 52 Indian girls, randomly selected from 261 boys and 260 girls in the third and fourth forms in junior schools and matched with the same number of English boys and girls by age, sex and classroom, were rated on Rutter's Child Behaviour Questionnaire by their teachers. Interviews were conducted also with 100 Indian and 98 English families to obtain parental assessments of behaviour. Fifty-four per cent of the Indian children's parents were Gujeratis, mainly Hindus, and 41 per cent Punjabis, mainly Sikhs. Only 20 per cent of the Indian children were UK born and a quarter had less than two years' schooling here. According to parents' assessments 4 per cent of the Indian pupils were considered to be maladjusted, compared with 19.4 per cent of English children according to their parents' ratings. Teachers gave higher ratings to both sets of pupils: 10 per cent of the Indian pupils and 26.5 per cent of the English pupils were considered by them to be maladjusted. There was a statistically significant difference in the maladjustment of the Indian and English children. There was no significant association between maladjustment and age, mothers' employment, family size, birth order or social class, but there was a tendency among both groups, for more boys than girls to be maladjusted and also for a proportionately higher percentage of the UK-born and long-stay Indian children to be maladjusted. It was hypothesized that the low prevalence of maladjusted behaviour among Indian children was due to the affectionate, strong and protective nature of Indian family life, the effective discipline and close supervision of children, as well as relative economic success, but also suggested that teachers might overlook some of the internalized emotional difficulties of some Asian pupils by focusing on their politeness, eagerness to please and deference to authority.

A second study largely confirmed these findings. Teachers in five ethnically diverse schools in Birmingham with proportions of 50–90 per cent ethnic minority pupils, completed Rutter's Child Behaviour Questionnaire for 301 Indian, Pakistani, West Indian and British nine-year-olds. Information from teachers and school record cards showed that the four groups were similar in sexual composition, age and father's occupational status (largely working class). Most of the Asian pupils were UK born: 81 per cent of the Indians, mainly Sikhs, fifty-two boys and forty-two girls, and 76 per cent of the Pakistanis, mainly Muslims, twenty boys and twenty-two girls. On the twenty-six item scale boys overall had significantly higher deviance scores than girls, although the mean scores for Pakistani children were higher for girls than boys, largely due to conduct disorders. Even so, Pakistanis score significantly lower than either West Indian or British children. Indian pupils also obtained lower scores than either of those two groups; the Indian girls' mean score was the lowest. There was a significant correlation for all groups between teachers' ratings of behaviour and school performance in comprehension, vocabulary, reading, written and number work. In fact 11 per cent of the Indian and 26 per cent of the Pakistani children attended remedial classes. Maladjustment was independent of the proportion of ethnic-minority pupils in the class and birthplace though it was suggested there might be increasing maladjustment among Asian pupils with growing integration into British society.

Research studies have investigated the personalities of secondary-school pupils, including pupils of Asian origin by using other reliable and well-validated measures. As part of a larger study Hill (1975) administered the Junior Eysenck Personality Inventory (a twenty-four extraversion scale, a twenty-four item neuroticism scale and a twelve-item lie scale) to fourteen-to-sixteen-year-old pupils in fourteen schools in the West Midlands. Of the total of 700 pupils there were in each group 100 English, West Indian and Indian boys and girls and Pakistani boys. It was not possible to include Pakistani girls in the sample because of the predominance of all-male Pakistani households in the West Midlands in the early 1970s when the study was conducted. The pupils all had a minimum reading age of ten years and came from working-class backgrounds. The ethnic-minority pupils were divided into equal groups according to length of stay: long (seven years plus) and short (five years or less). Indian and Pakistani pupils had the lowest extraversion scores which were significantly different from those of the English and West Indian pupils. Hill suggested that this was owing probably to the fact that Asian cultures do not actively encourage those traits associated with extraversion, i.e. sociability, activity and outgoing and impulsive behaviour. Within the group of Asian pupils the Indian pupils had a significantly higher extraversion score and the Pakistani boys, who had the lowest mean extraversion score of any group, were the only pupils to have a lower score with length of UK residence. Hill thought this was because the boys were not living in family households and might be subject to stricter control. Again English and West Indian pupils were significantly more neurotic than Asian pupils but the Indian pupils were also more neurotic than the Pakistani boys. However, Indian girls became more neurotic with length of residence in the UK. The Asian pupils' low neuroticism was again explained in cultural terms: Hill pointed to the individual's strong and valued identity within the family and suggested that Asian cultures seem to discourage extremes of neuroticism and extraversion. Findings on the lie scale were also interesting. Once again English and West Indian pupils scored significantly higher than Asian pupils and Indian pupils scored higher than the Pakistani pupils. However, although there was a tendency for the Pakistani boys' scores to increase slightly with length of stay, the lie scores of Indian girls and boys decreased significantly with length of stay. Hill suggested that the Asian pupils attained a high lie score because in fact they probably were responding truthfully in claiming they were not rude to their parents, their responses might also have reflected consciousness of expected behaviour and the desire that nothing detrimental to the family should be revealed. However, as length of stay increased so their need to be consciously socially sensitive might have decreased with increasing adoption of the British way of life.

　　Other studies are also worthy of mention in connection with the personality traits of pupils of Asian origin. A study in 1967 administered the New Junior Maudsley Personality Inventory (NJMPI), which assesses personality on the dimensions of extraversion–introversion and neuroticism–stability, to 95 Bangladeshi pupils in the UK and 200 age peers in Bangladesh. Although there was no significant difference between the two groups on the extraversion scale the immigrant group, who had been in the UK more than two years, were found to be significantly more neurotic, i.e. 'quiet, reserved, pessimistic, anxious, moody, etc.' and seemed to experience some stress in the school environment. It is also of interest to note findings for the NJMPI administered as one of a battery of tests as part of the assessment of attitudes to English by pupils of Asian origin. Overall the Gujerati-speaking girls seemed to be more neurotic, significantly more so than the Punjabi-speaking girls and Gujerati-speaking boys, but Punjabi boys were also more neurotic than Punjabi girls. Punjabi girls seemed to be the most extrovert, as both the Gujerati and Punjabi speakers were significantly more extrovert than Urdu speakers, Gujerati-speaking girls significantly more extrovert than Urdu-speaking girls, and Punjabi girls were significantly more extrovert than Gujerati-speaking girls. It is only possible to speculate whether migratory patterns or socialization practices might have influenced these findings. Finally, it was found that, like the English adolescents, Asian pupils were significantly more internal in their control orientation compared with West Indian adolescents and Asian girls more so than Asian boys.

These results from quantitative measures appear to support teachers' own observations and impressions and may perhaps begin to explain both teachers' and other pupils' attitudes to pupils of Asian origin. Teachers seem to welcome the apparent emotional stability which pupils of Asian origin often demonstrate in the classroom. In addition their low levels of observed behavioural deviance which, combined with qualities such as motivation to learn and positive attitudes to school, seem to make them more acceptable members of multiracial classes to teachers trying to teach. It is clear, moreover, that teachers have quite different views of the behaviour of Asian pupils compared with pupils of West Indian origin, that their views are to some extent less stereotyped and that they admit a greater range of behaviours, which are much more similar to behavioural dispositions manifested by white pupils, indeed probably quieter and certainly less forthcoming. On the other hand, Asian pupils clearly are not integrated socially in their classrooms according to both their teachers and peers. Findings from personality measures appear to indicate that Asian pupils are considerably less extrovert than their white or West Indian peers, and it seems likely that their less evident sociability compared with that of their West Indian peers is noticed by white pupils. On the other hand, Asian pupils display considerably less maladjustment in school compared with white or West Indian pupils and this generally has been attributed to cultural and social factors such as family cohesiveness and strong discipline. It is of interest that Pakistani girls have shown the highest, albeit relatively low, level of maladjustment amongst Asian pupils. Whether their conduct disorders can be attributed to greater self-expression in the possibly less restricted environment of the classroom compared with their homes is not known; it would be interesting to ascertain whether a similar subgroup of pupils display the kind of attention-seeking behaviour reported in some studies. Yet teachers may overlook some emotional stresses experienced by pupils of Asian origin because of their perceived mannerliness, polite and reserved behaviour, hard work and application. It seems possible that the inner strength, to which some of these personality measures point, together with considerable social sensitivity which enables some pupils of Asian origin to make 'multiple representations of the self' and engage in 'impression management' may be camouflaging the stresses and strains which may result, not only from certain experiences of cultural mismatch between home and school, but also from increasing social and educational aspirations on the part of both pupils and parents.

REFERENCES

Bagley, C. (1976) Behavioural deviance in ethnic minority children, *New Community*, Vol. V, No. 3, pp. 230–8.

Brittan, E. M. (1976) Multiracial education 2. Teacher opinion on aspects of school life. Part 2: pupils and teachers, *Educational Research*, Vol. 18, No. 3, pp. 182–94.

Burgin, T. and Edson, P. (1967) *Spring Grove, the Education of Immigrant Children*, OUP for IRR, London.

Coard, B. (1971) *How the West Indian Child is Made Educationally Sub-normal in the British School System*, New Beacon Books, London for Caribbean Education and Community Workers' Association.

Crishna, S. (1975) *Girls of Asian Origin in Britain*, YWCA, London.

Dosanjh, J. S. (1967) A study of the problems in educational and social adjustment of immigrant children from Punjab in Nottingham and Derby. Unpublished M.Ed. thesis, Nottingham University.

Driver, G. (1977) Cultural competence social power and school achievement: West Indian secondary school pupils in the West Midlands, *New Community*, Vol. V, No. 4, pp. 353–9.

Giles, R. (1977) *The West Indian Experience in British Schools. Multiracial Education and Social Disadvantage in London*, Heinemann, London.

Green, P. A. (1972) Attitudes of teachers to West Indian immigrant children. Unpublished M. Phil., Nottingham University.

Green, P. A. (1983) Teachers' influence on the self-concept of ethnic minority pupils. Unpublished Ph.D. thesis, University of Durham.

Hill, D. (1975) Personality factors among adolescents in minority ethnic groups, *Educational Studies*, Vol. 1, No. 1, pp. 43–54.

Jeffcoate, R. (1977) Looking in the wrong place, *Times Educational Supplement*, 24 June.

Kirp, D. (1977) Wrong problem, wrong solution, *Times Educational Supplement*, 24 June.

Mabey, C. (1980) ILEA Literacy Survey, *West Indian Attainment*, unpublished.

Mabey, C. (1981) Black British literacy: a study of reading attainment of London black children from 8 to 15 years, *Educational Research*, Vol. 23, No. 2, pp. 83–95.

McCrea, W. (1964) A study of some problems presented by immigrant children in the schools of one authority with additional reference to the work being done by other authorities. Dissertation for Diploma in Education, University of Liverpool.

Pollak, M. (1979) *Nine Years Old*, MTP Press, Lancaster.

Rex, J. and Tomlinson, S. (1979) *Colonial Immigrants in a British City. A Class Analysis*, Routledge & Kegan Paul, London.

Rosenthal, R. and Jacobson, L. (1968) *Pygmalion in the Classroom*, Holt, Rinehart & Winston, New York.

Rutter, M. *et al.* (1974) Children of West Indian immigrants: 1, rates of behavioural deviance and of psychiatric disorder, *Journal of Child Psychology and Psychiatry*, Vol. 15, No. 4, pp. 241–62.

Rutter, M. *et al.* (1979) *Fifteen Thousand Hours*, Open Books, London.

Saint, C. K. (1963) Adjustment problems of the Punjabi-speaking children in Smethwick. Unpublished M.Ed. thesis, University of Birmingham.

Seaver, W. B. (1973) Effects of naturally induced teacher expectancies, *Journal of Personality and Social Psychology*, Vol. 28, pp. 333–42.

Short, G. (1983) Rampton revisited: a study of racial stereotypes in the primary school, *Durham and Newcastle Research Review*, Vol. 10, No. 51, pp. 82–6.

Tomlinson, S. (1979) Decision-making in special education (ESN–M) with some reference to children of immigrant parentage. Ph.D. thesis, University of Warwick.

Tomlinson, S. (1981) Multi-racial schooling: parents' and teachers' views, *Education 3–13*, Vol. 9, No. 1, pp. 16–21.

Townsend, H.E.R. and Brittan, E.M. (1972) *Organization in Multiracial Schools*, NFER–Nelson, Windsor.

TOPICS FOR DISCUSSION

1. What are the causes of the reported confusion among teachers as to how to treat pupils of West Indian origin in relation to similarly socially disadvantaged white children?

2. What conclusions can be drawn about the incidence of disruptive behaviour among children of West Indian origin from the evidence reviewed in the extract? What criticisms can be levelled at that evidence?

3. Why is it that pupils of South Asian origin appear to be perceived so more favourably by teachers than their West Indian class mates?

SUGGESTIONS FOR FURTHER READING

1. Thomas, K. C. (1984)A study of stereotyping in a multicultural comprehensive school, *Educational Studies*, Vol. 10, No. 1, pp. 77–86.
   This is a study of the stereotypes of various ethnic and national groups held by pupils of Indian, Pakistani, West Indian and white British origins in an eleven-to-sixteen years comprehensive school in the East Midlands.

2. Short, G. (1981) Racial attitudes among Caucasian children: an empirical study of Allport's 'total rejection' hypothesis, *Educational Studies*, Vol. 7, No. 3, pp. 197–204.
   One-hundred-and-eighteen white children drawn from primary schools in Dagenham and Brighton were shown a picture of a black and a white boy fighting and another of a black or a white teacher punishing one of the boys. Dagenham boys were more ethnocentric (wanting the white boy to win) than those in Brighton. Girls were equally ethnocentric in both schools. The most interesting finding relates to the children's views of the black teacher punishing the white boy.

3. Denscombe, M. (1983) Ethnic group and friendship choice in the primary school, *Educational Research*, Vol. 25, No. 3, 184–190.
   A report of research on friendship choices between pupils from different ethnic groups that supplements the findings of similar studies by Jelinek and Brittan (1975) and Davey and Mullin (1982).

REFERENCES

Davey, A. G. and Mullin, P. N. (1982) Inter-ethnic friendship in British primary schools, *Education Research*, Vol. 5, February, pp. 83–92.
Jelinek, M.M. and Brittan, E.M. (1975) Multiracial education and inter-ethnic friendship patterns, *Education Research*, Vol. 5, November, pp. 44–53.

Reading 7
ETHNIC MINORITY CHILDREN IN SPECIAL EDUCATION
S. Tomlinson

The position of ethnic-minority children in special education, particularly those of West Indian origin, is one of the clearest indications that this type of education does not exist solely to cater for the needs of individual children, but is related to the way particular groups are regarded as potentially troublesome to schools and society. Given the history of

S. Tomlinson (1982) Ethnic minority children in special education, in *A Sociology of Special Education*, Routledge & Kegan Paul, London.

colonialism and white beliefs about the potential of black people, it was highly probable that when black immigrant children began entering the education system in the early 1960s they would be regarded as a problem. Liberal pedagogic ideologies have always been stretched to their utmost in the assumption that black children were equal to white in most of the educative processes. The general poor level of achievement of West Indian children in normal schools and their non-achievement through special schooling are not necessarily due to factors intrinsic to the children, but also to the ways in which the education administrators and practitioners regard, and deal with, black children.

While this chapter concentrates on the issue of the overplacement of children of West Indian origin in the non-normative categories of special education, the treatment of ethnic minority groups can raise questions about the whole nature of special education. For example, if 'special needs' are difficult to define for indigenous children, and the causal factors behind these needs are unconsidered, how can professionals and practitioners claim to understand the special needs of minority-group children? If the curriculum and its aims are unclarified for indigenous children, how can special schools deal adequately with minority children, particularly at a time when a multicultural curriculum is under consideration in education as a whole?

Those who work in special education are often unaware of the connotations that the phrase 'special education' has taken on for some minority-group parents in Britain. The number of West Indian children referred, assessed and placed in schools for the mildly educationally subnormal has, for a number of years, been a particular emotive issue for the West Indian community in that it became symbolic of the general under achievement of their children within the English school system and contributed to anxieties among first-generation immigrants that their children may be destined, through educational failure, to inferior employment and status. Toward the end of the 1970s, there has been similar anxiety about the numbers of West Indian children referred and placed in disruptive units and classes. Official anxiety over the general educational performance of children of West Indian origin contributed to the setting up of the Rampton Committee in 1979, and the Assessment of Performance Unit at the DES is considering a national survey on the issue.

The legislative changes that will bring remedial and disruptive children officially into special education even though largely as non-recorded children will have a profound effect on the education of children of West Indian origin in Britain; the symbolic significance of the ESN issue will certainly become redundant as special education would become a major form of education for this particular minority group. In the context of the equal and just provision of education for the children of ethnic minority groups this would seem to be an unacceptable facet of multi-ethnic education. Many West Indian parents have never accepted the rhetoric that their children have special needs, and have become one of the first sustained pressure groups to protest about this kind of classification. Their protests may well be followed by other social groups as the results of expanded special educational treatment become apparent in the form of rejection by the labour market.

PROBLEM OF NUMBERS

The current symbolic significance of the overplacement of children of West Indian origin in special (ESN-M) education can be better appreciated if the numbers in question are set against the total numbers of all children and the probable numbers of children of West Indian origin in maintained primary and secondary education. In 1972, when the total school population in England and Wales was around nine million, 4,397 children of West Indian origin and 1,101 children of Asian origin were officially in all types of special education. As collection of statistics on immigrant children was discontinued in 1972, calculating numbers of percentage has become problematic since then. However, the 1972 statistics showed that two-thirds of all 'immigrant' children in special education were of West Indian origin. Also in that year, although West Indian children as a whole constituted 1.1 per cent of all children in state schools, they constituted 4.9 per cent of all children in ESN-M schools. The overplacement of West Indian children in ESN-M schools is demonstrated further by the fact that in 1972, at a time when the total percentage of children in ESN-M schools constituted less than 1 per cent (0.6 per cent in fact), the value for West Indian children was almost 3 per cent.

Although there was a general decrease in referral and placement of all children in ESN-M schools in the mid-1970s, estimates indicated that West Indian children continued to be overplaced in proportion to their total numbers in the school population.There is thus no question that children of West Indian origin have been over-referred and placed in this form of special education, which offers a non-credentialling stigmatized form of education with much-reduced job prospects even for indigenous children.

Similarly, although numerical evidence is hard to acquire since collection of education statistics by ethnic origin ceased, it seems likely that children of West Indian origin are over-represented in the expanding existing statutory category of maladjustment and in the numbers of disruptive centres and units which have developed on an *ad hoc* basis during the 1970s. An HMI survey (Department of Education and Science, 1978) found that 69 local education authorities were operating a total of 239 units for nearly 4,000 pupils. An ACE survey (Advisory Centre for Education, 1980) found that 63 LEAs were offering 5,857 places in 386 units: an increase of 48 and 62 per cent respectively in 2 years.

This is particularly relevant for children of West Indian origin in Britain. They live in a society in which white racism has become more and more respectable and come from a culture which has been systematically down-graded. There are a variety of new forms of black-consciousness development among the young, the cult of Rastafarianism being one of the most important. However, the overt political overtones of West Indian assertiveness are currently creating much anxiety in urban schools; any disruption of normal classroom activity by West Indian children is regarded as a serious control problem by teachers and it is not particularly surprising that they should have become candidates for referral into 'disruptive' units. However, as Francis has pointed out:

> In the forefront of the sin-bin controversy has been the fear of black parents that the units could be turned into dumping-grounds, mirroring the ESN school battle of the 1960s. Units are one of the items under investigation by the Commission for Racial Equality in Birmingham and London. Many local community relations councils have expressed disquiet.
>
> (Francis, 1979)

WEST INDIAN GRIEVANCE

The West Indian community can be regarded as the first pressure group to sustain a protest and demand more clarity over the criteria used to decide on ESN-M placement. The North London West Indian Association expressed concern as early as 1965 that a disproportionate number of West Indian children was being placed in this form of special education. In 1967 an ILEA report noted that 28.4 per cent of children in ESN schools were 'immigrant', mainly of West Indian origin, and that in a survey of special schools the schools felt that a misplacement of these children was four times more likely due to methods and processes of assessment. In 1970 the North London West Indian Association lodged a complaint of racial discrimination against Haringey LEA and, although the Race Relations Board found no evidence of an unlawful act, they suggested that IQ tests might be unsuitable for the assessment of black children. It was interesting that in America in the same year the over-representation of black children in a similar type of special education, classes for the educably mentally retarded (EMR), was becoming a cause for black parental anxiety. In San Francisco, where some 28 per cent of the city schools contained black pupils, 66 per cent of children in classes for the EMR were black.

However, the complexity of the referral and assessment procedures in England has always made it problematic to point simply to the culture bias of IQ tests as a 'cause' of the overplacement of black children in ESN-M education. Asian children, who would be similarly handicapped by IQ tests, are not placed in disproportionate numbers in the non-normative categories of special education. Bernard Coard, who in 1971 published a polemical paper entitled 'How the West Indian child is made educationally subnormal in the British school system', suggested that low teacher expectations and stereotypes about black children could lead to their over-referral and the low self-esteem that black children acquire in a white racist society might influence their school performance. A letter sent to chief education officers by the DES in 1973 on 'the educational arrangements for immigrant children who may need special education' mentioned the use of dialect English as a possible cause of education difficulties, and also teachers who could not cope with the learning problems and disciplinary of West Indian children in normal schools.

The ESN issue continued to be a cause for concern throughout the 1970s, voiced in the columns of the black press and in evidence to government select committees. Articles in *Race Today* in 1974 and 1975 pointed out that the issue had become symptomatic of the general failure of the school system to incorporate children of West Indian origin, and criticized the variety of explanations offered for the poor educational performance of West Indian children, particularly those centring on innate explanations, or 'deprivation' hypotheses.

The evidence to the Select Committee on Race Relations and Immigration for their 1972–3 report took evidence from sixteen official bodies concerned with the overplacement of West Indian children in ESN-M schools. Evidence from the Caribbean educationalists and community workers claimed that

Many children are packed off to ESN-M schools on the basis of inadequate assessment procedures. Very little consultation between

the parents and the authorities takes place. Many parents are given inaccurate information as to the nature and purpose of ESN schools.
(Select Committee on Race Relations and Immigration, 1973, Vol. 3)

Despite a recommendation in this report that an annual review of the placement of immigrant children in special schools should take place, no action was taken and nine official bodies gave evidence to the Select Committee for its 1976 report, *The West Indian Community*, again complaining about ESN schools. A witness from the West Indian Standing Conference wrote that 'this was one of the very bitter areas' for West Indians, and the Select Committee wrote in its report that

It is clear that the West Indian Community is disturbed by the under-achievement of West Indian children at school, and continues to be seriously disturbed by the high proportion of West Indian children in ESN schools.
(Select Committee on Race Relations, 1976, Vol. 1)

Evidence from Brent West Indian Standing Committee to this committee indicated that while the ESN issue was largely symbolic, the large numbers of children who were placed in low streams or remedial classes in normal schools (those who will now form a large number of non-recorded children in special education) also created anxiety.

Do not go away with the impression that our major interest is with ESN schools. We are concerned about them, but we are concerned more with the point that the majority of youngsters who have been to the so-called normal schools came out having achieved as little on the academic side as the children who went to ESN schools.
(Select Committee on Race Relations, 1976, Vol. 3)

Explanations for the generally poorer educational performance of children of West Indian origin have merged with explanations for their overplacement in ESN-M schools. In a review of thirty-three studies of West Indian school performance (Tomlinson, 1980) in which twenty-seven studies indicated a lower performance than whites, explanations ranged through migration stress, family difference and disorganization, child minding, domestic responsibility, dialect interference, low self-esteem, disadvantage, culturally biased tests, low teacher expectations, unsuitable curricula, low socio-economic class and racial hostility. However, it does appear that, when challenged, the education system will defend itself by reverting to innate individualistic explanations stressing the pupils' deficiencies. Thus, for example, in the aftermath of the Bristol 'riots' the chairman of Avon County Council announced that black children were 'less academically inclined' and 'could not acquit themselves in ways which were attractive to employers'.

The West Indian community has a legitimate 'grievance' concerning the education of their children and has certainly not agreed that the placement of numbers of black children in the non-normative categories of special education has been a response to the children's special needs. Rather, they feel that the education system has a 'need' to deal with the children in this manner.

TABLE 7.1   Accounts of educational subnormality

Subnormality	Account
Functional	Child cannot do X (X may be social, educational technological, but is usually connected to attainment, 'learning' or intellectual functioning). Child cannot communicate adequately
Statistical	Child has a 'low' IQ as measured on standardized tests. Child falls into lowest 1% (or 20%) of school population in school achievement
Behavioural	Child is disruptive, troublesome, uncontrolled. Child exhibits bizarre, odd, non-conformist behaviour. Child unable to behave 'appropriately'
Organic	Child has: genetic disorder or 'innate incapacity' pre-natal or birth 'damage' organic or metabolic disorder medically demonstrable 'illness' or 'condition'
Psychological	Child is 'emotionaly disturbed'
Social	Child has: family with low socio-economic status; father semi- or un-skilled family 'disorganized' (poor maternal care, single parent, working mother, etc.) poor or different socialization techniques adverse material factors (poor housing, bad physical environment) cultural deficiency (poor cultural milieux; poor preparation for school)
School	Unsatisfactory school conditions Normal school rejects child Child rejects school, i.e. truants
Statutory	Child may be 'certified' as in need of special education
Intuitive	Child has 'something wrong with him'
Tautological	Child is in need of special educational treatment

PROFESSIONALS AND WEST INDIAN CHILDREN

The social and cultural beliefs of professionals have always been reflected in the decisions and judgments they make when assessing children for the non-normative categories of special education. In the study of referral and assessment of ESN-M children undertaken in the mid–1970s (Tomlinson, 1981) an attempt was made to demonstrate that professionals also made decisions based on beliefs about the racial characteristics of particular children. It attempted to collect some empirical evidence as to why schools tended to over-refer children of West Indian origin and why other professionals concur with the schools' judgments. In a study described elsewhere, it was noted that all the professional people who had made a decision about the forty children (eighteen of them of 'immigrant' parentage) passing into special education were interviewed and a series of accounts (Table 7.1) was abstracted to describe and explain 'ESN-M' children.

The referring headteachers are the people who actually make the initial decision to institute the process of ascertainment for special education, although usually after consultation with teachers. It was noted that in terms of accounting for ESN-M children, heads overwhelmingly used functional and behavioural criteria. Figure 7.1 demonstrates the variety of replies that the heads gave, the percentage of replies being shown in histogram form.

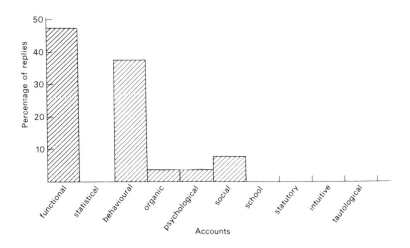

FIGURE 7.1   Referring headteachers' accounts of ESN-M children

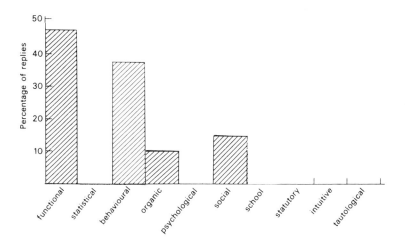

FIGURE 7.2   Referring headteachers' perceptions of the problems of West Indian children

Headteachers were also asked what they considered the educational problems of West Indian children to be. The result of this question is documented in Figure 7.2 and it is at once apparent that the criteria heads use to account for ESN-M children correspond almost exactly to their perceptions of the problem of West Indian children. The comments of the head teachers also indicated that they considered children of West Indian origin to possess 'natural' educational handicaps: the children were 'bound to be slower — it's their personalities' or they were described as 'a representative bunch, slow, docile and low-functioning', they were also 'less keen on education' than other children. Their behavioural problems were also taken to be a 'natural' characteristic, as one head said, 'They have the usual problems — hyperactivity and anti-authority.' All in all, the close correspondence between the headteachers' referral criteria for ESN-M education and their cultural perceptions of the 'natural' problems of West Indian children made it highly probable that West Indian children would be regarded by heads of normal schools as likely candidates both for ESN-M education and, latterly, for 'special' education in behavioural units.

Once in the ascertainment process, 'immigrant' children appeared to be processed more speedily than indigenous children. The indigenous children in this study waited a mean of two years between referral and

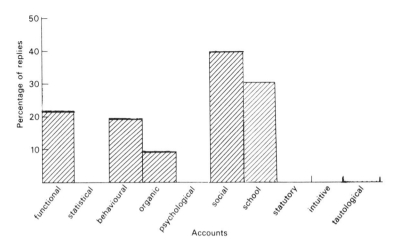

FIGURE 7.3 Educational psychologists' perceptions of the problems of West Indian children

placement in special school; the immigrant children waited only eleven months. Decisions appeared to be made more speedily in the case of black children. Educational psychologists and medical officers, although more cautious than heads in attributing natural racial characteristics to West Indian children, did seem more likely to proceed with assessment on the basis of their beliefs. Psychologists, who rejected accounts of ESN-M children as behaviour problems, did think that West Indian children were more likely to have behaviour problems and also social problems connected to 'disadvantage', as Figure 7.3 demonstrates.

Psychologists who relied on IQ test results, and believed that West Indian children had family problems and different developmental norms, were more likely to recommend ESN-M schooling. Those who were dubious about the value of IQ testing and the way in which normal schools went about educating West Indian children were less likely to recommend placement. However, one psychologist, who refused to test a West Indian boy on the grounds that the tests were culturally biased, did not, despite his liberal intentions, help the boy. The pupil, referred by his secondary school for low educational performance and bad behaviour, was sent to a guidance centre, then a suspension unit and then, at sixteen years, was allowed to leave the education system with no follow-up and was soon in trouble with the police. Had he arrived in the ESN process he would have had a medical examination and the fact that he was deaf would presumably have been discovered.

Medical officers, in common with other auxiliary professionals, also regarded West Indian children as potential behaviour problems. As one doctor said, 'They have ebullient natures, they can go berserk at school.' In general this study demonstrated that, despite the issue of their children being categorized out of normal education into special education causing acute anxiety to the black community, the professionals were not overtly informed or concerned. The actual referral and assessment procedures, based as they are on the cultural and racial beliefs of professionals, would certainly seem to work against the children of West Indian origin as far as the consideration of their 'special needs' is concerned.

ASIAN CHILDREN IN SPECIAL EDUCATION

The 'under-representation' of children of Asian origin in ESN-M education and in disruptive units has caused some comment among professionals and practitioners although there are some indications that they are increasingly, in particular parts of the country, being put forward as candidates for the normative categories of special education, particularly deaf, partially sighted, physically and severely mentally handicapped. In Bradford in 1980 Asian children constituted 19.4 per cent of the general school population, but took 31 per cent of places in deaf schools and 22 per cent of places in schools for the partially sighted. Asian children in Britain, reportedly, have a higher death rate from congenital abnormalities: 8.7 per thousand, compared with 3.4 per thousand among the indigenous population. Explanations put forward to explain this include poor nutrition of mothers, larger families, reluctance to abort any abnormal foetus and recessive genes due to cousin intermarriage.

However, in 1972 0.5 per cent of Indian and Pakistani children were in ESN-M schools compared with 0.6 per cent of the indigenous population and 2.9 per cent of West Indian children. Explanations for their under-referral into this type of special education would seem to centre on the professionals' perceptions of the school problems of Asian children. As shown in Figure 7.4, Asians do not meet the headteachers' criteria for referral into ESN-M education. Their functional problems were considered to be related to language, but they were not considered to have any 'natural' or intransigent educational or behavioural problems. Asian children are regarded as 'keen on education' and their parents are perceived as valuing the educative process. Heads stressed what

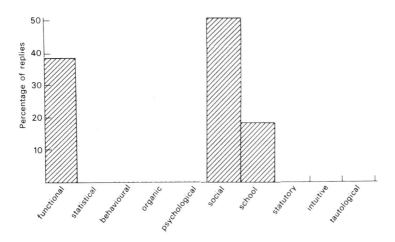

FIGURE 7.4   Headteachers' perceptions of the problems of Asian children

they perceived as the social deficiencies of Asian families, cultural and language problems, but these do not constitute referral criteria into special education. Similarly, Asian children are not, as a group, perceived as a threat to the normal order of schools by 'bad' or disruptive behaviour and there has, so far, been no evidence that numbers of Asian children are placed in behavioural units.

It does not seem likely that Asian children will be particularly affected as a group by new legislation in special education. Although special educational needs are equated with 'learning difficulty' in the 1981 Education Bill, and language problems might be thought to lead to 'learning difficulty', the Bill specifically lays down that 'a child is not to be taken as having a learning difficulty solely because the language (or form of language) in which hc is taught is different from a language (or form of language) which at any time has been spoken in his home'.

WEST INDIAN CHILDREN AND NEW LEGISLATION

The recommendation of the Warnock Committee and the embodiment of some of these recommendations in proposed new legislation will have far-reaching consequences for a large number of children of West Indian origin in schools. The Warnock Report touched on the issue of the disproportionate number of West Indian children in ESN-M schools in one paragraph, out of 416 pages, and noted that 'any tendency for educational difficulties to be assessed without proper reference to a child's cultural and ethnic background and its effect on his education can result in a category of handicap becoming correlated with a particular group in society' and that the 'uncertain relationship between remedial and special education' might prove to be a problem for certain ethnic groups. However, the paragraph went on optimistically to comment that no variation in assessment procedures should be envisaged for ethnic minority children as, provided that cultural factors were taken into consideration, parents would come to view assessment 'not with suspicion, but as offering the possibility of enhanced educational opportunity for their children'.

In the light of evidence over the past fifteen years it seems unlikely that the West Indian community will view any form of special education for their children as enhanced educational opportunity. The Warnock Report recommended that:

1. a meaningful distinction between remedial and special education can no longer be maintained and that former remedial children should be described as children with learning difficulties
2. special education embraces educational help for children with emotional and behavioural disorders who have previously been regarded as disruptive.

If children of West Indian origin continue to be over-represented in the non-normative categories of special education, it would seem that around one-third or more of all West Indian children in schools would in the future be candidates for some form of special educational provision.

The basis for calculation of these numerical possibilities must lie in the examination of the current referral and assessment criteria for the non-normative categories of special education, in the current placement in remedial classes of a number of West Indian children in schools, and in the schools' perception of disruptive behaviour. To recapitulate on these: the stereotyped beliefs that professionals and practitioners, particularly teachers, hold about West Indian children's ability, behaviour and attitudes to education, together with an acceptance that these are somehow 'natural' racial attributes, have in the past made it likely that West Indian children would meet the criteria for referral into the non-normative areas of special education. The assumption that black children start 'equal' in the referral and assessment processes, with no account being taken of the fact that these children are being educated in a largely hostile white society, in which even professionals are influenced by postcolonial beliefs, have further 'disadvantaged' West Indian children in the processes leading into special education. There is no reason to suppose that, under new legislation, beliefs and assumptions made by professionals will be changed. Indeed, teachers, who hold the most stereotyped beliefs about black children will be the people who will initiate and participate in the first three stages of decision making as to whether children have special educational needs. It also seems likely that similar beliefs and assumptions, which have influenced over-referral into ESN-M education, have also influenced the categorization of numbers of West Indian children as remedial. Teachers have tended to regard the learning problems of West Indian children as somehow 'natural' and intransigent, and have had lower expectations of good academic performance. There is no reason to suppose that the numbers of 'remedial' West Indian children in schools will diminish. The inclusion of disruptive units and centres in new legislation as answering special educational needs certainly offers official recognition on what is already happening: these units are already looked on as a form of special education to which children can be referred more quickly than use of the long-drawn-out old assessment procedures for the old statutory non-normative categories of ESN-M and maladjusted.

The terms of the White Paper proposing new legislation, that it 'will include not only those difficulties which arise from physical or mental disability, but also those which may be due to some other cause', are ominous words when applied to West Indian children. There has been, and will be, considerable disagreement over the 'cause' of the poorer educational performance of West Indian children and their disruptive behaviour in schools. Under new legislation, the exclusion of even larger numbers of these children from normal education and their placement in special education, even in 'non-recorded' special education, may mean that special education becomes a major form of education for children of West Indian origin.

While some writers have been concerned to demonstrate what one of them considered to be the 'real purpose of British schools — the maintenance of white supremacy' by the overplacement of black children in the stigmatized non-normative parts of the education system to ensure their low socio-economic status, this chapter has been included to provide evidence that there are groups in the society who vehemently oppose the benevolent rhetoric that their children have 'special needs', and point instead to the 'needs' of a society that denies certain groups of children a normal education.

REFERENCES

Advisory Centre for Education (1980) *Survey of Disruptive Units*, Mimeograph, London.

Department of Education and Science (1978) *Behavioural Units: a Survey of Special Units for Pupils with Behavioural Problems*, HMSO, London.

Francis , M. (1979) Disruptive units: labelling a new generation, *New Approaches in Multi-racial Education*, Vol. 8, p. 1.

Select Committee on Race Relations and Immigration (1973) *Education*, 3 vols., HMSO, London.

Select Committee on Race Relations (1976) *The West Indian Community*, 3 vols., HMSO, London.

Tomlinson, S. (1980) The educational performance of ethnic minority children, *New Community*, Vol. 8, p. 3.

TOPICS FOR DISCUSSSION

1. Discuss the explanations that have been advanced (p. 97) to account for West Indian children's generally poorer educational performance.
2. What evidence does Tomlinson adduce in support of her assertion that referral and assessment procedures used in classifying children of West Indian origin are based on the cultural and racial beliefs of the professionals involved?
3. How is the 'under-representation' of children of Asian origin in ESN-M schools accounted for?

SUGGESTIONS FOR FURTHER READING

1. Carrington, B. (1983) Sport as a side track: an analysis of West Indian involvement in extracurricular sport, pp. 40–65, in L. Barton and S. Walker (eds.) *Race, Class and Education*, Croom Helm, London.

This is a case study of Hillsview Comprehensive School in which the author adduces evidence to support his contention that, despite state interventions to curb racism, the structural position of West Indians in contemporary Britain has scarcely changed since the initial phases of immigration some thirty years ago. Carrington's particular interest is in the thesis that West Indians have been cast as the 'twentieth-century gladiators for white Britain'. His analysis of sporting activities at Hillview Comprehensive reveals that the over-representation of pupils of West Indian origin in the school's sports teams is in part the result of channelling by teachers whose stereotypic perceptions of this particular ethnic group in terms of 'body skills' rather than 'mind skills' reinforces West Indian academic failure. The consequence of this, Carrington argues, is the 'reproduction of the black worker as wage labour at the lower end of employment production and skill'.

2. Cohen, L. and Manion, L. (1983) Underachievement: some differing perspectives, pp. 53–76, in *Multicultural Classrooms: Perspectives for Teachers*, Croom Helm, London.

A number of key issues in connection with the underachievement of certain ethnic minority groups, in particular, children of West Indian origin, are reviewed. The debate on the relation of race to intelligence is summarized, the ideas of Jensen and Eysenck being matched by critical commentary from Hebb and Bynner. A section on teacher attitudes and pupil underachievement touches on the processes involved in categorization and stereotyping and contains a summary of the study by Green (1983) who showed the differential treatment accorded to West Indian pupils in classrooms of highly intolerant teachers. The reading ends with an account of the deleterious home circumstances of many black children as revealed in Home Office research statistics and the association between such disadvantage and underachievement in school.

3. Commission For Racial Equality (1985) *Birmingham Local Education Authority and Schools: Referral and Suspension of Pupils*, CRE, London.

An investigation of suspension within the schools of the Birminghan LEA reveals two distinct patterns of behaviour between black and white pupils suspended from schools. The black pupils were characterized by more violent confrontational offences against teachers in contrast to their white peers' greater association with disruption, vandalism and truancy. The report has comments on the difficulties that arise in black pupil–teacher relations when teachers misinterpret black pupils' behaviour as insolence (the lowering of eyes when confronted by a teacher as a sign of respect is quoted as one such example). Further comment focuses on the view widely held in ethnic-minority organizations that attitudes toward blacks in some schools are dismissive. The issue of Rastafari is raised in the report as one aspect of confrontation in schools over the question of hair-style. There appears to be a considerable mistrust of the school system in the black community although it is conceded that over the past few years schools appear to have become more tolerant of their black pupils' affiliation to Rastafari. Concern over suspension procedures within the authority is expressed. Irrespective of the nature of their offending behaviour, it was found that black pupils were more likely to be recommended for and placed subsequently in a suspension unit placement than white pupils.

REFERENCE

Green , P.A. (1983) Teachers' influence on the self-concept of ethnic minority pupils. Unpublished Ph.D. thesis, University of Durham.

Reading 8
THE TWO CURRICULA OF SCHOOLING
D. H. Hargreaves

Our present secondary-school system, largely through the hidden curriculum, exerts on many pupils, particularly but by no means exclusively from the working class, a destruction of their dignity which is so massive and pervasive that few subsequently recover from it. To have dignity means to have a sense of being worthy, of possessing creative, inventive and critical capacities, of having the power to achieve personal and social change. When dignity is damaged, one's deepest experience is of being inferior, unable and powerless. My argument is that our secondary schools inflict such damage, in varying degrees, on many of their pupils. It is not intended by the teachers, the vast majority of whom seek and strive hard to give their pupils dignity as I have defined it.

To find convincing evidence for this argument will be difficult. Most of the hidden-curriculum literature offers two related propositions: that the hidden curriculum makes a greater impact on pupils than does the formal curriculum and that this is true for most, if not all, pupils. It is not at all clear what should or could count as evidence to verify or refute that argument. Over the years it has proved to be extremely difficult to evaluate the effectiveness with which the formal curriculum is taught and learned; these problems are greatly magnified with the much more nebulous concept of the hidden curriculum. So it must be conceded that we are very far from being able to make comparisons between the two in terms of their relative impact on pupils. Hitherto the propositions have been furthered by persuasive argument which introduces new and indirect evidence, usually in a rather weak form, or by interpreting established evidence in a new way.

For a few, the arguments presented so far will be sufficiently persuasive, but there is much more relevant material to be discussed, and not merely to strengthen the argument, necessary though that is. The literature on the hidden curriculum draws attention to some of the unnoticed and unintended consequences of schooling; it tells us one part, a neglected part to be sure, but only one part of a complex educational story. Yet it gives surprisingly few indications of how we might change schools for the better. I shall take it that Illich's radical cure for the ills that schools induce, the 'de-schooling of society', is either mistaken or not a feasible

D. H. Hargreaves (1982) The two curricula of schooling, in *The Challenge for the Comprehensive School: Culture, Curriculum and Community*, Routledge & Kegan Paul, London.

reform. We must therefore give ourselves wider terms of reference in the hope that, through a close look at British secondary education, we can specify more precisely the undesirable aspects of schooling *and* the ways in which schools might be reformed. Reform is not just a negative process of discarding those elements of which we disapprove; we might then too readily throw out the baby with the bathwater, as does Illich. We must also detect what schools could and should do and explore how such tasks can be grafted on to the best of what schools currently achieve.

The work on the hidden curriculum makes depressing reading because it concentrates so heavily on the undesirable features and functions of school. Though you would not know it from much of the sociological literature, schools yield the most astonishing achievements consistently. They, too, often pass unnoticed and uncelebrated, but they must not be forgotten, even though they are not 'news'. Bearing this in mind, we must continue for a while to scrutinize the darker side of schooling.

We can begin where all analysis begins, with a commonsense objection to my argument about the destruction of pupil dignity. Most pupils in school simply do not give the impression of lacking dignity. In most secondary schools today, even with the most difficult classes, teachers' relations with their pupils frequently are characterized by friendliness and good humour, a remarkable tolerance and patience, and a genuine concern to get the best out of pupils. There has been a marked change in teacher–pupil relations over the last twenty years. The humourless army-sergeant authoritarian is fast disappearing. Teachers, it can be argued, have never in the history of British education been more concerned with the promotion of pupil dignity. Certainly, it would be very rare for a pupil to protest overtly that school is damaging his dignity. This is, however, the subtlety (and difficulty) of the hidden-curriculum argument: that it can be effective only as long as it remains hidden and unintended and the fact that it is for the most part hidden blinds us all, including most pupils, to its existence and power. Most pupils accept school with varying degrees of resignation as their lot; there is very little they can do about it. But there is a distinct minority which reacts with overt bitterness and hostility and the issue at stake is how we interpret that reaction.

In school this minority comprises those pupils who turn against school in explicit opposition. This group is predominantly but not exclusively urban working class in composition. It is also largely male, though the number of girls in this category is rising rapidly. When I was earning my academic 'colours' by coining sociological neologisms, I called it the 'delinquescent subculture' of the school: a group with delinquent-prone values and attitudes, Hargreaves (1967). In the conventional language of teachers they are the 'awkward squad', the 'trouble-makers'. Their opposition to schooling expresses itself in an aversion to schoolwork and lack of co-operation with teachers. This is the immediate and 'obvious' way to interpret such conduct and it is an interpretation that anyone who tries to teach such a class of pupils will find difficult to deny. I shall argue, however, that these pupils' protest is only incidentally against learning, against the formal curriculum, against the teachers as persons (though ironically teachers have tried to defuse the opposition by revamping the formal curriculum and cultivating more informal social relations as well as by, in other cases, becoming more authoritarian). The argument is that the opposition can be interpreted as an attempt to remove and negate the indignities meted out to them by the hidden curriculum. No writers have expressed this contention more succinctly than Sennett and Cobb (1972).

> There is a counterculture of dignity that springs up among these ordinary working-class boys, a culture that seeks in male solidarity what cannot be found in the suspended time that comprises classroom experience. This solidarity also sets them off from 'suck-ups'. Hanging around together, the boys share their incipient sexual exploits, real and imagined; sex becomes a way to compete in the group. What most cements them as a group, however, is the breaking of rules — smoking, drinking, or taking drugs together, cutting classes. Breaking the rules is an act 'nobodies' can share with each other. This counterculture does not come to grips with the labels their teachers have imposed on these kids; it is rather an attempt to create among themselves badges of dignity that those in authority can't destroy.

This argument is a fairly simple one: that this pupil opposition is a rejection of school because schooling destroys their dignity. In response, the pupils set up an *alternative* means of achieving dignity and status by turning the school's dignity system upside down. In the opposition's counterculture dignity and status are earned by active hostility to school and teachers, whenever this is possible. The teachers contribute to this alternative system, paradoxically, by trying to subvert it, for whenever a teacher seeks to undermine it, he provides the opposition with yet a further opportunity of achieving status in the alternative system. The counterculture requires and depends for its existence on teachers' attempts to eradicate it. As a solution to the dignity problem it is exceedingly clever, for the harder teachers try to make these pupils conform, the more the counterculture thrives. On this interpretation we must recognize that the counterculture is strongly *rational* in its own terms and sophisticated. From the teachers' point of view, however, the opposition seems irrational, since teachers are operating quite different criteria of what constitutes rationality. Because teachers often do not recognize this rationality, the opposition is genuinely puzzling; it seems pointless. It must therefore be explained and the explanations preferred by teachers are ones which are heavily deterministic, that is to say, ones in which the oppositional pupils do not *choose* to behave in this way but are driven and constrained into opposition. Commonsense and some social science conjoin to provide excellent rationales: oppositional pupils may be driven by psychological forces ('He's seriously disturbed and in need of psychological help — a good case of maladjustment') or by sociological forces ('What can you expect of a girl who comes from a home like that?'). There is, of course, some truth in these explanations; they would not appear so frequently in teachers' and social scientific explanations if they were patently false.

My argument is not that they are entirely mistaken, but that a partial explanation is being taken to be the whole explanation. I am not, of course, suggesting that pupil misconduct in the classroom is somehow not really misconduct at all, but a kind of political protest which teachers simply repress. These pupils can be very naughty, and intentionally so, sometimes showing themselves to be shockingly cruel and vindictive to teachers and to other pupils. And often the pupils will (at least privately) condemn their own behaviour as heartily as do their teachers. We have to be careful, on the one hand, that we do not 'read' too much into pupil opposition and, on the other, that we do not interpret it in too narrow and simplistic a fashion. Countercultural opposition has some highly specific features: misconduct is not directed simply against the teacher but also toward the audience of countercultural peers, because it represents a social solution to a personal problem. Whilst it is true that social scientists have been prominent in offering these interpretations, they are by no means incompatible with teachers' own experiences. Many teachers can readily recognize the difference between individual misconduct and countercultural opposition, and they often have ambivalent feelings towards the latter, having a partial sympathy with it.

Neat psychological or sociological explanations, of defective personality or defective home background, nevertheless remain popular as explanations. There are two main faults to this approach. The first is that such explanations attribute the blame for pupil opposition to forces in the pupil (psychological) or in the home or social background (sociological) and distract attention away from any part the school may play in the generation of the opposition. In so averting criticism from themselves, teachers sustain their own interests and avoid the need for any self-analysis. That such explanations support teachers' self-interest is not in itself sufficient to demonstrate that the theories on which they draw are false; but it alerts a suspicion in us. The second fault by the argument is that in every school there are many pupils who have similar family and social backgrounds to those of oppositional pupils but who do not join the counterculture. If the teachers' explanations were sound, many more pupils would be in opposition than is in fact the case. These two faults suggest that the explanation lies in some complex *interaction* between, on the one hand, certain psychological and sociological forces affecting the pupils and, on the other, certain processes occurring within the school itself. Both are necessary conditions to the emergence of the counter-culture of opposition, but neither is sufficient in isolation from the other.

Oppositional pupils do not *appear* to lack dignity because their conduct so often is not merely rebellious, but also precocious, self-confident, arrogant. So it is. At other times teachers catch a glimpse of the carefully hidden low level of self-esteem, when the mask of adult self-assurance looks like a paper-thin veneer. Behind the assertive toughness stands a pathetic little boy lost. But the abrasiveness of the counterculture under-standably irritates many teachers more often than it arouses their pity. In consequence, we often fail to see it as the very tentative, vulnerable and only partially successful attempt to resore dignity that is its true nature. The counterculture is heavily dependent on teachers' opposition to it for much of its life blood; it is a symbiotic relationship in which the counter-culture rarely evolves above the level of a lowly parasite which irritates its host but yet cannot break free into an independent cultural system. In the end it is the teachers' version of a culture of dignity which prevails because theirs mirrors society at large. However big and powerful the counterculture becomes in some schools, it can never lose its essentially parasitic qualities.

That the counterculture has no more than limited success in creating an alternative means of conferring dignity is not, however, its most startling characteristic. The wonder is that it exists at all. Pupils who create the counterculture of dignity must find that their dignity is damaged in school and elsewhere to generate the need for the counterculture. But the destruction of dignity cannot be so severe that the urge to promote an alternative system is itself damaged. The counterculture can flourish among pupils who retain some *sense of dignity* on which to build; the pupils must somewhere find the resources with which to build a new system. If it is the hidden curriculum of schooling that largely perpetrates the damage to dignity (a thesis still not adequately documented) then it is only partially successful in its unintended effects; the pupils can defend themselves against the force of the hidden curriculum sufficiently to offer an alternative which will then act as a barrier of resistance against further effects of the hidden curriculum. Perhaps the hidden curriculum is not as pervasive or overwhelming at least with oppositional pupils, as some of the writers allege. With deviant pupils, the hidden curriculum, like the formal curriculum, is partially inculcated and partially rejected.

To the teacher who has the persistent daily task of coping with difficult pupils it is very natural to live a kind of double life. The first, in the classroom at the front line of the battle, is organized around the immediate tasks of discipline and control and of seeking to educate these pupils as best one can in the circumstances. The second life is one in which the teacher reflects on these events and seeks explanations for them. It is natural that many teachers should resort to relatively simple and deterministic explanations in terms of constraining psychological and sociological forces; it is not merely that they wish to deflect criticism and blame from themselves. Rather it is difficult to see and integrate the many different layers of interpretation by which the counterculture is more adequately understood.

In a brilliant study of these working-class boys in a Midlands school, Paul Willis (1977) has carefully unravelled some of the strands of this alternative culture of dignity. More successfully than any other writer he shows that it is not, as some sociological accounts suggest, that lower-working-class boys become oppositional *because* they come from a certain kind of home and social background. Rather we can interpret the 'class values' of these boys as an important *resource* on which they can creatively draw to erect the counterculture as a means of salvaging their dignity which is diminished in school. Pupils in British schools are judged against a measuring rod in which mental qualities are regarded as superior to manual qualities. Schooling may not ignore the physical, but it is the mind and intellect which are cultivated most carefully: for most people that is what education is self-evidently about. Willis shows, as earlier studies have also shown, that by this measuring rod some pupils are relative failures. These are the pupils in the lowest streams in the third–fifth years at secondary school, where the counterculture normally emerges. The counterculture inverts this measuring rod by which they are judged failures: the physical is now held to be superior to the intellectual. It has been argued for many years by sociologists that among 'working-class values' there is an emphasis on aggressiveness and masculinity. Such values provide a resource to pupils with damaged dignity, for they can draw on the culture of masculinity to sustain their inversion of the mental–manual distinction which their teachers operate. Status within the counterculture is achieved through an aggressive and 'hard' masculinity, which is now associated with adulthood and maturity. Mental labour and all that is theoretical, all that is so highly valued to be successful in school, is associated with femininity and the effeminate. It is no accident that these pupils refer commonly to the 'bright' boys in school as 'poufs'. Willis goes on to show how this has important consequences in the preparation of these boys for shop-floor culture, for the maintenance of working-class sexism and for the encouragement of fascist attitudes to the new underclass of immigrants, especially Asians who are seen as 'soft'.

We can see in Willis' account a clear reflection of what Miller (1968) has defined as the 'focal concerns' or values of the lower working class. These are: *trouble* and *toughness*, which offer an obvious model for the male as a 'tough guy' who is hard, fearless, emotionally undemonstrative and skilled in physical fights, as portrayed in the cinema by Clint Eastwood; *smartness*, or a shrewdness shown in a capacity for quick repartee and the ability to outsmart, 'con' or dupe the stranger or outsider who is a 'sucker'; *excitement*, which breeds a constant search for immediate thrills or 'kicks' and the taking of risks; *fate*, or the attribution of the causality of events to good or bad luck; *freedom* and *independence*, the deep resistance to those in authority, accompanied by assertions such as 'Nobody pushes me around' or 'I know how to take care of myself'. It may well be, of course, that such values are rational adaptations of the lower working class to their lot in life. The suggestion is that they form a cultural heritage available to young people brought up in certain inner-city environments.

The problem is how we interpret the clear parallel between such working-class values and the expression of them by certain pupils in school. We may take an 'input' view which argues that pupils simply import such values into school because lower-working-class pupils are so heavily imbued with them that they cannot leave them at home as they pass through the school gates. Or we take a 'process' view which suggests that these values are expressed in a strong form in school only when they are activated by certain conditions which arise within the school itself; that is, under normal conditions these values would appear in no more than a weak form in school, since they are highly incongruent with the values of teachers and are usually suppressed by teachers. The classical or 'input' view argues that working-class boys do badly at school and join the counterculture because their values (for example, the emphasis on aggressiveness) make them resistant to schooling. An alternative or 'process' interpretation argues that, of the boys who fail in school, those with a working-class background have at their disposal a latent set of values to which they can and do turn when they need to find an alternative source of dignity. Neither view is probably adequate in itself; the generation of the counterculture requires us to make both arguments, though exactly how the two should be combined is still far from clear. But even a limited acceptance of the second view greatly undermines the neat deterministic sociological accounts that are associated with the first view, which so often reduce to the simplistic proposition that these pupils fail *and* become difficult in school because they come from deprived working-class homes.

Moreover, if we combine the two views, some interesting possibilities and problems emerge. Does the counterculture rely on the pupils coming from homes where the traditional working-class values appear in a strong form? Some of Willis's material, in which he makes a parallel between the experiences of the boys in school with those of their fathers at work, is consonant with such a view. If that is so, then when a group of pupils all experience the same assault on their dignity in school, and when all or most of the group members have, through their family and community, a common pool of working-class values on which they can draw, the counterculture of dignity will emerge in its classic and most successful form. This is a possibility that could be investigated. But there is also the problem: what happens to pupils who experience an assault on their dignity but lack the resources or working-class values that are important to the creation of a counterculture? How do they respond? Are these the boys and girls who hang around the fringes of counterculture groups, struggling to tune into the culture of aggressive masculinity? Such boys, and girls, are familiar in many classrooms; their conduct strikes the observer as an exaggerated imitation of some of the group's leaders, a desperate attempt to find acceptance. In practice, they are often not accepted, but are seen as a source of amusement, for after all they add to the fun by disrupting the lessons. Frequently, their frenetic displays merely confirm their status, to teachers and oppositional pupils alike, as 'nutters' for whom teachers can provide complex psychological explanations as 'maladjusted'. It is possible that they are pupils who simply lack the requisite working-class values and so do not understand the complex rules of the games in the counterculture, thus lacking the qualifications for admission to the counterculture. If this is so, then such pupils would find their dignity more profoundly threatened, since they can participate in neither the official status system of the school nor the alternative counterculture. Are these the pupils who withdraw psychologically, because they dare not run away physically? Is it they, rather than the members of the counterculture, who are truly deprived of dignity?

It has been known for many years that teachers, in contrast to psychiatrists, see withdrawn children as a much less serious cause for concern than aggressive noisy pupils for the obvious reason that oppositionals disrupt the lesson and require immediate attention from the teacher. Is it the 'silent opposition', so easily escaping the teacher's attention, who are the most important problem? Because such pupils who withdraw are so silent, their objections to schooling are unvoiced; it is the oppositionals who make the angry objections and endless complaints. In this they are aided and abetted by their friends; the counterculture has a collective strength from which oppositionals derive the courage and social support that is needed to rebel. In this do they speak only for themselves, or are they the spokesmen for other pupils too?

These are bold questions to which we have no clear answers; at present we lack the evidence to say. But, if there is *some* truth in the argument that the counterculture represents not merely an expression in school of attitudes originating in defective or 'culturally deprived' homes, but rather a creative opposition to school with its own sources of dignity, yet open only to those who possess the admission price of relevant cultural resources, then we have some grounds for at least listening to the criticism they may make of school. When teachers and pupils give us conflicting accounts of schooling, it is the teachers' voices which are usually granted credibility. When the pupils are defined as deviants, their accounts are double suspect. There are always at least two sides to every story; we know, understand and often rightly sympathize with the teachers' story. If we are to understand schools, we must listen to some of the other accounts, albeit with a proper scepticism. But before looking at school from their point of view, our most difficult task, we must consider some more of the ingredients that comprise the perspective on school of those who join the counterculture.

REFERENCES

Hargreaves, D. H. (1967) *Social Relations in a Secondary School*, Routledge & Kegan Paul, London.

Miller, W. B. (1968) Lower class culture as a generating milieu of gang delinquency, *Journal of Social Issues*, Vol. 14, pp. 5–19.

Sennett, R. and Cobb, J. (1972) *The Hidden Injuries of Class*, Cambridge University Press.

Willis, P. (1977) *Learning to Labour*, Saxon House, Farnborough.

TOPICS FOR DISCUSSION

1. How strong a case does Hargreaves make for the assertion that 'our secondary schools inflict damage (loss of dignity) in varying degrees on many of their pupils'?

2. Comment on Hargreaves' suggestion that behind the assertive toughness of the disruptive pupil 'stands a pathetic little boy lost'?
3. Discuss the explanatory power of input and process interpretations (p. 114) of lower working class boys' values.

SUGGESTIONS FOR FURTHER READING

1. Bird, C., Chessum, R., Furlong, V. J. and Johnson, D. (1980) *Disaffected Pupils: a Report to the Department of Education and Science by the Education Studies Unit, Brunel University*, Brunel University, Uxbridge.
This account of a study conducted in six secondary schools in two outer-London boroughs not only looks at the differing definitions that pupils and teachers have of particular behaviour but goes on to show how teachers' differential perceptions (i.e. their contrasting theories of pupil disaffection) are operationalized within the six schools and have markedly different consequences for school policy. The report is particularly useful in its discussion of differences in the schools' climates of pastoral care and disciplinary procedures.

2. Burden, R. (1981) Systems theory and its relevance to schools, pp. 28–36, in, B. Gillham (ed.) *Problem Behaviour in the Secondary School*, Croom Helm, London.
A *system* can be thought of as comprising a number of components each related to at least some others in a more or less stable way within a specific time period. Applied to schools, system theory offers a framework for thinking about the ways in which complex organizations such as comprehensive schools function. Applied to deviant behaviour, it suggests that deviance can be understood within any specific context and that various behavioural outcomes might be predicted as a result of systems analysis and systems change.

3. Her Majesty's Stationery Office (1985) *Better Schools*, Cmnd 9469, HMSO, London.
This report deals with the quality of education in primary and secondary schools. Chapter 6, 'Discipline', identifies the responsibility of the school to create an atmosphere that encourages good behaviour and self-discipline. Imaginative teaching, together with a determination to actively involve and interest pupils in their work are proposed as one remedy for indifference and disaffection.

Reading 9
DISRUPTIVE PUPILS AND EFFECTIVE PASTORAL CARE
D. Galloway

INTRODUCTION

In a study of pupils whose behaviour had resulted in exclusion from Sheffield schools, Galloway (1982) showed that the pupils tended to: be educationally backward; be exceptionally vulnerable on constitutional and/or medical grounds; come from acutely stressful home backgrounds. Yet more than half the pupils in the sample had attended only five of the city's thirty-nine mixed comprehensive schools. Over a four-year period some schools had consistently had high exclusion rates and others low rates.

Although the relation was not altogether consistent, teachers in schools with high exclusion rates tended to report relatively few problems from disruptive behaviour and vice versa. More important, it was clear that the amount of disruptive behaviour in school was not related in any obvious way to factors in a school's catchment area. Frequently, teachers attributed disruptive behaviour to home and community influences; yet of twenty-two catchment-area variables studied, none was found to predict exclusion rates. The conclusion of these studies was that factors in the catchment area have much less influence on children's behaviour at school than the policies and practices of the school itself.

Other research, too, has demonstrated differences between schools which could not satisfactorily be attributed to family or social background. Thus, Reynolds (1976) emphasized the influence of the schools' rules and the way teachers applied them, while Rutter *et al.* (1979) described a range of factors reflecting a school's climate or ethos. In a detailed case study Hargreaves (1967) drew attention to the effect of streaming policies on the pupil's attitudes and behaviour.

One common feature in these studies has been their emphasis on variables within the school. None, though, has focused in much detail on the influence of a school's pastoral care system. This is surprising for two reasons. First, disruptive pupils are invariably a source of concern to teachers with posts of responsibility for pastoral care. Secondly, the development of a comprehensive secondary education system has witnessed a huge increase in the number of posts carrying special

D. Galloway (1983) Disruptive pupils and effective pastoral care, *School Organization*, Vol. 3, No. 3, pp. 245–54.

responsibility for pastoral care. Best, Jarvis and Ribbins (1980) have criticized both the concept and process of pastoral care. Reynolds and Murgatroyd (1977) have suggested that truancy problems may have increased as a result of a policy in many comprehensive schools of basing pastoral care on 'middle-management' personnel, such as year tutors. Such criticisms, though, have been relatively infrequent. Pastoral care clearly is an established part of the secondary education scene.

Systematic studies of pastoral care have been infrequent remarkably. There seems nevertheless to be some consensus on at least two issues. First, pastoral care is not seen as a specialist's activity, but as an essential part of the work of all teachers. The basic unit of pastoral care therefore is the form tutor; the function of senior staff is to co-ordinate, or lead, a pastoral team. Secondly, the primary function of pastoral care is to help the school attain its objectives. Teachers have little or no control over their children's home backgrounds. Hence, the focus should be on adjustment and progress at school. Teachers who get overinvolved in the family problems of their pupils become frustrated and exhausted. As a result they may overlook what they themselves can do to help a child at school.

The existence of a broad consensus on what constitutes 'good' pastoral care tells us nothing about what actually happens in schools. Nor does it tell us anything about the effects of what happens. Specifically, research on the relation between pupils' behaviour and the organization and practice of pastoral care is conspicuously lacking. The present article describes characteristics of pastoral care in four secondary schools in England and in New Zealand. Each school was selected for its low level of disruptive behaviour. This report is not, however, a comparative study. Rather, it aims to describe effective pastoral care for potentially disruptive pupils in four schools.

METHODOLOGY

The four schools were identified from the results of two research programmes. The first was based in Sheffield, and included ten comprehensive schools. Seven of the schools had established a special group to cater for their disruptive pupils. Three had decided, as a matter of policy, not to establish any such group. Three schools had exceptionally high rates of exclusion for disruptive behaviour. Three had exceptionally low rates. Information was collected by observation and by interviews with senior teachers, class teachers and pupils about the prevalence and nature of disruptive behaviour. This information was supplemented by data from school and LEA records on attendance and exclusion rates and on a range of school and catchment-area variables. The second study took place in New Zealand. Four mixed comprehensive schools were selected for study on account of their high reputation locally in catering for their potentially disturbing pupils. Information was obtained by observation and by interviews with senior teachers and class teachers. This was supplemented by data from school and central records.

Of the fourteen schools, four stood out for the relative infrequency with which teachers reported incidents of disruptive behaviour. Also, three schools had exceptionally low suspension rates. The fourth had a higher suspension rate, having suspended, on average, three pupils each year over a four-year period. One school served a predominantly working-class catchment area. Two had a socially mixed intake, ranging across the five categories of the Registrar General's classification. In one of these schools, 30 per cent of pupils belonged to a minority ethnic group. The remaining school served a mainly middle-class catchment area.

Information on the formal organization of pastoral care was obtained from the headteacher. The headteacher also explained his conception of the aims of pastoral care and the philosophy behind it. Information on the actual practice of pastoral care was obtained from other teachers in the school. In the case of the English schools this was supplemented by interviews with the pupils.

Information from each of the four schools was examined to identify characteristics of the organization and practice of pastoral care. Six characteristics were identified, all of them present in varying degrees in each of the four schools. Some differences between the schools were also noted and are reported where they have obvious implications for pastoral care.

ORGANIZATION AND PRACTICE OF PASTORAL CARE

Underlying philosophy

Each headteacher was quite clear that the principal aim of pastoral care was to enhance children's educational progress and/or adjustment at school. They differed, though, in how they expressed this. Two head-teachers emphasized the importance of pastoral care in promoting a child's educational progress; each child needed a sense of achievement. Effective pastoral care should therefore aim to identify factors at school or at home which might militate against this. Thus, if circumstances made it impossible for a child to complete homework at home, the school should make alternative arrangements. Similarly, if a group of pupils was developing hostile attitudes toward individual teachers, or toward the school in general, this too must be investigated and tackled at source.

In contrast, one headteacher saw the central function of pastoral care as promoting the child's social adjustment. His aim seemed to be that pupils should see the school as a caring, stable place in which they were valued as individuals irrespective of their academic ability or social background. He saw membership of a stable school community as a valuable goal in itself and regarded pressure from the pro-social majority as the most powerful sanction against a potentially disruptive minority.

The fourth headteacher differed from the first two by placing an even stronger emphasis on the curriculum and teaching methods. The solution to disruptive behaviour, in his view, lay in removing sources of tension that arose from ineffective or inappropriate teaching. No classes in this school were ability banded or streamed. Consequently, much energy was devoted to provision of a resource bank of materials suitable for children with a wide range of abilities. This headteacher was also clear that effective pastoral care implied setting realistic goals. A minority of pupils had little or no chance of success in the existing public examination system. For these pupils the goal of the final year of compulsory schooling was successful entry to employment.

Pastoral care and discipline

The distinction between pastoral care and discipline was regarded as spurious in all four schools. Disruptive behaviour would interfere with the pupil's progress and/or adjustment at school. To respond effectively, teachers needed to understand the reasons for the problem. These might lie in the pupil, for example learning difficulties, in the family, in school organization or in classroom teaching programmes. Further, a response that would motivate one pupil, whether behaviourally or academically, might be ineffective for another.

This did not imply that teachers at these schools made interminable inquiries before dealing with incidents of disruptive behaviour. Often they felt that swift and decisive action was necessary. The point was that their responsibility did not end there. Prevention of such incidents occurring again would require investigation and a more considered response.

Other schools in both studies encouraged teachers, either as a matter of policy or by default, to distinguish between 'pastoral' and 'discipline' problems. Some schools, for example, required class teachers to refer discipline problems to the head of department and pastoral problems to the year tutor. Senior teachers in these schools were quite happy to acknowledge that discipline problems in the classroom could reflect stress in the child's home life. They could even see that emotional problems, such as withdrawn or tearful behaviour, could reflect stress resulting from poor teaching. Yet they saw no contradiction in expecting a teacher, who might see the child only for one or two lessons a week, to distinguish between discipline and pastoral problems. Not surprisingly, teachers and pupils alike seemed to feel a degree of confusion.

Referral to senior staff discouraged

Class teachers were not encouraged to pass problems to senior staff for investigation and subsequent action. They were expected to seek help in dealing with these matters, but in general they could not simply pass them on to someone else. This did not imply that serious matters had to be dealt with by the class teacher. One school even specified certain problems which should *immediately* be referred to a senior staff member. Because these occurred so seldom, however, they were seen as serious by pupils and teachers alike.

There were two common results of the policy, adopted in other schools, of referral of disruptive pupils routinely to middle or senior management. One was that year tutors and heads of departments spent an enormous amount of time investigating and dealing with the pupils referred to them. In the process they became exhausted and frustrated. They developed a problem of role conflict, complaining that most of the problems referred to them were caused by home background, which they felt, quite rightly, they could do nothing about. At the same time, illogically, they resented the way their colleagues referred these children to them, claiming that they were dealing with teachers' problems, not children's. The second result of referral of problems to senior staff was that the problem escalated. The act of referral meant that the conflict was now between the pupil and a member of the school hierarchy and was no longer a matter to be resolved between the pupil and the class teacher. Lawrence, Steed and Young (1977) describe the effects of this process in a London school. Galloway *et al.* (1982) also show how relatively minor incidents could escalate in some schools into a major confrontation resulting in suspension.

Class tutor

Senior staff in all four schools recognized the impossibility of one or two year-tutors knowing every pupil in their year. Consequently, pastoral care had to be based on form tutors, who in turn would receive support and guidance from year tutors and/or members of the school's senior management team. This had implications for the policy that teachers should deal with discipline problems themselves, albeit with advice and help from colleagues. The first person from whom to seek advice or information about a pupil was the form tutor, rather than a member of middle management.

Emphasizing of the class tutor's role also implied that the class tutor would be consulted in decisions affecting a pupil's welfare or educational progress. It meant that senior staff did not see as their own sole prerogative discussions with members of the support services such as educational psychologists, social workers or educational welfare officers. Similarly, class teachers expected to be consulted about matters such as a change of class or option.

Interestingly, the headteachers of all fourteen schools in the original studies emphasized the class tutor's importance in pastoral care. In practice, however, school policy and organization could defeat this goal. The most frequent ways in which this happened were:
1. class tutors changed each year
2. class tutors seldom taught pupils in their tutor groups
3. class tutors only saw their tutor group for ten minutes once or twice daily, and had to spend virtually all this time in administrative chores, such as completing attendance registers
4. class tutors felt that year tutors were paid to do pastoral care and saw no reason for accepting the responsibility themselves
5. the year tutor's job was defined in terms of investigation and the dealing with problems, rather than as leader of a pastoral team.

Perhaps the most important of these points was the feeling of class tutors in some schools that year tutors were paid to do pastoral care. This attitude both reflected and helped to create a climate of resentment in some staffrooms. The formal organization of a class-tutor system may be relatively unimportant. Indeed, the head of one of the four schools expressed concern that the form-tutor system was not operating satisfactorily. In this school and in one other form tutors changed their tutor group each year. Yet in both schools there was general acceptance of the principle that inexperience as a teacher did not prevent a person carrying out effective pastoral care.

Pastoral care for teachers

Although teachers were not encouraged to refer problems to senior staff, they were expected to seek advice and assistance. One headteacher commented that needing help was not a sign of failure, but failing to ask for it was. There was a widespread acceptance at this school that teachers could benefit from watching each other teach. The school's special education department (which the headteacher, explicitly, did not call the remedial department) was based on the principle that specialist teachers would help children in the ordinary classroom, working alongside the class teacher.

Teaching can be a very private activity. Moreover, teachers tend to be highly defensive about their classroom performance. Defensiveness makes it as hard to seek help, implying an admission of failure, as to offer help, implying doubt about a colleague's competence. This depressing cycle was evident in some of the other schools in each study.

One result of teachers seeking help in dealing with disruptive behaviour, was to increase stress in the short term; the problem cannot be passed to someone else, but must be faced. In the longer term, finding a solution, or at least a *modus vivendi*, enhanced a teacher's self-esteem by demonstrating professional development and growth. It was striking in several other schools that teachers had little confidence in the ability or willingness of senior staff to tackle problems referred to them. Moreover, the fact that they were expected to refer disruptive pupils to senior staff was taken, often correctly, to imply that senior staff saw referral as reflective of their inexperience or incompetence.

Failure of teaching or a failure in learning?

Generally, the climate in the four schools enabled teachers to discuss a child's disruptive behaviour or slow progress openly, without actual or implied recrimination. In this climate it became possible to discuss these matters as problems of teaching, rather than as problems of learning.

The climate in some of the other schools seemed almost to compel teachers to individualize a problem in the child or the child's family. To do otherwise was felt by the teacher to be an admission of personal or professional inadequacy. Worse, it was seen as such by the teacher's colleagues. To accept personal responsibility for a classroom problem could threaten the individual's status in, and acceptance by, the staffroom group. Thus, lack of professional support generated a defensive reaction, in which deviance was individualized on pupils or their families. Moreover, lack of professional support increased a teacher's need for personal acceptance by colleagues, thus increasing pressure to conform to the majority view.

Peer-group pressure has as powerful an effect on teachers as on pupils.

The prevailing ethos among the staff could pressure teachers into individualizing the problem. Alternatively, it could encourage them to review their own responses.

Three of the four headteachers remarked in interview that most disruptive behaviour was teacher induced. In other words, disruptive behaviour could result from teaching problems, as well as causing them. No headteacher said explicitly that disruptive behaviour and/or poor scholastic progress enabled them to identify weaknesses in school organization or classroom practice. Yet the way the schools investigated behaviour and learning problems often enabled them to identify weaknesses in school organization or classroom practice. In other schools the response tended to conceal such weaknesses.

Contact with parents

Two of the four schools encouraged teachers to make home visits when parents were unable or unwilling to come to the school. The headteachers of all four schools placed a high priority on contact with parents. That, however, was also true of all the other headteachers in both studies. The difference lay in the way contact with parents was organized and the attitude with which teachers approached it.

Generally, teachers at the four schools set out to enlist the parents' advice and co-operation in tackling a problem. The generally correct assumption was that parents would co-operate if they felt that their advice and opinions were valued. It was rare relatively to hear teachers at these schools complaining of lack of co-operation from parents.

Contact tended to be informal, frequently in one school by handwritten note, or by a log-book in which teachers made notes on the child's progress. Care was taken to make positive as well as critical comments in the log-book, which had to be seen and signed each week by the child's parents. In contrast, contact with parents at some of the other schools tended to be formal and infrequent. Only senior teachers would interview parents, except on routine occasions such as the twice-yearly open night.

SOME DIFFERENCES BETWEEN THE FOUR SCHOOLS

Academic outcome

Three of the four schools enjoyed a reputation in the community and in their controlling authority for high academic standards, based on results in public examinations. The fourth school did not enjoy this reputation. On the headteacher's appointment the school had had the highest rate in the district of persistent pupil absenteeism. Disruptive behaviour had been rife. Within three years the persistent absentee rate was around the median for the city, and the school stood out for the high level of co-operation between pupils, and between teachers and pupils. As the headteacher admitted, however, these changes had not been accompanied by a similar improvement in academic results.

Leadership style

Democratic leadership characterized only one of the four schools. Teachers at this school felt that they would be consulted on matters of school policy. They also felt that they could contribute actively in forming policy. An example occurred shortly before the research visits. A group of young teachers had decided to use each other as resources in managing disruptive pupils. When an incident occurred they would send the pupil to a colleague for a cooling off period. At the end of the session they would take the matter up with the pupil again. This initiative was welcomed by senior staff.

By comparison, leadership style in two schools was autocratic. In these schools, too, teachers generally felt that they would be consulted on matters of policy. There was little doubt, though, that the decision rested with the headteacher and senior management. Leadership style in the fourth school was midway between these two points.

Irrespective of style, leadership in all four schools was strong and accepted. The headteacher communicated his philosophy and goals to teachers and through them to pupils and to the community. Mostly, teachers felt that their problems were understood, and their efforts and achievements respected. Decisions might be autocratic, but they were not arbitrary.

Sanctions

All four schools used conventional sanctions such as detentions and daily report forms. They tended to involve parents at an earlier stage than many of the other schools in the studies. One school had abandoned use of corporal punishment and at another it was only used on very rare occasions by the headteacher. At a third school, corporal punishment was available for use by members of the school's middle and senior management, but was in fact used relatively seldom, at least by comparison with other schools in the study. At the fourth, use of this sanction was slightly above the median for the ten schools in the study.

Behavioural units

Two headteachers were strongly opposed to behavioural units as a response to disruptive behaviour. The other two had established a unit and saw it as a valuable resource in helping teachers to cater for pupils they found disturbing. These units were not seen as a long-term educational alternative. Indeed, one unit admitted pupils strictly on a part-time basis, allowing full-time attendance only for an initial day or two. Thus contact with the mainstream was never lost. Admission also was based on a clear assumption, understood by all concerned, that the pupil would shortly be returning to *all* ordinary classes.

DISCUSSION AND CONCLUSIONS

These observations on the pastoral care of schools with low rates of disruptive behaviour raise questions relevant to recent debate on school effectiveness. Rutter *et al.* (1979) found that, in general, schools with good pupil outcomes on one measure, for example examination results, also did well on the other measures, for example delinquency rates. Three of the four schools described in the present article had legitimate cause for satisfaction with their examination results. The fourth did not.

Further work is needed on the relation between pupils' social attitudes and behaviour and their educational progress. It is noteworthy, however, that the head of the school with poor examination results placed greater emphasis on social adjustment than on educational progress in defining the aims of pastoral care. Grace (1978) had noted a tendency in heads of inner-city primary schools to define 'good' teachers in terms of their pastoral orientation rather than by their classroom programmes. That could also have been true in the school with poor academic outcomes. In the other three schools there seemed to be an assumption that effective pastoral care and effective teaching were interdependent, since each was logically impossible without the other: effective classroom teaching would depend on understanding the needs of individual pupils; conversely, understanding and meeting individual needs would affect classroom practice.

A seldom stated but important characteristic of the four schools was that the principle of pastoral care was extended to include teachers. In each school, teachers seemed, on the whole, to feel that support was available when they encountered disciplinary problems. They also seemed to feel that their successes were recognized and appreciated.

Evidence from the four schools suggests that leadership style and organizational details may be relatively unimportant. In each case consistency of leadership seemed to be the crucial element. The essential ingredients in effective pastoral care may be clear goals, membership of a wider group in which support and advice are available, an opportunity to contribute to the group and recognition of achievement. This applies as much to the pastoral care teachers offer each other as to the pastoral care they offer their pupils.

REFERENCES

Best, R. E., Jarvis, C. B. and Ribbins, P. M. (1980) *Perspectives on Pastoral Care*, Heinemann, London.

Galloway, D. (1982) A study of pupils suspended from school, *British Journal of Educational Psychology*, Vol. 52, pp. 205–12.

Galloway, D., Ball, T., Blomfield, D. and Seyd, R. (1982) *Schools and Disruptive Pupils*, Longman, London.

Grace, G. (1978) *Teachers, Ideology and Control: Studies of Urban Education*, Routledge & Kegan Paul, London.

Hargreaves, D. H. (1967) *Social Relationships in a Secondary School*, Routledge & Kegan Paul, London.

Lawrence, J., Steed, D. and Young, P. (1977) *Disruptive Behaviour in a Secondary School*, University of London, Goldsmiths' College.

Reynolds, D. (1976) When pupils and teachers refuse a truce: the secondary school and the creation of delinquency, in G. Mungham and G. Pearson (eds.) *Working Class Youth Culture*, Routledge & Kegan Paul, London.

Reynolds, D. and Murgatroyd, S. (1977) The sociology of schooling and the absent pupil: the school as a factor in the generation of truancy, in H. C. M. Carroll (ed.) *Absenteeism in South Wales: Studies of Pupils, their Homes and their Secondary Schools*, Faculty of Education, University College of Swansea.

Rutter, M., Maughan, B., Mortimore, P. and Ouston, J. (1979) *Fifteen Thousand Hours: Secondary Schools and their Effects on Children*, Open Books, London.

TOPICS FOR DISCUSSION

1. Why should referral of disruptive occurrences to year tutors or heads of departments result in (a) role conflict for senior staff and (b) the escalation of the original incidents?
2. In what ways were schools' organizational policies found to work against class tutors' involvement in pastoral care?
3. Discuss the observation that, 'evidence from the four schools suggests that leadership style ... may be relatively unimportant [but that] ... consistency of leadership seemed to be the crucial element'.

SUGGESTIONS FOR FURTHER READING

1. Grace, G. (1978) Pupils, localities and the experience of teaching, pp. 170–89, in *Teachers, Ideology and Control: a Study in Urban Education*, Routledge & Kegan Paul, London.

Grace analyses the ways in which many inner-city teachers in London comprehensive schools characterize their pupils and the experience of teaching. Typifications of inner-city pupils as *victims* and teachers as *ameliorators*, he argues, have their origin in social and historical contexts which suggest that contemporary urban teachers are as unlikely as their nineteenth century predecessors to bring about radical changes in the educational experiences of their pupils. Historically, Grace contends, schools have been preoccupied with maintaining system order and minimizing change. Clearly, many teachers regard this as being in the best interests of their pupils; some, however, see in this the continuing and unacceptable face of social control in urban education.

2. Galloway, D., Martin, R. and Wilcox, B. (1985) Persistent absence from school and exclusion from school: the predictive power of school and community variables, *British Educational Research Journal*, Vol. 11, No. 1, pp. 51– 61.

This is a somewhat technical report of a study of thirty-three Sheffield secondary schools that sought to investigate the association between (a) persistent absenteeism and (b) pupil exclusion from school, with some fifty-eight other variables, twenty-two of which described the catchment areas of the schools (type of housing, standard of amenities, socio-economic background of occupants, percentage of pupils on free school meals, etc.) and thirty-six of which described structural and organizational aspects of the schools themselves (pastoral care, remedial teaching, streaming policy, careers guidance, etc.). Of particular interest is the reported finding that neither catchment area nor structural/organizational variables were helpful in predicting pupil exclusion rates. The authors of this study suggest that there is a need to initiate intensive studies of individual schools if factors involved in pupil exclusion are to be understood more clearly.

3. Evans, J. (1982) *Fifteen Thousand Hours*: where do we go from here?, *School Organization*, Vol. 2. No. 3, pp. 239–53.

In the aftermath of the publicity attached to Rutter's book on school effectiveness (*Fifteen Thousand Hours*) the author reviews major studies in the area and makes a plea for the development of what he calls *conceptual maps*, that is to say, a list of those factors that the researcher(s) consider(s) relevant to a target (or dependent variable), often as not pupil attainment. The presentation of an explicit conceptual map, he argues, can go a long way toward dispelling confusion about a particular study's conclusions. A second question that is raised concerns the ability of quasi-experimental studies such as Rutter's to give any understanding of the *processes* by which school climate (or *school ethos*) is actually linked with effects such as better attainment or better attendance, etc. The need for ethnographic methods in future research is self-evident.

IMPROVING SECONDARY SCHOOLS
Inner London Education Authority

The ILEA (1984) report (*Improving Secondary Schools*) is specifically concerned with underachievement in secondary schools. Where it breaks new ground is in its emphasis on the needs of all pupils, not just the least able or the most disaffected. It focuses attention on the importance of looking at the curriculum as a whole both in terms of its content and its structure; moreover, it invites a close scrutiny of the association between *curriculum, underachievement* and *disaffection*. A selection of paragraphs (3.9–3.11 and 3.16) from the report is provided for discussion.

FOURTH AND FIFTH YEARS CORE AND OPTIONS

The vast majority of schools adopt for the first three years a policy of imposing a broad common curriculum with little choice for pupils. In some schools this begins to vary in the third year. We consider that there is considerable scope for redirecting the third-year curriculum. It is at the beginning of the fourth year that the sharp differences between schools emerge, with the introduction of option schemes that last throughout the next two years. It is for this reason that the recent discussions about the secondary-school curriculum have focused so heavily on the fourth and fifth years. That virtually no two schools are alike in the structure and content of the curriculum in the fourth and fifth years has been a source of concern to many, including HMI and the DES. This diversity between schools is held to be undesirable and efforts have been made to create greater consensus between schools on this matter. It has been argued by HMI that there should be more 'breadth, balance and coherence' in the secondary curriculum (*A View of the Curriculum*; HMI, 1980). They argue that there should be greater national agreement that all pupils in the comprehensive school should be offered a formal curriculum which provides opportunities to engage in a largely comparable range of learning.

'Extending the amount of common ground implies in practice a broader coverage of subjects than many pupils now sustain to the age of 16, and a substantially larger compulsory element in the final two years. Both the number of optional subjects and the range of which they are chosen would be correspondingly smaller. ...'

Inner London Education Authority, *Improving Secondary Schools: Report of the Committee on the Curriculum and Organization of Secondary Schools* (the Hargreaves Report), ILEA, London.

A similar note is struck in HMI (1981) *The School Curriculum*:

'There is an overwhelming case for providing all pupils between 11 and 16 with curricula of a broadly common character, designed so as to ensure a balanced education during this period ... At present, for the first three years in most secondary schools pupils follow broadly similar programmes ... In the fourth and fifth years, the numbers of subjects studied by all pupils is much reduced. Some subjects are dropped, others added, with varying degrees of guidance and control. The result is that a balanced curriculum for each individual pupil is not always assured ... Although choices are made, and have to be made, at the end of the third year, every pupil up to 16 should sustain a broad curriculum.'

The ILEA inspectorate document on the curriculum shows the same preference for a broad curriculum up to the age of sixteen years. At the present time our thinking about the structure and content of the secondary-school curriculum must be influenced by this recent national discussion on the degree to which the school curriculum, especially in the fourth and fifth years, should be a *common* curriculum, that is, a curriculum which is compulsory for all pupils. Put another way, how much curriculum time (of some forty periods a week) should be devoted to options, and what should be the content of those options? In England and Wales there is today considerable diversity between schools in the extent and contents of the common (or 'core') curriculum and of the optional areas. In principle, a school might adopt a wholly common curriculum, i.e. a compulsory curriculum for all pupils with no options, or a wholly optional curriculum, i.e. one in which no element is compulsory for all pupils. In practice these extreme cases do not exist; the differences between schools are in the amounts of time allocated to the commom curriculum and to the optional subjects. HMIs *The Secondary Survey* in 1979 found that, in full range comprehensive schools, on average some 42 per cent of curriculum time was allocated to the common curriculum in the fourth year: over half these schools allocated between 40 and 49 per cent curriculum time to the core. At the extremes, one school allocated over 70 per cent curriculum time to the common curriculum and three schools less than 30 per cent.

There is a clear trend in the advice offered to schools that there should be an increase in the common curriculum in the fourth and fifth years, and a corresponding reduction in option choices. Among ILEA secondary schools, some currently are offering an extensive common curriculum in the fourth and fifth years along the lines advocated by HMI, the

DES and the ILEA inspectorate; others, however, have a relatively small compulsory element, usually English and mathematics, some with physical education and/or religious education in addition. Arguments can be made on both sides, but we can find no document which makes a neutral exposition of both sets of arguments. Recent official documents from HMI and the DES are, quite properly, attempts to persuade the relevant parties to increase the compulsory elements and reduce the number of options and so, naturally, do not make the best possible case on the other side. Since ILEA schools vary considerably in the extent of the compulsory curriculum in the fourth and fifth years, we feel that, before presenting our own conclusions, we should first set out both arguments as best we can.

Arguments in favour of a larger common curriculum in the fourth and fifth years

Unless the broad curriculum of the first three years of secondary schooling is extended into the fourth and fifth years, the educational diet of older pupils will lack balance and breadth. In *The Secondary Survey,* HMI cite the case of a boy with a programme of study which consisted of English, mathematics, religious education, physical education, physics, chemistry, computer studies, geology and metalwork; thus the humanities (history and geography), aesthetic subjects (art, music, drama and dance) and modern and classical languages had all been abandoned at the end of the third year. The first three years of secondary schooling introduce pupils to the basic elements of the subjects of the curriculum, sometimes in the form of distinct subjects, sometimes in an integrated form (e.g. humanities). It is far too early, at the age of thirteen to fourteen years, for pupils to abandon any of these subjects entirely. The subjects of the eleven-to-thirteen-years curriculum are placed there precisely because in our society we regard them as the most important forms of knowledge into which all should be initiated. If these are the subjects that society considers to be worthwhile knowledge, they are worthwhile knowledge for all pupils throughout their period of compulsory schooling. If pupils are permitted to drop any of these subjects, they will be partially, not fully, educated. Moreover, if pupils are permitted to elect against one or more of these subjects, there will be a hidden form of selection. Some pupils, perhaps particularly those from working-class homes, will make an unbalanced selection of options: such pupils may be tempted toward a very limited range of subjects and those which they consider to be 'easier', i.e. less academic. There is a real danger that the tripartite system may reappear within the comprehensive school and an important social injustice will ensue. The comprehensive principle requires that all pupils follow a comprehensive (i.e. broad and balanced) curriculum up to the age of sixteen years.

A common curriculum is the only means by which all pupils can be led to keep their opportunities for the future fully open. The defect of option systems is that subjects selected at the age of thirteen to fourteen years constrain very heavily possibilities within the educational system beyond sixteen years; they often constrain vocational choices too. At the age of thirteen to fourteen years pupils are not in a position to understand the nature and power of these longer-term constraints. Of course, some parents do understand them and guide their children accordingly. Working-class parents, who often have no personal experience of further and higher education, or without occupations which demand specific qualifications, may be at a serious disadvantage in guiding their children or in interpreting the advice provided by teachers. It is irresponsible of the school to permit young people to make choices which they, and perhaps their parents, may later come to regret. Pupils at this age lack the maturity to make the most sensible choices: they are too likely to be influenced unduly by whether or not they like a subject or their current teacher, or by the subject preferences of their close friends. Some pupils do not show to the full their talents for a particular subject, or come to develop a real interest in it, until well into the fourth or even the fifth year. If pupils are allowed to drop subjects at too early an age, they may well make choices which will inhibit or deny their talents and interests.

There is evidence that some subjects are associated with deep-seated and barely acknowledged sex stereotypes. If given the choice, boys in most schools drop modern languages, which have an entirely unwarranted 'feminine' image. If a modern language were part of the common curriculum until the end of the fifth year, more boys would achieve a far higher standard than at present in languages. An even stronger argument, perhaps, can be made in the case of girls and science. When science becomes optional, many girls drop the subject entirely; if the pupils are permitted to choose between sciences, then girls predominantly opt for biology and against the physical sciences (physics and chemistry). In effect, at the age of thirteen to fourteen years far too many girls are closing off the possibility of specialization in science and technology and the opportunity to enter a wide range of occupations for which some qualification in the physical sciences is necessary. By allowing girls to opt against science, we serve to maintain the male dominance of science and technology (and thus much of our industry). We also, of course, ensure that the majority of our science teachers will continue to be men.

The argument for an extension of the common curriculum in the fourth and fifth years does not entail a denial of the principle of choice within our education system. It means that some important choices will simply be postponed until the age of sixteen years when pupils have a more mature and informed assessment of their abilities and preferences, of their aspirations for educational and occupational futures, and of the advice tendered by parents and teachers. Moreover, a school may make a subject part of the common curriculum but still permit a degree of choice within a subject area. Thus if science is part of the compulsory curriculum, pupils may still be free to choose between, say, a relatively short course of integrated science or a more time-consuming course of the separate subjects of physics, chemistry and biology. A pupil who opts for the integrated science course is then better able, at the age of sixteen years, to choose to do further work in science than is the pupil who abandons the subject entirely at the age of thirteen to fourteen years, and who at sixteen years feels it is far too late to begin science again. The case for an extension of common curriculum is not based on the denial of choice; rather it seeks to prevent the making or irrevocable choices at too early an age. To argue that some of the basic choices must be postponed until sixteen years is to accept in a realistic way some of the major changes in our educational system of recent years. We must now, in the light of massive youth unemployment, think in terms not of the eleven-to-sixteen-years curriculum, but of the fourteen-to-eighteen-years *curriculum*, for most young people will receive some form of education and training in the sixteen-to-eighteen-years period. When the majority of pupils left school at sixteen years, the end of the third year was perhaps the appropriate age for choice. Now that most continue with their education beyond sixteen years, it is sixteen which is the most appropriate age for choice.

The immense variation between schools in the fourteen-to-sixteen-years curriculum is a source of considerable disturbance and difficulty when pupils transfer from one school to another during this period. If schools were more similar because they adopted a more extensive and agreed common curriculum in the fourth and fifth years, transfers between schools would be accomplished much more easily. This is of particular significance in inner London, and all our major cities, where there is often a considerable movement of the population. It must be added that, if there were a larger agreed common element to the school curriculum, amalgamations between secondary schools (which have been necessitated by falling rolls) would be substantially less fraught with difficulty for both pupils and teachers.

It is claimed that a large degree of subject choice at thirteen-years plus increases pupil motivation and inhibits potential disaffection and alienation. Yet so far as we know there is no evidence to substantiate this alleged link between degree of subject choice and pupil disaffection. When pupils display hostility toward or dislike of a particular subject, it is often not the subject as such which is being rejected: rather, it is the particular syllabus which is at fault, and/or the methods the teacher adopts in the teaching of that subject. For every subject it is possible to find examples of teachers who have found or developed an appropriate syllabus and effective methods of teaching it. The purported link between disaffection and lack of subject choice is often merely an excuse for poor teaching.

One major weakness of schemes of extensive subject choice is the unpredictable relation of supply and demand between options. Some subjects are oversubscribed and some are undersubscribed, so some pupils have to be 'guided' away from the former to the latter. In effect this gives considerable powers of selection to the teachers of the oversubscribed subjects. In practice, and for understandable reasons, they favour pupils with superior ability and achievement, with high motivation, and with a good record of behaviour. Lower achieving and 'less able' pupils, those with lower levels of commitment and with less favourable records of behaviour are thus 'guided' to the undersubscribed subjects. Such hidden selection is not compatible with the principles of comprehensive education. Furthermore the teachers of the undersubscribed subjects feel that they are being left with 'rejected' pupils and this can seriously lower their morale. Even more important, the lower-achieving and less-motivated pupils are very aware that their choices are being denied; they feel cheated by the option system and the effect is often to increase their disaffection with school, and even to increase their truancy from the subjects they are now compelled to take, but for which they did not opt. Choices that have to be made from within an arbitrary set of options are never, from a pupil point of view, 'equal'; some pupils see themselves as 'choosing' the least undesirable dish from the proffered menu, which hardly stimulates their appetite. Pupils accept compulsory subjects less reluctantly than the pseudo-choices of option schemes. The changing membership of teaching groups which is associated with option schemes has social side-effects. 'Problem' pupils may find themselves in the same options and the likelihood of 'sink' classes is increased. Teaching groups that have remained relatively stable over the previous three years are now upset and some pupils find they are no longer in the same classes as their friends. Such isolation and unhappiness make for a poor start to the fourth year.

It is much easier to make a persuasive argument for an extended common curriculum in the fourth and fifth years than to implement it. Even if the power of the case is conceded, some schools would experience considerable difficulties in implementation in the short term; for some schools it would be virtually impossible. In certain subjects there is already a considerable shortage of suitably qualified teachers. Many schools are simply not in a position to ensure that all, or even most, pupils follow a modern language through until the end of the fifth year. In other subjects there is often a lack of physical and material resources to allow such plans to be implemented. Many schools, for example, do not have sufficient laboratory space to countenance compulsory science for all pupils in the fourth and fifth years. Facilities take time to change; some of the current option schemes have had effects on the allocation of resources which cannot be easily or quickly undone: in some cases the options were themselves adaptations to scarce resources. A common curriculum may also be difficult to maintain at a time of falling rolls, when schools lose staff in unpredictable and often undesirable ways. Option systems are by no means immune to the effects of falling rolls and teacher losses, but they possess a degree of flexibility which allows them to adapt in difficult times.

A major weakness of some of the arguments for an extension to the common curriculum is that, whilst in principle the arguments for greater balance in the curriculum are persuasive, in practice it is the conventional academic subjects which tend to dominate the common curriculum. Now the kind of academic curriculum proposed would unquestionably have considerable breadth; it would be broader than was the academic curriculum of the former grammar schools, where sometimes pupils found themselves making a virtually irrevocable choice between the arts and the sciences at the end of the third year. Within the comprehensive school, however, the breadth must be more than just academic breadth; such a school must give recognition and prestige to areas which the grammar schools neglected, such as technical knowledge and skill. A truly comprehensive school must have a truly comprehensive curriculum: it must offer all its pupils full opportunities to display and exercise the whole range of abilities, talents and skills, not merely the academic. Many pupils have abilities, talents and skills which are not primarily academic in the grammar-school sense. The traditional academic curriculum emphasized memorization, abstract theory and written expression: it gave a much lower priority to the practical application of knowledge; physical and manual skills; social and oral skills; technical subjects; subjects with a clear vocational relevance. The comprehensive school must achieve a much better balance between these different emphases and that goal cannot be reached unless pupils can exercise considerable choice in the fourth and fifth years. The first three years in the secondary school introduce all pupils to the academic curriculum. Thereafter, while no pupil should be permitted to choose too narrow an academic curriculum, and no pupil should be permitted to abandon entirely the academic elements, pupils should be free to select an educational emphasis in accordance with their abilities, preferences and aspirations. Most of all, pupils must be able to follow a curriculum in which they can experience a real degree of success in most aspects. It is laudable to argue that the curriculum must be more coherent and more balanced. Yet it is impossible to find a coherent and balanced common curriculum that meets the very different needs of all young people. Coherence and balance must be experienced as such by the individual pupil if the curriculum is to be one in which success can be achieved. Because of the considerable differences between pupils in their abilities, interests and aspirations, a substantial degree of choice is essential.

What general advice, then, should we give to schools about the curriculum in the fourth or fifth years? We have presented as fully and fairly as we can the arguments in favour of an enlarged common curriculum and those in favour of a retention of the substantial optional elements now favoured by most schools. There are powerful arguments on both sides, and there is no simple way in which the two can be reconciled to create a curriculum structure and content by which we achieve the strengths of both and the disadvantages of neither; it is impossible, for example, to retain a substantial amount of choice while seeking to meet the issues raised concerned with pupil transfer as discussed previously. We favour a degree of choice in the fourth and fifth years, i.e. a common curriculum of not more than 60–70 per cent. However, we believe that the option system should not be entirely 'free'. There are two basic types of option system. In the *free option* system pupils are entitled to choose a number from the total set of available options, with no constraints on choice, except perhaps those of the timetable and staff availability. In the *constrained option* system subjects are grouped on some principle and pupils must choose one from each group. In one version of the constrained option system subjects are grouped on the basis of similarity, e.g. aesthetic subjects, and the pupil is then required to select at least one aesthetic subject, e.g. one from art, music, drama and dance. Thus, in a constrained option system an area of study, such as science or aesthetic subjects, is made compulsory, but the pupil is free to choose a subject *within* the area. We shall argue that some of the option choices should be constrained in this way.

TABLE 10.1   Ideal ILEA Secondary-school Fourth- and Fifth-year Compulsory Curriculum

Elements	Suggested minimum-time allocation	
	periods	%
English language and literature	5	$12\frac{1}{2}$
Mathematics	5	$12\frac{1}{2}$
Science	4	10
Personal and social education ⎱ Religious education ⎰	3	$7\frac{1}{2}$
At least one 'aesthetic' subject (a constrained option)	4	10
At least one 'technical' subject (a constrained option)	4	10
Total	25	$62\frac{1}{2}$

Compulsory curriculum

The compulsory curriculum toward which, in our view, ILEA secondary schools should be moving for fourth-and fifth-year pupils contains six elements (Table 10.1). This leaves fifteen out of forty periods (37.5 per cent) for either additional periods in compulsory subjects or the free options or some of each. Pupils would thus be free to make choices for these fifteen periods from among the following:

1. classical and modern languages
2. history
3. geography
4. economics
5. commercial and business studies
6. physical education
7. additional science subjects
8. additional 'aesthetic' subjects
9. additional 'technical' subjects
10. additional English and mathematics.

In our view, it is particularly important that single-sex schools move toward the curriculum structure we recommend, since at present in some of these schools pupils are presented with a fourth- and fifth-year curriculum which lends itself to programmes of study lacking balance and breadth.

Active learning

Much of the boredom cited by ILEA pupils relates to this view that too little effort is made to engage them in active learning, that they are required to spend too much time listening or copying, or completing worksheets. A negative effect of the trend toward individualized learning materials has been a preponderance of worksheet materials across the curriculum. While we endorse the need for materials suited to the individual's current level of attainment and designed to lead him or her on to a further level of knowledge or achievement, we believe that pupils need to experience variety of activity and a range of modes of learning if their interest is to be sustained. As stated by the Schools Council (1981):

> 'a teacher needs to be able to call on an extensive repertoire of teaching and learning methods. Crude descriptions of teaching as progressive or traditional, exploratory or didactic fail to convey the variety and range of modes of teaching and learning teachers have at their command. Some pupils will respond well to one mode, and others to different modes. They and their teachers are more likely to enjoy school, and stay on their toes, if their days and weeks are varied by skilful choice of mode. Sometimes the mode or process of learning has its own lessons, more potent than the formal subject matter of the lesson.'

Boredom leads to resentment and that resentment is expressed either by passive withdrawal of attention or by disruptive behaviour. In the case of the latter a 'double-bind' situation is all too often created: rebellious pupils are seen as too irresponsible to be given opportunities for discussion, working in pairs, or in small groups and are meted out with yet more of the very kind of silent solitary activity that has stimulated their original rebellion. From our talks with disaffected pupils, from watching them at work, and from the evidence we have received about various 'sanctuary' or withdrawal facilities for disaffected or disruptive pupils, it is clear that, supervised by a sympathetic but firm teacher, they settle down to the tasks in hand, sometimes continuing through breaktime. Their enthusiasm seems to arise from being given the opportunity to pace themselves and to elect to change activity. This convinces us of the need for teachers to achieve a balance between individual work and work which involves interaction with peers, allowing pupils to make their own individual contribution, and which requires a variety of intellectual and practical responses. Thus our evidence suggests that pupils wish to be given much more responsibility for their own learning and to have the opportunity to negotiate much more of both its content and its process. For example, pupils could be offered choices in the literature studied in English; of topics in social studies; between individual, pair and group work in a wide range of subjects and of ways of presenting their work. Curriculum, organization, teaching methods and assessment are welded into a coherent whole. In current educational developments there is a tendency to separate these four dimensions, and we believe this should be resisted.

A proposal for change

The task is this. How are we to resolve the problems raised and also design courses and methods of recording which permit a combination of public-examination courses, graded tests and profiles/records of achievement, and do so *in a manner which is economical in terms of teachers' time and efforts*? We believe that a critical change is the restructuring of the two-year courses in the fourth and fifth years into *half-term units.* Instead of setting out on a vague two-year educational journey toward nebulous and distant goals, pupils should, from the beginning of the fourth year embark on a series of six- to eight-week learning units, each of which has a more readily defined and perceived purpose, content and method of recording. The two-year course would thus be subdivided into eleven or twelve interconnected units, each of which is meaningful in itself and adapted to the time perspective of fourteen year olds and especially many of those with a working-class background. Indeed, there are precedents in university, polytechnic and adult education which suggest that a curriculum organized around shorter-term objectives appeals to *all* learners, regardless of age, sex, class and ethnicity.

A half-term unit permits a form of pupil involvement which is very difficult to achieve in a two-year course. The syllabus content is relatively small, so the pupils can clearly see the knowledge and skills they need to acquire over the next few weeks. Course objectives, instead of existing only in the teacher's mind or the course design, can now be shared with the pupils. If pupils see clearly where they are going, they are more likely to be motivated to make the journey. Once unit objectives have been shared between teacher and pupil, it is easier for teacher and pupils to negotiate the *means* by which unit goals can be reached. In other words, there can be joint planning of methods and procedures of work. This takes pupils out of passive roles into active and collaborative roles with the teacher. At the end of the unit, teachers and pupils can overtly and jointly evaluate the extent to which unit objectives have been achieved. This helps to motivate pupils for the beginning of the next unit. It also makes it genuinely possible for the pupils to play an active role in curriculum development and evaluation.

At the end of each unit, all pupils can be offered a clear and tangible assessment: each unit must give the pupil 'something to show' for the six to eight weeks work. In other words, we believe that some form of assessment should be devised for every area of the curriculum in the immediate future. The unit *credit* may take a variety of forms. It might be a certificate which specifies the ground covered and what has been achieved. The advantage here is that pupils can be shown the certificate at the beginning of the unit and thus be made aware of the unit content and have a clear target to aim for. Alternatively the unit credit might be a graded test/assessment or profile. In developing unit credits, each school can draw upon its own experience and preferences and also the distinctive needs of different subjects, whilst also taking account of developments relating to the London Record of Achievement (which we see as complementary to our proposals) as well as innovations arising from DES initiatives. Whatever the format of the unit credit, its existence will, we believe, enhance pupil motivation for the unit as well as for the succeeding units, since the units are cumulative. Moreover, the unit credit is a permanent record of achievement (and the quality of the credit format should reflect this) so that even if a pupil does not ultimately enter for a public examination, the credit remains. It is essential that pupils see the potential value of the credit for use in seeking employment and/or for entry into further education. The credit also serves as a form of school record, which can be the basis for reports to parents, especially if the unit credits are assembled to form the main part of a 'cheque book' format. Thus the unit credit can serve several purposes.

ALTERNATIVE PROVISION

We believe that our proposals for the curriculum and organization of the fourth and fifth years in secondary schools should, if implemented, greatly help to reduce underachievement and disaffection among the pupils in this age-group. Prevention is always better than cure and the measures we have proposed are clearly directed at prevention. However, we recognize that these measures will not solve all the problems with which we are here concerned. Some pupils would, in spite of these measures, continue to be disaffected by their experience of school, to be disruptive and to underachieve. What provision are we to make for these pupils?

The most urgent need, we believe, is to change the way in which we perceive these pupils. At present in this country we tend to treat the pupils who do not fit into the secondary school as problems: they are pupils who are labelled as 'difficult', as 'deviants' or as 'misfits'. There is, it is said, nothing wrong with the school, but there is something wrong with the pupils who reject the school. Quite rightly, we try all we can to help such pupils to adjust to school like the majority of their peers but, when our attempts to integrate them fail, we tend to respond in one of two ways. The first response is often to be punitive by suspending the disruptive pupil. Schools may use suspension also to demonstrate that continued disruptive or antisocial behaviour is unacceptable to the school community and to enable teachers and the other pupils in the class to get on with their work without disturbance while discussions take place with the parents. The second response is to reject them. The misfits are best catered for if they are placed outside the normal school, in a special class or a special unit, where people with the appropriate expertise, skill or interest can cope with these pupils, leaving ordinary teachers or ordinary pupils free to get on with the normal business of schooling

We are not unsympathetic to these responses. Disaffected and disruptive pupils do indeed create real problems for teachers and other pupils. Not unnaturally, teachers often feel relieved when such pupils are absent. All this is true. But it is also true that the response of punishment and rejection tends to make the pupils worse, not better. They know they are being rejected and they resent it. They feel they have their own valid point of view, their own criticisms of the school and the teachers and their own unmet needs none of which they believe are being taken seriously. The ensuing stalemate between frustrated and rejecting teachers and resentful and rejected pupils is clearly unsatisfactory. Relationships can at this point only deteriorate. It is possible, we think, to break out of this vicious circle only by changing our general approach to these young people. The school's initial response to disaffection and disruptive behaviour should always be to seek the support and co-operation of the parents and to reintegrate the pupil into the normal life of the classroom. But when these attempts fail, as they do with a minority of pupils, there is no point in rejecting the pupils and blaming them for their refusal to conform or fit in. Instead it seems more realistic and more productive to accept that the school has in some sense failed them rather than insisting that it is they who have failed us. Our school system can work for the majority, but we need not be afraid of recognizing that for a minority the ordinary school, with its curriculum, teaching methods and organization, is simply inappropriate. Instead of blaming and rejecting this minority, we can, if we recognize the limitations of the school to cater for the needs of every child, be ready to treat their rejection of school as legitimate and thus seek *positive alternatives* by which their needs can be met. The theme of our remarks on the severely disaffected and disruptive is this: first, seek to integrate and, when that fails, find a positive alternative.

It is often argued that the needs of these pupils are best met in the positive way we advocate by providing them with a distinctive vocational education. We do not deny that vocational alternatives can have beneficial effects, but we believe this to be a very dangerous solution. Earlier in this report we rejected the creation of 'vocational streams' in comprehensive schools: all pupils, we repeat, have rights before the age of sixteen years to a broad education and many of our recommendations are designed to make that curriculum more practical and more relevant; nor are we opposed to vocational elements in the 'free-options' section of the curriculum for older pupils. In place of vocational streams, or even vocational schools, we believe it is better to build on and extend the positive approaches which are already being adopted within the authority.

Many schools have created an on-site support unit or 'sanctuary' for children who experience difficulties of various kinds which result in disruptive classroom behaviour. Though it is exceptionally difficult to ensure that these units are not seen as 'sin bins', we think that many schools are striving hard to give them a positive image whereby they are seen as positive opportunities for pupils to withdraw from the ordinary classroom, for a few hours, a few days or a few weeks. It takes time and care, both for the teacher who refers these pupils and for the teacher who receives them, to impress on them that the unit is not a punishment. On our visits to schools we have seen that pupils often behave well and work hard in the units, using their period of strategic withdrawal from all or some of their normal lessons as a period of reflection, self-assessment and recovery. Many of the staff in charge of these units have impressed us by their determination to reintegrate the pupils into normal lessons as soon as possible, taking care that the pupils do not fall behind or out of step with the rest of the pupils in their classes. A carefully planned and staggered return to normal lessons is often very successful.

Two points stand out from our inquiries into these on-site units or sanctuaries. First, successful reintegration is more likely to be achieved if there is full consultation with the home and the help and support of parents is obtained. It seems essential to invite the parents to school to talk with the pastoral tutor, the sanctuary staff and the classroom teachers. When the parents prove unwilling to come to school, it is important that the teacher visits the home and/or that the Education Welfare Officer (EWO) contacts the parents on behalf of the school. This is achieved more readily if there is a school-attached EWO. Secondly, it is important that the skills of sanctuary teachers become disseminated to ordinary classroom teachers. Most of the sanctuary staff whom we consulted told us that referrals to the sanctuary tend to come disproportionately from some teachers. This is a delicate matter, of course, but we feel that too often this fact is simply acknowledged in a half-embarrassed way with no further action being taken. We believe it to be an important element of long-term policy that staff who refer large numbers of pupils to a sanctuary should be given more constructive help by colleagues. It can be done quietly and efficiently. At several points in our report we emphasize the need for teachers to co-operate and offer one another mutual support by sharing skills. In a school where this obtains, the dissemination of skills from sanctuary teachers to others can be achieved naturally and unobtrusively.

The effective on-site support unit or sanctuary thus plays an extremely important preventative role in relation to both underachievement and disaffection. When it succeeds, the pupils are successfully reintegrated into ordinary schooling. But this will not be sufficient to meet the needs of some pupils, for whom more direct measures have to be taken.

REFERENCES

HMI (1979) *Aspects of Secondary Education in England: A Survey*, HMSO, London.

HMI (1980) *A View of the Curriculum*, Matters for Discussion Series No. 11, HMSO, London.

HMI (1981) *The School Curriculum*, HMSO, London.

Schools Council (1981) *The Practical Curriculum*, Working Paper 70, Schools Council, London.

TOPICS FOR DISCUSSION

1. What in your view are the most persuasive arguments for a common curriculum in fourth- and fifth-year secondary-school classes?
2. What advantages does the constrained option system contain both for pupils, teachers and school planners?
3. How might a system of half-term units prove especially helpful with disaffected secondary-school students?

SUGGESTIONS FOR FURTHER READING

1. Schostak, J. F. (1983) The reformation of maladjusted schooling, pp. 187–215, in *Maladjusted Schooling: Deviance, Social Control and Individuality in Secondary Schooling*, Falmer Press, London.

   The author looks at the possibilities for innovation and change both in curriculum and interpersonal relations in the *self-elected school* in contrast to the *conscript school*. His detailed study of Slumptown Comprehensive raises a number of key issues to do with organizational reform, curriculum reform, professionalization of teaching, and the role of support groups and pressure groups in the process of change.

2. Fontana, D. (1985) Causes of problems: the schools and the teachers, pp. 49–64, in *Classroom Control*, British Psychological Society and Methuen, London.

   Ways in which the curriculum can be responsible partly for certain of the class-control problems that many teachers encounter are discussed. A radical rethinking of the curriculum is recommended with the introduction of more vocationally orientated and life-skills subjects as one step toward reducing conditions that breed apathy and misbehaviour in the classroom. The author then goes on to discuss the school examination system as it relates to problems of classroom behaviour. Current moves to reform the present system are welcomed. Changes to criterion-referenced tests as opposed to norm-referenced tests suggest that the large percentage of secondary-school pupils doomed to failure under current examination conditions will be reduced with consequent changes in their attitudes to school and involvement in the full life of the school.

3. Docking, J. W. (1980) The curriculum; pastoral care, and special provision, pp. 161–98, in *Control and Discipline in Schools: Perspectives and Approaches*, Harper and Row, London.

   The author considers some ways in which curriculum arrangements are related to behaviour problems. In particular, the degree of pupil involvement in school is explored and the challenge of designing appropriate curriculum experiences for those pupils who do not respond to traditional 'academic learning'. There follows a brief discussion on pastoral care and counselling in relation to questions of discipline and control and to curricular aims. Finally, attention is given to the minority of very disruptive pupils in school and to ways of dealing with them by suspension, expulsion and the use of special behavioural units attached to the school.

COPING WITH
DISRUPTIVE BEHAVIOUR

INTRODUCTION

Each reading in the third section of the sourcebook has been selected on the basis of the practical insights and advice that it offers to hard-pressed teachers. Reading 11 not only traces the course of events in a number of classroom confrontations but attempts to understand the deeply uncomfortable feelings that disruptive incidents arouse in most teachers. Reading 12 offers clear guidelines for changing unwanted behaviour. These are based on reinforcement theory and have proved successful in many educational settings. Reading 13, too, outlines behavioural modification techniques that can be employed with disruptive children and it illustrates the strategies in a detailed case study of one very disruptive primary-school child. Reading 13 is supported by further references to the application of reinforcement techniques in classrooms. Beynon's contribution (Reading 14) deals with the problems that arise in initial encounters with classroom groups. It surveys both strategies that pupils commonly employ in meeting the demands made on them by teachers, peers and parents and the techniques used by teachers by way of inducting pupils into ways of behaving sensibly and responsibly. The supporting readings complement Beynon's outline with their illustrations of 'mucking about' and 'stirrers and clowns' (McPherson, 1983).

Reading 15 is concerned with coping strategies in the face of disruptive classroom behaviour. The focus of Reading 15 is the 'child with difficulties of adjustment', the 'underachieving child' and the 'trapped-in-role-child', each of whom manifests a different form of unwanted behaviour. The final reading by Docking (Reading 16) provides a review of research on the effects and the effectiveness of punishment in school, concluding with a timely and salutory list of suggestions for the dealing with infractions and misbehaviour.

REFERENCES

McPherson, J. (1983) *The Feral Classroom: High-School Students' Construction of Reality*, London, Routledge & Kegan Paul.

Reading 11
CONFRONTATION SITUATIONS AND TEACHER SUPPORT SYSTEMS
R. Pik

By a confrontation situation, I mean the tense 'showdown' that occurs when, in response to what the *teacher* considers to be a reasonable request for a pupil to either do something or stop doing something, he (or she) 'digs in his heels', shows open defiance and communicates either verbally or non-verbally 'I won't, you can't make me and I dare you to try'. The following are examples of confrontations drawn from suspension letters sent to an LEA:

> I asked Mark (aged 15) in a quiet and friendly manner to sit down and get to work. He continued to run around the classroom ... I asked him, still very quietly, to leave the room ... but all he did say was 'Piss off' and 'I'm not going'.

> Denise (aged 14) screwed up (her) paper and threw her book on the floor. I replaced the book back on her desk and re-opened the paper and told her that she would have to write on it. Denise screwed up the paper and threw the book on the floor again ...

> Steven said he wouldn't go to detention (for an incomplete homework assignment). I said, 'Very well then, you will come with me to see Mr B. (Deputy Head) right now!' He then sat down in his seat and replied, 'I'm fucking not going anywhere!'.

Talking to teachers, it is apparent to me that confrontations such as these have an intense and unforgettable quality which makes them very difficult

R. Pik, Confrontation situations and teacher support systems, in B. Gillham (ed.) *Problem Behaviour in the Secondary School*, Croom Helm, London, pp. 129–42.

to dismiss at the end of the school day. Although the slow learner in the classroom can be the source of endless frustration for the teacher, most teachers are able to 'switch off' from the slow learner's problems when the teaching sessions are over. The teacher feels that he/she has given his/her professional best and will try again tomorrow. There is seldom a feeling of apprehension about having to face the slow learner and his class again. By contrast, a teacher who has had a confrontation with a pupil usually experiences the great anxiety about the prospect of having to face that child and the class the next day and possibly for the rest of the term. The incident may be replayed many times in the teacher's mind.

There are three related questions that are seldom discussed with teachers by the professionals who are meant to be offering support and advice either as part of the in-school support network or as members of support services available to schools, e.g. educational psychologists. The questions are: Why do confrontations provoke such strong, uncomfortable feelings in teachers? What precisely are these feelings? What measures do teachers usually take to reduce these feelings? By failing to tackle these questions with teachers, professionals have failed to understand or appreciate the pressures on teachers, or they have failed to communicate to teachers that they really understand and appreciate these pressures. It is therefore hardly surprising that many teachers are often unable or unwilling to implement the advice being offered, because the tone of the advice is unsympathetic, or because the actual content of the advice is judged to be irrelevant, ineffective or impractical.

Before going on to outline specific management strategies I should like to explore the three questions in turn.

WHY DO CONFRONTATIONS PROVOKE SUCH STRONG UNCOMFORTABLE FEELINGS IN TEACHERS?

I suggest that it is because in a confrontation there is more of the teacher *as a person* 'on the line', that is, exposed and vulnerable. The slow learner may sometimes cause the teacher to question his own expertise as a master purveyor of his subject; the openly defiant student challenges the teacher's authority *and* severely dents the image the adult has of him/herself as a reasonable and sensitive person. The student puts a strong doubt in the teacher's mind about his ability to cope.

The following example ilustrates this notion of the teacher as a person feeling devalued during a confrontation.

This incident began around 11.45 a.m. Denise was provided with paper and a text for a writing exercise after a discussion period (in which she participated sensibly).

1. Denise screwed up her paper and threw her book on the floor.

2. I replaced the book back on the desk and re-opened the paper and told her she would have to write on it.

3. Denise screwed up the paper and threw the book on the floor again. I replaced it again and explained she was being asked to do something and should learn to do what she was told without getting angry about it. Denise's response to this was a chain of swear words ending in a clenched fist swung towards my face. But Denise's action at this point was clearly not intended to hurt me as she stopped her fist before it made contact with my face.

4. I walked away at this point in order to give my attention to the rest of the class. A book thrown by Denise hit my back, followed by several screwed balls of paper.

5. I picked up the book and returned it to Denise, taking the opportunity to explain to her that she could not behave in this way or do whatever she wanted to do when she felt like it. She replied that I couldn't make her do anything and I insisted that she had to learn to do what she was told to do. She threw the book at me again. I said that there was no point in being aggressive as it would not achieve anything. She swore at me again and I said I did not have conversations with people in that sort of language. I asked her whether she wanted me to hit her and I explained that I don't talk to people in that way. She replied that I wouldn't dare to hit her, and I replied that I didn't want to. I explained to the class that hitting someone did not achieve anything. Some of the rest of the class laughed, apparently seeing this a sign that I was too scared to face up to Denise. I turned to Denise and asked her to come out in front of the rest of the class. She refused and said I would have to make her. I asked her again more firmly. I said I was not prepared to drag her. I continued to fix her in her eyes and she came out to the front. She faced me and before I could speak attempted to hit me in the face with her fist, and then went and sat down again. I went over to Denise and shouted at her that she could not treat people like that. I shouted that there was no reason to hit me since I liked her and did not want to hurt her.

6. At this point I resumed my efforts to start the class on their written work, before dealing with Denise. The class were all hushed in expectation at this point. Denise got up and proceeded to pick up all the paper on the rest of the class's desks and then screwed them all up

and threw them on the desk at the front of the class. I asked the class to read the first act of the play whilst I left the room (I was going to find a senior member of staff to remove her from the class). As I was walking out of the room, Denise followed me and shouted at me that I could not leave the class as I was supposed to be teaching them. I replied that as a teacher I was free to leave the room when I wished. She asked me where I was going and I replied that it was none of her business and told her to return to the room. She said I was going to tell on her and then hit me in the back as I continued to walk on. The bell for the end of the lesson rang as I was crossing the playground. Denise ran up to me and said ****. I turned to walk on and she hit me with some force in the back again. Mrs L. later dismissed the class, after discussing the incident with them (12.30).

Notice, in the above example, how the teacher tries first to secure Denise's co-operation by invoking the teacher–pupil framework of rules, e.g. I am the teacher and you are the pupil; you must do as I say. It seems, however, that Denise does not share the same basic understanding of teacher and pupil roles. She refuses to obey the teacher merely because she is the teacher. When attempts to control Denise by appealing to teacher–pupil roles fail, the teacher resorts to appeals on a person-to-person level, e.g. 'I don't talk to people that way ... I shouted at her that she could not treat people like that ... Do you understand Denise, I like you and do not want to hurt you?'. These statements are attempts to convey the message, 'I am a reasonable person and so are you. Let us try to work out our differences in a more sensible and less hurtful way'. Having these personal appeals rebuffed is very painful to one's self-esteem. Not only does the teacher now feel a failure because of her inability to shift Denise on either the professional or the personal level, also she is acutely aware of having somehow made a fool of herself in front of the class, e.g. 'Some of the rest of the class laughed, apparently seeing this as a sign that I was too scared to face up to Denise'.

The notion of how a 'class hushed in expectation' adds tremendous tension to a confrontation will be discussed under the second question.

WHAT ARE THE FEELINGS EXPERIENCED BY TEACHERS DURING AND AFTER CONFRONTATIONS?

There are likely to be three main feelings aroused: anger, fear and embarrassment. There is sometimes also a feeling of sadness after a confrontation.

Anger

The teacher may begin by experiencing annoyance because one pupil is taking his/her time and attention which he/she feels ought, at that moment, to be devoted to the other twenty-five children in the class. Annoyance quickly turns to anger when appeals for co-operation on either the professional or the personal level fail (as in the Denise example).

Fear

There is fear of aggression and fear of losing respect. The fear of aggression often is, I feel, mistakenly, only viewed as the teacher being afraid of physical or verbal abuse by the student. It is important to recognize, however, that teachers, like parents, are often afraid of their own aggressive impulses when disciplining children. Just as a parent worries that his/her child may have provoked him/her to the point where he/she might hit too hard or say something too hurtful and irretrievable so, too, teachers are afraid of letting loose their full fury on even the most provocative pupil. Loss of temper is a double-edged sword: the teacher often fears loss of temper in her/himself more than in his pupils during a confrontation. This is because as a teacher one is meant to be the example-setting adult.

Teachers tend to speak about fear of losing control of the class more openly than they do about the fear of loss of self-control. There is fear of losing the individual pupil's respect and, more commonly, fear of losing 'the class's respect'. To a large extent, the degree of control that a teacher is able to exert over a class is dependent on the degree of respect accorded to him/her by the pupils. Today, it seems, teachers are more aware than their counterparts twenty years ago that respect from the pupils needs to be earned. Perhaps this is because many of the props which supported the idea of automatic obedience to the teachers have disappeared over the past two decades. Increasingly, children are aware of themselves as people with power, rights and privileges who are entitled to respect. They resent being talked down to by adults in general and by teachers and parents in particular. Teachers, however, still fear being seen as 'weak'. Therefore, when discussing a confrontation, a teacher will usually say, 'If I let the child get away with it he will try it again' or, more commonly, 'If the class see him getting away with it then others in the class will have a go next time'.

Embarrassment

Clearly, confrontations produce embarrassment for the same reasons they produce anger and fear. When professional and personal appeals for co-operation are rebuffed, the teacher worries that this may signify a personal weakness or failing. By definition, it is impossible for the teacher to fail privately, because an essential feature of the confrontation is the audience. (The notion of public failure is, of course, equally important in understanding the *pupil's* increasing stake in the confrontation and this will be discussed later on.)

A further and less widely recognized source of embarrassment is the teacher's apprehension that someone above him/her in the school's hierarchy might well need to be involved, either during or after the incident. Teachers often experience acute embarrassment when they have to call a colleague out of the classroom to help with a tricky situation. But even if no other teacher needs to be summoned at the time, and even if the pupil is not sent out of the class to go to another member of staff, the teacher may feel obliged to report a serious incident to his head of department or to a senior teacher later on. Actions taken during a confrontation that seemed reasonable and imperative to take at the time, are sometimes difficult to explain and to justify to colleagues *and to oneself* later on. Once the dust has settled, the events that triggered the incident may, in retrospect, seen petty, trivial or infinitely ignorable. In any case the need to involve another teacher is often construed as an admission of one's inability to cope with a class. I have found teachers in their probationary year of teaching most vulnerable to this pressure. Because probationers know that the senior staff are recording their progress, they are often unduly and unrealistically worried about having to ask for help with an unruly class. They fear that asking for help in this way will somehow go down as a black mark on their record. Further, if a probationer does call on a senior member of staff to help handle a serious incident, e.g. a pupil flatly refusing to leave the classroom despite the teacher's insistence that he/she do so, the senior teacher sometimes appears to succeed so easily where the probationer has failed, that the younger teacher finds it difficult to imagine the senior colleague ever being non-plussed by a child. What is often not realized is that the confident veteran has probably, in the past, made every mistake in the book but has learned from experience which strategies are most likely to work in certain situations; he/she also has the 'formal status' of his/her position as senior tutor, deputy head, etc. To the probationer, however, it appears that it is only he who cannot cope.

However, it would be wrong to suggest that only young inexperienced teachers feel embarrassment when asking a colleague for help. More often than not, a teacher with many years of teaching experience is assumed to be able to control a class. If this teacher encounters difficulty it may be embarrassing for him/her to admit the situation and even more embarrassing for him/her to have to ask for help.

Sadness

Although less commonly experienced than anger, fear and embarrassment, many teachers have, in reflecting on confrontations, expressed feelings of sadness. There is feeling sorry for oneself, often tinged with bitterness, e.g. 'Why did I have to get landed with 3C for a double period on Friday afternoon?'. Interestingly, however, a teacher may also feel sorry for the pupil after a confrontation. This usually occurs when the incident has led to the pupil being severely punished, perhaps more severely than the teacher had expected, e.g. suspension or expulsion. There is a feeling that if only he had handled the situation better, the outburst and its consequence might not have occurred. A teacher may also feel sorry for a pupil when he/she has some intimate knowledge of the child's home background. For example, when the teacher is aware that the child receives very harsh treatment at home, the teacher may well feel that he/she has in some way 'let down' the pupil by acting overpunitively, just like the child's parents.

WHAT MEASURES DO TEACHERS USUALLY TAKE TO REDUCE THE UNCOMFORTABLE FEELINGS?

It is not the place here to discuss the range of possible disciplinary actions available to teachers. Rather, I want to consider how teachers deal with the personal feelings of anger, fear, embarrassment and possibly sadness which are evoked by confrontations.

The most dramatic effect of a confrontation on a teacher may be avoidance of the pupil and/or the class. Teachers may refuse to have a particular class or, more likely, insist that the pupil with whom the confrontation took place 'be excused' from that class. In taking this type of action the teacher must openly ask for help from the senior staff or the headteacher. A much more difficult situation arises when the teacher takes time off 'due to illness'. I have observed the vicious circle of stress leading to time off in many schools. What happens is that a teacher who has difficulty controlling a class (or classes) succumbs to the stress by taking days off school, ostensibly because of colds or flu. After several such absences, however, the other teachers begin to be slightly resentful about having to cover in their 'free' lessons. The antipathy which builds up toward the absent teacher usually makes it *less likely* that he/she will get the support needed to cope with the difficult situation on his/her return. This leads to greater strain and isolation necessitating more time off and so on. It is important therefore for senior staff to be sensitive to this developing situation and to intervene quickly and positively with support for the teacher and not leave him to struggle along on his/her own.

By far the most common reaction to a confrontation which helps the teacher reduce uncomfortable feelings is absolving oneself by attributing the child's disobedient behaviour to 'something wrong with the child' (usually 'inside his/her head') or blaming the child's parents (usually referred to as 'home background'). Many schools want those children frequently involved in confrontations referred to the psychologist or psychiatrist because they 'require treatment' to enable them to return to the classroom 'cured'. Teachers are often surprised to hear that a child whom they consider 'a thorough pest' in school may be quite well behaved at home. Although children and their families may value the out-of-school support and interest shown by a psychologist, it is difficult to see how this contact will lead to dramatic and enduring behaviour change in the classroom.

In the second half of this reading I will go on to discuss various strategies for prevention and defusing of those situations which can prove so traumatic for teachers and pupils alike. These strategies will involve the school as a system on three levels: the class teacher, the in-school support network and the out-of-school support services.

STRATEGIES AVAILABLE TO THE CLASS TEACHER

From my own teaching experience and from discussions with teachers I believe that confrontations develop and progress in four, possibly overlapping, phases: a build-up, a trigger event, a rapid escalation and a finale. The responsibility for the build-up or the trigger event may lie with either the teacher or the pupil but both are responsible for the escalation. Consider the following account of a confrontation:

> [the headteacher writes] On December 12th, Arthur, together with two other boys, was very late for school. Mr H. saw him, sent him off to assembly and told him to report later. All three boys were given 300 words to write as an imposition.
>
> When Mr H. checked up on their record he found that Arthur and one other boy had not been late for a month and so he decided to excuse them because of their good record. When they reported he said

he would excuse them from doing the writing since they had not been late for many weeks and asked them for the paper back. It then became clear that they had gone off without any intention of doing the imposition anyway because the paper was later found torn up in the school's Christmas card post box. Because of this attitude, Mr H. decided that the imposition should stand after all.

Arthur refused to do this imposition. When he was told he would work in isolation to get it done in school, he refused. When he was brought before me and I told him that he would do it or be suspended, he still refused and I, therefore, have no alternative but to suspend him.

In this case the build-up is clear, i.e. coming late to school and having to report to the teacher after assembly. Although the teacher then decided to excuse Arthur from the imposition, it later became clear that Arthur already had excused himself from doing it. Was Arthur's tearing up the paper for the imposition the trigger event? Obviously, the teacher thought it serious enough to warrant punishing him for his 'attitude'. On the other hand, might not one construe the teacher's action of retracting the exemption he had given already as the trigger event? In any case, what follows is a fairly common pattern of escalating punishment and refusal to accept the punishment leading to more severe punishment, etc. The finale is the suspension. The headmaster states that he had 'no alternative' and I believe that Mr H. would also claim that he had no alternative to the action he took. This feeling of 'having no alternative' is an important feature of confrontations. In the rapid-escalation phase both teacher and pupil 'stake in' more and more, thus increasing the temperature, pressure and pace of the interaction. Note that at this stage in a confrontation, 'winning' and 'losing' become increasingly important to both participants while the notions of winning and losing become more narrowly defined by them. Things reach such a pitch that the teacher can only construe winning as getting the pupil to do precisely what he says at that moment; anything less is losing. The pupil, meanwhile, defines winning as refusing to 'knuckle under' to the teacher's demands; losing is giving in and obeying the teacher. In Arthur's case, even the headteacher gets drawn into a very narrow definition of winning which, in fact, is the same as Mr H.'s definition, i.e. making Arthur do his imposition is winning and no other alternative is even considered.

What rules about the prevention and handling of confrontations can we derive from Arthur's case? *Rule No. 1* must be: *decide first whether it is worth risking a confrontation over a particular incident. Has there been a*

breach of school rules or principles important enough to warrant intervention at that moment or would a quiet word with the pupil later on perhaps
be a better course to follow? I am not advocating looking the other way
when school rules are broken. I am advocating 'weighing up' the pros and
cons of taking certain actions at certain times. In Arthur's case, the issue
of lateness to school became a non-issue by the teacher's own admission.
If the teacher felt that Arthur's attitude warranted punishment, why
choose the same instrument of punishment, i.e. the imposition, which
had already been judged by both teacher and pupil to be unfair?

Rule No. 2 is a paraphrase of Dr Benjamin Spock's well-known
formula: *leave yourself and the pupil a gracious way out.* When there are
no visible outlets or graceful exits available for either the teacher or the
pupil, there is pressure on both to continue escalating the confrontation.
The idea of saving face, discussed already with regard to teachers, is
equally important with regard to children. There is always the danger of
the pupil being pushed by the audience toward greater acts of bravado
and defiance. The further the confrontation develops the harder it is for
both pupil and teacher to back down. Often, therefore, the best move the
teacher can make is to refuse to 'stake in' during the build-up stage
or to refuse to increase his stake during the escalation phase. This may
sometimes require the teacher taking the lead by admitting that he was
wrong. It should have been clear to Mr H. that trying to force Arthur to
do the imposition in isolation would be a further escalation. An alternative strategy, still available to Mr H. at that time, could have been to
dismiss the event while still making his point. For instance, he might have
said something to this effect: 'Arthur, you were wrong not to do the
imposition I gave you but perhaps I was wrong in giving it to you in the
first place. Make things easier for us both by keeping up your good record
of punctuality.'

Here is another example of a confrontation:

At lunchtime today the Deputy Head reported serious trouble with a
teacher over misbehaviour in the House block.

Clive was in the House area with three other boys who were from
another house and shouldn't have been there. They made raucous
comments in the hearing of a young teacher and then ran off. The
teacher followed and found these 13-year-old boys hiding like children
in lockers in a cloakroom alcove.

He told them to get out and they sauntered off in the direction of
the exit. He followed them to see if they had gone out and hearing a
noise in the toilets, he looked inside to see that three of the lavatory

cabinets were occupied, but that Clive was waiting outside. When the teacher entered, Clive went into another toilet cabinet, sat down on the seat and made a coarse and obscene remark. The teacher told him to get out once more and had to repeat this order at least three times. Clive did not go and was quite obviously deliberately provoking a situation.

Finally the teacher had to warn him, 'If you will not go and I have to take hold of you to get you out you will regret it'.

Clive replied, 'Go on, mark me, I would love that'.

Consequently the teacher had to take hold of Clive and with considerable difficulty began to lead him out of the building. By the time other staff arrived, Clive was reduced to tears of rage and frustration at not being allowed to have his own way. He continued to be loud, abusive and obscene as he was escorted from the building. When he finally left he threatened the teacher concerned with violence, saying something to the effect, 'That is the way to get your neck broken'.

The other boys admit that they were all being provocative and refer to the incident as 'aggro'.

I believe that the young male teacher involved in this incident was lured into a confrontation. The toilets, cloakrooms and locker rooms are generally areas that adolescent pupils tend to consider their own 'ground', or at least not the teacher's ground. The teacher is usually in a 'one-down' position when trying to remove them from these areas. Note that it was the teacher, and not Clive, who first made threatening remarks about using physical force, i.e. 'If you will not go and I have to take hold of you to get you out, you will regret it'. I believe that this teacher was very fortunate not to have been assaulted by the pupil. (Referring back to the Denise incident, the reader will recall that again it was the teacher who first suggested physical force, i.e. 'I asked her whether she wanted me to hit her ... ')

Rule No. 3 is therefore: *remember that threats by a teacher to use physical force or the actual use of physical force will nearly always escalate a conflict very quickly and dramatically and will greatly increase the probability of the pupil reacting violently.* A situation that is especially important to avoid is a male teacher physically handling or restraining a female pupil. Consider the example of Mary:

At the beginning of the fifth period on a Friday, Mr S. was standing at the door of Room J20 to control the movement of the pupils out and in when Mary, holding a plastic bag, tried to push past him in order to give the bag to a friend already in J20. Mary should have been in another room and was behaving characteristically in being where she ought not to be at that particular time. The (male) teacher restrained her, intending to call over the friend to collect the bag at the door. When restrained, Mary kicked out at the teacher, hit him twice in the face, tearing off his spectacles. The teacher made no attempt to retaliate, but Mary then pulled his hair and kicked out.

Even though the impression given is that the teacher's physical contact with Mary seemed quite spontaneous and not intended to be threatening, Mary over-reacted instantly. Physical handling, even something so slight as catching at the sleeve of a child's jacket, may trigger a violent response.

Rule No. 4 is: *a reasonable time after confrontation, the teacher involved should take the opportunity to talk privately with the pupil before they are next scheduled to come into contact with one another in the classroom.* There is obviously little point in trying to have a conversation while either the teacher or the pupil is still 'high' after a confrontation and so one must allow a reasonable 'cooling-off' period. In practice, what often happens is that the pupil is sent to a senior teacher who is left to deal with the situation without further involvement by the class teacher. Although this is a useful manoeuvre in that it allows for a cooling-off period for both teacher and child, it does little to reduce the teacher's apprehension about the next contact he will have with the child in the classroom. In a quiet moment, away from the audience, it is usually much easier for teacher and pupil to make the kind of contact in which they come over as 'themselves'. In this conversation there is little point getting hung up on the issues of who was right and who was wrong. It is better for the teacher to concede that both he/she and the pupil seem to get rather carried away sometimes. The message for the teacher to try to get across is: 'I regret that this happened; let us try not to force each other into a difficult position again.'

Some teachers may regard this as merely 'humouring' or 'placating' the child, when a 'firm stand' would be more correct. But desired behaviour is not brought about by confrontation: putting a child in a position he/she cannot move from is to confirm him/her in a deviant role. A child, like an adult, becomes what he/she does. Some children may need a good deal of humouring in this fashion but, at the very least, it enables them to keep out of a role that they would then feel they had to defend. A brief 'backstage' contact will greatly reduce the teacher's anxiety about the next contact he/she will have with the child when both will again be 'on stage'. The personal appeals made by the teacher and rejected by the child in the heat of the confrontation are more likely to be responded to by the child later on.

The reader will recall that in defining a confrontation I stated previously that the pupil reacted with defiance to *what the teacher considered to be a reasonable demand*. Often, however, in the aftermath, the teacher's eyes may be opened to the fact that what he/she considered a reasonable demand was, in fact, very *unreasonable* from a child's point of view. One dramatic example of this was evident in an account a teacher related to me. The teacher had, in his own words, 'a real dust-up' with a thirteen-year-old boy.

In covering a class for an absent colleague, he asked the class to read aloud from their geography books. The second boy he called on to read was still fumbling around in his desk for the correct book. The teacher waited patiently, not wanting to let the boy off the hook by calling on someone else to read. When the boy said that he did not have his book, the teacher went over to his desk and found it for him. Feeling that the boy was 'trying it on' and testing him out, and increasingly aware of the giggles and titters from the rest of the class, the teacher demanded that the boy stand up and read immediately. At this point the boy slammed his desk shut, sat back in his chair and folded his arms in a gesture of defiance. A rapid and intense escalation followed. Ultimately, the boy was sent to wait outside the headteacher's office. Two periods later the teacher chanced on the boy still waiting to see the head. He asked the boy to have a chat with him in the medical room adjacent to the office. He felt that both he and the lad appeared calmer to each other. From this conversation it became apparent to the teacher that the boy had refused to read because he was almost unable to read. The boy had managed to keep his illiteracy fairly secret to all but his closest friends. Clearly, what seemed to the teacher to be a reasonable demand for the boy to read was totally *unreasonable* and embarrassing from the boy's point of view. The confrontation had provided an effective 'smokescreen' for the boy's problem.

STRATEGIES AVAILABLE TO THE IN-SCHOOL SUPPORT NETWORK

Many schools have a specially designated pastoral-care team comprising heads of year, senior masters and mistresses and/or heads of department. Very often these staff are paid an extra allowance for their pastoral-care duties. However, a school need not necessarily have a formal pastoral-care team as such; sometimes it can even be a disadvantage. The least-effective pastoral-care teams I have encountered are those that are construed by the staff as dealing exclusively with discipline problems, i.e. handing out punishment to 'troublemakers' sent to them by class teachers and form teachers. By contrast, the most effective senior staff, whether they are called a pastoral-care team or not, are those who make it clear to the staff that pastoral care is something worthwhile for all children and for all teachers. The role is one of support and guidance for pupils and staff. Matters to do with the curriculum, in-service training courses and academic standards in the school are seen to be just as much their concern as the issue of children's behaviour in the classroom. Teachers are seen to be receiving advice and back-up by the senior staff while being encouraged to take on greater responsibility for dealing with disruptive behaviour themselves rather than passing routine problems on.

Senior staff have an important role to play in the management of confrontation situations. To begin with it is essential that all the teachers know who the senior staff are and how they may be contacted at short notice. Although this may sound almost absurdly elementary, I have found several schools which were so large and with such frequent staff turnover, that many of the newest teachers asked me, the visiting psychologist, for some kind of list or chart to clarify the staff structure of their school! No-one had ever told them who to turn to in the complicated school hierarchy if they required help in a difficult situation. Pupils sometimes received more formal induction into the school structure than did the teachers. Senior staff need to hold regular meetings and support groups for the probationer teachers and they should include in these groups teachers who are new to the school and its particular characteristics, even though they may have had a few years of previous teaching experience.

All staff, especially the probationers, should be encouraged to ask for help from the senior staff, sooner rather than later, if they are experiencing difficulties in controlling a class. Senior staff are in the best position to explain some of the points covered in this chapter with regard to the nature of confrontations and the feelings they evoke in teachers. Many teachers have told me that it would have helped them very much if they had heard from their senior colleagues that they too sometimes experienced difficulty in controlling a class. In fact, it took them some time to find out that they were not the only ones who sometimes found it difficult to cope with a class. This discovery, really more of a revelation to many of them, was acknowledged to be greatly reassuring.

As well as a support and advisory role, senior staff need to take an intervention role. That is, they should fulfil a 'call-out' function that class teachers can make use of if a confrontation escalates to a dangerous stage (I sometimes refer to 'calling out the cavalry'). Mark's case illustrates some useful points with regard to a teacher's summoning help during a confrontation.

> When Mark came in, he immediately started to fight (not seriously) with Gary. I asked him many times, in a very quiet and friendly manner, to sit down and get to work. He continued to run around the classroom directing Kung Fu kicks at various people and jumping over the furniture. Eventually I asked him, still very quietly, to leave the room. He did leave, but returned very shortly and stood behind me. I again asked him to leave but he stopped listening to me and went and appropriated David's chair. I went over to him and tried to persuade him to leave, but all he did say was 'Piss off' and 'I'm not going'. He would not come out of the room with me and I decided not to touch him or use any force at all. I tried to phone a senior member of staff but could not contact anyone. I then went to ask Mr R. for assistance, and I had to stay to supervise his class.
>
> Signed: Mr S. [probationer]

> At approximately 14.00 hours today I was teaching 3C in D27 when Mr S. came in and said that Mark had entered his room, had hit some of the others and refused to leave. Mr S. asked me to intervene. I left him with my class and went to the class next door where Mark was sitting quietly in the far corner. I asked him to leave and his reply, as accurately as I can recall, was 'No, I'm not going to pick up any books.' This puzzled me and I said I didn't know anything of any books. I again asked him to leave and he refused. I said, 'Mark, I will ask you three times to leave'. This I did and each time he refused. I then took hold of the back of his chair to turn it (he was sitting with his back to me). He stood up and lashed backwards with his foot. By accident or design he struck the chair which hit my leg. He then turned and swung a punch at my body. This I parried and he backed up against the wall. We faced each other for several moments during which I asked him several times to leave. The Senior Master then arrived and took over.
>
> Signed: Mr R. [2-year veteran]

The class teacher's initial handling of the situation seemed quite reasonable. He did, however, make one mistake in sending Mark out of the room without either sending him *to* someone or otherwise 'attaching' him. Just sending a child out in this manner usually invites him to stand outside the door making funny faces, much to the amusement of the class, and of course does not prevent his coming back in again to carry on the argument if he so desires. Unfortunately, in the present example, the system lets the teacher down badly, with disastrous consequences: 'I tried to phone a senior member of staff but could not contact anyone'. This should never happen. At worst, it should always be possible to contact a secretary and leave it to her to summon a senior staff member to a classroom as a matter of urgency. Or, a colleague in the next classroom could be asked to do this. Calling in a colleague who is not much more experienced than oneself (like Mr R.) will often only escalate the confrontation. There is a definite face-saving element for the pupil in being removed from the classroom by a senior member of staff and not by a junior member of staff. There is a feeling that 'anyone would go out if Mr B. ordered them to'.

A further mistake made by Mark's teacher, however, was sending his colleague next door to deal with the situation for him. If the two teachers had gone in together to deal with Mark at least they would have had strength of numbers. Instead, Mr R. is asked to deal with the difficult situation on his own and is easily confused when he sees Mark sitting quietly in the corner; he is even more puzzled by Mark's reference to 'picking up books', about which Mr R. clearly knows nothing. Why did Mr S. feel that he needed to cover Mr R.'s class during all this?

One other point worth noting is Mr R.'s tactical error in saying to Mark, 'I will ask you three times to leave'. Less experienced teachers often fall into this trap not realizing that by stating that they will ask three times, they are begging the student to defy the first two requests! Only by waiting for the third request will the pupil get the confrontation back to the stage it was already at before the first two requests were made. Usually, teachers make three requests to stall for time. Like Mr Micawber there is the magical hope that 'something will turn up', e.g. a senior member of staff will suddenly materialize to help out, or the bell will ring for break. Senior staff need to be available to intervene in these situations. Furthermore, they should make it clear that they would prefer to be called out *immediately* rather than have to deal with a situation that has escalated into something more serious. Probationer teachers, in particular, will need reassurance that it is reasonable to ask for help in this way; that it is better to accept help than lose control.

STRATEGIES AVAILABLE TO THE SUPPORT SERVICES

In terms of preventing and handling confrontations the educational psychologist may have a good deal to offer but only if he/she visits the school on a regular basis and is seen by the staff as being a useful adjunct to the in-school support network. Inviting the psychologist to attend occasional staff meetings or, more importantly, pastoral-care meetings, may often prove helpful. A psychologist who knows a school well, is familiar with its physical layout and its staff resources, is in a good position to suggest possible alternative management strategies for dealing with pupils frequently involved in confrontations. He/she can encourage staff to look for patterns in the confrontations; to explore such questions as:

1. Does the pupil tend to have more confrontations with male or female staff?
2. Are there more confrontations with junior staff and, if so, does the pupil's timetable show a large number of lessons with junior staff?
3. Do there appear to be more confrontations during the more formal lessons or during the more 'free-ranging' lessons such as art, physical education and home economics, in which movement around the room, gym or kitchen is essential?
4. Does the class size appear to be a significant factor?
5. Is there a small group of his or her peers who might be providing a suitably provocative audience for the pupil in several of the classes during which confrontations take place?
6. Is there a pattern of failure or difficulty with certain subjects which might be a contributing factor to confrontations during these lessons? (often signified by the days of the week on which the pupil poses difficulties or is absent from school.)
7. With which teacher(s) does the pupil get on particularly well in and out of the classroom? (this person, even if he or she doesn't actually teach the child could be useful in a counselling role).

These kinds of questions may provide answers which will suggest possible management strategies. These may range from altering an individual pupil's timetable to co-ordinating a clear plan of action for teachers to take in the event of misbehaviour. In cases where the staff feel that counselling for a particular child may be beneficial it is better for the psychologist not to take on the counselling him/herself; rather, he/she can offer supervision and support to a staff member with whom the child already has a good relation if that teacher is willing to try counselling the child. The staff member need not necessarily be a member of the senior staff nor a trained counsellor. The important qualification is that he or she is the person with whom the child feels able to talk. If a teacher is willing to make this commitment, the psychologist must devote fifteen to twenty minutes of his/her time on each visit to the school during which he can conduct a private supervision session with the teacher.

It would be naïve to give the impression that schools are crying out for psychologists to work in this sort of way. Similarly, this form of intervention would not appeal to every psychologist. Some schools and psychologists still get bogged down with the idea of individual referral, assessment and treatment by the support services and prefer a more 'traditional' approach; clearly, the psychologist must first establish his own credibility with the school staff. One way to do this is to organize in-school talks with the teachers, perhaps during the lunch hour, to cover topics *chosen by them*, e.g. social-skills training groups for teenagers. In this way he can make contact with all the staff, not just those senior members responsible directly for 'pastoral care' who usually liaise with outside agencies.

If this reading has one main theme it is that of co-operation, mutual support and shared understanding in the management of behaviour problems in school. The educational psychologist is the most obvious, and the most usually available outside agent for such a co-operative enterprise, but his/her role is not exclusive. An adviser, a social worker or a psychiatrist could fulfil a similar function. Shared responsibility is a characteristic of successful secondary schools; it doesn't eliminate all the problems but helps to keep them under control and, more importantly, reduces the stressful sense of isolation experienced by many teachers.

TOPICS FOR DISCUSSION

1. Anger, fear and embarrassment are the three most likely teacher reactions to a confrontation. How might teachers best cope with these feelings?
2. Discuss the course of an actual confrontation that you or your colleagues have witnessed or experienced. To what extent is Pik's description of its progress correct? (a build-up, a trigger event, a rapid escalation, a finale).
3. Comment on Rule No. 2, 'Leave yourself and the pupil a gracious way out', as a useful and a necessary tactic in any confrontation.

SUGGESTIONS FOR FURTHER READING

1. Bond, J. (1982) Pupil-tutoring: the educational conjuring trick, *Educational Review*, Vol. 34, No. 3, pp. 241–52.
This is a fascinating account of six adolescents with records of disruptive behaviour and persistent truanting who were placed in a primary school to tutor twelve young children (five to eight years of age) described by their teacher as 'slow learners'. Each fifteen-year-old pupil-tutor (two girls and four boys) was required to attend eight two-and-a-half-hour sessions in the primary school. The

author reports improvements in the pupil-tutors' attitudes to school and to teachers, in their self-concepts, their basic skills in reading and writing and in their understanding of child-rearing practices. 'The adolescents', she observes, 'turn into reliable, conscientious, caring individuals who are concerned about the educational progress of their future offspring, who can sympathize to some extent with their teachers and who begin to show some insight into their problems'. The cameos of the truants' personal backgrounds (pp. 250–2) lead the author to the same conclusions as most other researchers on truancy that 'these young people are more sinned against than sinning'.

2. Hoghughi, M. (1983) The clinical option: treatment, pp. 238–60, in *The Delinquent: Directions for Social Control*, Burnett Books, London.
This is a comprehensive review of the treatment of young offenders. The concept of *treatment* is discussed first before a variety of *treatment settings* in residential institutions are looked at. *Treatment methods* are then reviewed under the headings of physical, cognitive, behavioural, talking, group and environmental. A discussion of necessary ingredients of *optimal treatment* concludes the chapter.

3. Calley, E. (1982) Special provision for disruptive pupils: a school-based unit, pp. 229–47, in D.P. Tattum (ed.) *Disruptive Pupils in Schools and Units*, Wiley, Chichester.
One way of dealing with problem children in the ordinary school involves setting up a school-based unit which functions as an integral part of the school's pastoral system. This is an account of just such a unit within a large comprehensive school of some 1,850 girls. A detailed discussion of the referral procedures and the aims and organization of the disruptive unit are given.

Reading 12
CHANGING CHILDREN'S BEHAVIOUR
K. Wheldall and F. Merrett

All of us behave in different ways in different settings. Compare your own behaviour in the headteacher's room, in the staffroom and in your own classroom. Think how you behave at a concert, at a political meeting and in a restaurant. Much can be done by ensuring that children know the rules for behaviour in different situations and by being consistent. At one time schools used to have clear rules for behaviour in certain places like corridors, stairs and so on. If we have none at all, some children find the situation confusing in that they do not know what behaviour is appropriate and what is expected of them. A lot of the behaviour of children that

K. Wheldall and F. Merrett (1984) Changing children's behaviour, in *Positive Teaching: the Behavioural Approach*, Allen & Unwin, London.

parents and teachers find annoying arises because there is no agreement about what kinds of behaviour are appropriate and acceptable in given situations. An example, a real one, will illustrate. A little girl was observed standing with her mother in a queue in a very busy post office just before Christmas. The child remained near her mother but was jigging up and down, sometimes skipping a few yards away. This was obviously upsetting the mother because she kept grasping the child's arm to keep her by her side. When the child inquired, 'Are we going to see Granny after this?', she replied, 'I shall not take you at all if you are naughty'. This is a clear case of a mis-match in the definition of what is acceptable behaviour. The mother thought that the child's behaviour was inappropriate, although nobody else around seemed to notice what the child was doing or to be upset by it, nor was the child made aware of what was 'naughty' about her behaviour. This sort of thing can happen in the school situation too. There, however, the other children will often transmit rule expectations to their peers but this may not happen with the isolated, renegade type of child, which is one reason why he tends to be involved so frequently in confrontations with authority. Adults do children no favours, however, when they fail to spell out the rules for appropriate behaviour.

CHANGING BEHAVIOUR BY CHANGING THE CONSEQUENCES

It is not always possible to change a behaviour by changing the situation in which it occurs. Moreover, children, as we have said, have to learn what are the appropriate behaviours for a given situation, and the way in which they learn these is as a result of the consequences following their behaviour in different situations. In the ABC model, C, the consequences, describe what happens to the child after the behaviour occurs. Systematically altering the consequences is the most powerful and most direct method of changing behaviour.

CATEGORIES OF BEHAVIOUR TO BE CHANGED

We will assume that having looked at a child's behaviour in the classroom context we can justify an attempt to change it. Before we decide which strategy to adopt it is important to classify behaviour change into three broad categories. We need to decide whether:

1. There is a deficit in behaviour, that is, the desired behaviour never occurs at all.

2. the behaviour is acceptable but does not occur often enough; or
3. the behaviour is unacceptable and we wish to reduce it or eliminate its occurrence altogether.

So our problem may be one of teaching a completely new behaviour, encouraging wanted behaviours, or eliminating certain other unwanted behaviours. Another way of putting this would be to say that some behaviours we wish to increase and some we wish to decrease and that for each of these the behavioural approach has a different remedy.

Teaching new behaviour

In this section we are assuming that we have a complete deficit in the behavioural repertoire. We have a child who is completely lacking in some social skill. For example, Susan never contributes to class discussion, and Charlie never says 'Thank you'. This really is the basic problem of teaching: producing a behaviour where none existed before.

Shaping

If we wait passively for the behaviour to occur to apply reinforcement then we shall wait for ever. Somehow, we have got to arrange for the behaviour to occur; *to make it occur* if need be. However, if we expect a perfect example of the behaviour from the child before reinforcing him, then we shall fail. What we have to do is to apply the technique known as *shaping* or, more technically, as *successive approximations*. In using this technique we begin to apply positive reinforcement to any response which begins to approach, by however small a degree, the final behaviour we have in mind. For example, the first stage in getting Charlie to say 'Thank you' would be to establish eye contact at the moment of giving him something. When this has been done we would concentrate on getting him to copy our 'Thank you'. Then we could encourage his 'Thank you' with a smile, withholding the object until his response was complete. Finally, all our prompts and cues would be removed, although praise and encouragement would still be given immediately his response occurred.

Fading

In the example just given we can see two processes in operation. Shaping refers to manipulation of the child's responses gradually toward some criterion of performance. *Fading* is the term applied to the gradual reduction of prompts, cues, frequency of reinforcement and so on. You can see that shaping calls for a great deal of insight, skill and patience. It is necessary to recognize small changes in behaviour that can be used as steps on the way to the final desired outcome and to reinforce these, but not for a period long enough to establish them. We shall constantly be looking for further approximations toward better performance and withholding reinforcement (another aspect of fading) until these are produced. At the same time we have to keep up the rate of reinforcement, otherwise we risk the child losing interest altogether and refusing to co-operate. Generally, with normal children progress is rapid. Working with children who have gross motor or intellectual defects calls for much greater skill and patience and is outside the scope of this book.

Guiding

If we cannot get a child to respond at all we may have to produce the necessary response by *guiding*. This means that the child's limbs are held and pushed or guided through the process. To begin with, the teacher of young children who wants his/her class to raise their hands when they wish to speak to him/her may physically lift the arms of individuals, guiding them in the production of the appropriate response. Similarly, parents help their children to hold and swing a cricket bat or to cup their hands to catch a ball.

Prompting

At a later stage guiding may be replaced by *prompting*. When the guided responses are learned so as to require minimal intervention by the teacher or parent then physical contact may no longer be necessary and a cue or prompt substituted. So, for example, the teacher will now merely have to signal with an upward movement of his/her hand that the children must raise their hands when they wish to speak. Parents may indicate actions by demonstrating the cupping of the hands for the children to copy or they may use a verbal prompt, like 'Hands ready'.

Modelling

Sometimes subskills are present but are not being properly sequenced. Here, *modelling* may be the answer. Another child, or an adult for that matter, demonstrates the sequence and the subject is invited to copy. It is easy enough for the teacher to call the attention of his/her class to an individual social skill which has just been performed expertly. He/she may comment on some action, as in 'Look how quietly Ben and Peter are working together and what a lovely rocket they are making'. Some teachers find that to refer to an individual or group who are behaving well at that moment is the best way to bring the whole class to order. They may say something like 'I'm glad to see that red group are ready for the next step'. In other cases it may be necessary to have a skilled child go through the whole process and to draw attention to particular subskills and sequences. An example of this might be when teaching young children how to take a message to another member of staff. The whole process may then be acted through with the teacher pointing out the proper mode of address and so on. At a later stage we might see a similar process being employed when children are being taught to cope with being interviewed or taking an oral or practical examination. Much athletic and other skill training is done in this way by learning subskills and then learning and improving sequences. The coach is there to guide and model and then to fade prompts and give positive reinforcement for successful outcomes.

These techniques constitute *real* teaching and *real* learning. Much of what goes on in schools is a matter of presenting a succession of hurdles and providing evidence (results) to show who has jumped over them and who has failed to do so. This process does not teach. As the old saying has it, 'Teaching is not telling'. The teacher's job should be concerned more with structuring the task, arranging for success and providing positive reinforcement until the natural and intrinsic rewards, which come from the mastery of the skill and the completion of the task itself, take over. Once the batsman is scoring centuries he needs no one to tell him how good he is. Once the child is able to read an exciting story she needs no one to urge her to go back to the library. It is at the early stages, when progress is slow and much less obvious, when rewards provided by the natural environment are meagre and hard won, that *real* teaching comes in to provide artificial (extrinsic) rewards for effort and for progress, however small.

Increasing infrequent behaviour

In behavioural terms, to increase the rate at which a certain behaviour occurs we usually have to alter the consequences so as to provide outcomes that are consistent and more positively reinforcing. If a child is able to work quietly but does not do so very often we could say that the consequences which follow his/her working quietly are not sufficiently reinforcing. We can only find out what will reinforce him/her by experimenting with different consequences and observing their effect on his/her behaviour. It is possible that the very fact that the teacher begins to pay attention to his/her quiet behaviour (by commenting favourably on it) will be reinforcing to the child. He/she will then be more likely to work quietly in the future.

Sometimes, an increase in the rate of a behaviour can be brought about by changing the circumstances, that is, the setting. The effect of changing seating patterns has already been referred to. Making certain that children know exactly what they are expected to do, where equipment is kept and how and when they are to have access to it, how they are to recognize that the given task is complete and what they are to do next, are all part of the total setting. Children need to know whether interaction with others is permitted or encouraged in particular circumstances. All these, and many other factors which will occur to practising teachers, are part of the setting or the antecedent situation in the classroom. They are all subject to the teacher's manipulation which forms part of his/her professional competence.

Cueing

A child who can speak quite well but who seldom does so may need *cueing*. This involves the signalling of, either verbally or non-verbally, appropriate opportunities to the child and encouraging him/her to try to respond. All his/her attempts would then be reinforced appropriately. Once he/she begins to contribute to class discussion at a level comparable with his/her peers the cues would be faded. Alternatively, we may have a child who very rarely speaks in class through shyness or fear of failure. A quiet word with such a child could establish an agreed private cue to be given when he/she feels that he/she has something to contribute. When he/she uses this you could go up to him/her to receive an almost private communication. If, and when, you feel it appropriate, this could be exhibited to the rest of the class, not only as the shy child's contribution, but a worthy one at that. By degrees the child could be encouraged to speak more audibly and more often, once he/she realizes that his/her contribution to the class discussion is accepted and valued by the group as a whole. Finally, he will be able to conform to class custom for taking part generally. Both of these procedures exemplify the basic solution for increasing the rates of infrequent behaviour: to give the response every opportunity to occur and, when it does, to give appropriate positive reinforcement. The last stage is to fade out the extra prompts or other aids.

Social reinforcement

Adults, especially parents and teachers, who have close contact with them, find that children respond very well to the use of attention and praise. This is called *social reinforcement* and is very effective, especially with young children. On the whole teachers say that they believe in encouraging children by means of praise and attention and they doubtless mean what they say, but we have found in our research that most teachers use social reinforcement much less than they think they do and certainly much less than they could. Of course, some people find it easy to use praise whereas others find it very difficult, but we all do it sometimes and so we could all learn to use praise more frequently and effectively.

This does not mean the use of praise all the time and whatever the outcomes. When we were speaking to a male teacher about this recently he recalled that he had once worked in a school where the headmaster was always praising his staff and that this had resulted in a falling off in effort and in standards. This illustrates very well the point that we are making that reinforcement must be used *contingently* and *only contingently* to be really effective. If it is to work best, it must also, at the outset at any rate, be immediate and abundant. It is no good waiting until the next day to reinforce a young child in the early stages of increasing a behaviour. Moreover, the more abundant the reinforcement, the more effective it will be, at first, in increasing the frequency of the behaviour.

Now, although we have been stressing throughout the need for accuracy and objectivity in observing and recording, this does not mean that our interactions with the children have to be clinical, scientific and cold. Not a bit of it! A great deal of this work can be fun and would seem like a game to the child. Many of the interventions described in the second part of this book have been enjoyed by the children involved to the extent that they often reminded their teacher of the game they were using to improve some aspect of classroom social behaviour, if he or she forgot.

Rules

By and large, our society recognizes the necessity for *rules* to guide the behaviour of its members and proceeds to write laws and rules to provide a framework. Almost exclusively, however, these rules are framed in negative terms: 'Thou shalt not steal' and so on. Whether it is a matter of dealing truthfully with one's neighbour, rules for the safety and convenience of others, or just a matter of appearances, the result is always the same: rules are inevitably expressed negatively. We are told 'Do not walk on the grass' or 'Do not touch'. To ensure that people keep these rules, society appoints officers like policemen, traffic wardens, museum and park keepers. In the last resort, they report misdemeanours and the guilty are punished, probably, as in Voltaire's phrase, 'Pour encourager les autres'. But punishment, by itself, does not teach any alternative acceptable behaviours.

The behavioural approach is contrary to this. Rules are formulated in a way that sets out the behaviour that is desired. That is to say, they are put positively not negatively. In the classroom we might have 'We try to work quietly', 'We stay in our seats unless we have permission to move', 'We put up our hands when we have something to say' and so on. We have found that this procedure works better if children are involved and encouraged to generate a set of rules acceptable to teacher and class. (But beware, some of their suggestions can be *very* negative.) The teacher's task is then to ignore any failure to keep the rules, unless someone else is really at risk, to catch the children who are being good (that is, keeping the rules) and to provide positive reinforcement for them contingently, abundantly and immediately. This is a formula that has been used widely in research and has been found to be very effective. We usually refer to it as 'rules, praise and ignoring'.

Tokens

A good intervention strategy will give the child an achievable target from the start and will also provide a means by which he/she can see his/her progress toward it. One way of doing this is by using *tokens*. These can take the form of any objects or visible marks which are easy to handle and see, but not easy to copy nor readily available from elsewhere. Plastic discs or counters, buttons, draughts pieces or cards with the official school stamp on them have all been used successfully. Most teachers already use stars, points, order marks and so on as rewards, sometimes as part of the school system, so the idea is far from new. Tokens or tallies can be collected and then counted up at set times or they may be fixed to a chart so that they can be seen clearly all the time. The visual display is especially important where there is a target to be achieved, as in the case referred to in the preceding paragraph. As the target is changed so the display can vary also. For example, one teacher used a cardboard cut-out train which was moved along a track toward the station to indicate progress toward a rewarding situation. The track could then be lengthened to accommodate changes in the rewarding strategy.

Tokens have other advantages. They allow us to reward immediately for small incremental changes in behaviour, another aspect of thinking small. Many rewards used in interventions cannot be subdivided into small units. For example, in the classroom the reward could well be a period for using some special apparatus or a chosen activity which involves the rest of the group. The use of tokens allows us to give, as it were, a small portion of the reward immediately for a small unit of behaviour, the sort of unit we shall be observing and recording. In addition, the use of tokens allows us to vary the reward and/or the 'cost' of the reward without the tokens themselves losing currency. Some intervention strategies involve the use of a *token economy* where tokens become the currency for all sorts of privileges and activities throughout the classroom or school. In such situations a tariff or price list is published so that children can see what their tokens will buy. This is mentioned by way of illustration only, since we are not advocating token economies for normal schools. Such a powerful (and complicated) procedure can seldom be justified as strictly necessary, although tokens can be used in ordinary classrooms in a number of ways. They are very useful in that they provide a visual aid at the beginning of a programme and a ready means for fading the programme once behaviour change has been achieved.

Contracting

Contracting can be a very powerful device, especially with older children who have a problem (whether behavioural or academic), are aware of it and who want help in solving it. Contracts are based on the same principles as other interventions. Early goals must be realizable. Criteria must be defined so that all parties understand exactly what is involved and the consequences must be clearly spelled out. Because of the necessity of changing criteria, reward schedules, and so on, contracts should be made for short periods of a week or so to allow for such revision. They should always be written and formally signed by all the participants. An example might be:

> Each day of the week I, Sidney Jones, will write at least ten lines in my exercise book. Each line must start within half an inch from the margin and must contain at least six words. For each day that this is done I, Mrs Smith, will give Sidney a star. When Sidney has four stars he will be allowed half an hour on Friday afternoon to use any of the apparatus in the classroom cupboard with the help of any friend he chooses.
>
> *Signed*   Mrs G Smith   Sidney Jones
>
> 2 April 1981

It should not be forgotten that children are interacting with other adults both in school and outside and that some of the behaviours we are concerned with occur both in and out of school. There is no reason at all why some or all of these people may not be involved in intervention programmes and contracting is a very good way of bringing them in. Parents, for example, control some very powerful reinforcers for their children at home and they will probably be just as interested as the child's teacher in helping him/her to progress academically or improve his/her social behaviour in the school situation. There is no reason why improved behaviour in school should not carry over into the home but it will do so only if similiar behavioural strategies are used to control it. Where adults other than the teacher are active in the classroom/school it is essential that they are involved in interventions and given clear instructions, otherwise the consistency so essential to a behavioural programme can be destroyed. For instance, where bullying is a problem, much of it will take place in the playground or in the road outside the school where the co-operation of duty teachers, lunch-hour supervisors and even lollipop people will be necessary.

Self-recording

Again with older children who recognize their problem and who want to do something about it, *self-recording* may be a possibility. This is particularly so when the behaviours are covert, or partly so, like day dreaming, nail biting, chewing or smoking. Quite young children are capable of self-recording the results of academic outcomes like the numbers of spellings they have correct or the number of pages read in a given period. As with all behavioural events, careful objective definition is of great importance. When self-recording is attempted, at least in the early stages, it will probably be necessary to have some means of checking the accuracy of the recording. Self-recording may well lead to greater self-awareness, a recognition of one's own behaviour patterns, and it is a small step from there to self-control through self-reinforcement. Planning to arrange reinforcing events for oneself is not far removed from the joint planning involved in contracting, nor from the self-awareness brought about through self-recording. Logically, perhaps, this is the place for *teachers* to start, since in order to bring about behavioural change in children they have first to change their own behaviour.

At least one teacher began to use behavioural methods by allowing his class of secondary-aged boys to modify his behaviour first. He asked the children which of his behaviours annoyed them the most and found, to his chagrin, that it was his use of sarcasm. He allowed the class to help him to record the incidence of this behaviour and it was agreed with them that if he could reduce it below a certain level by the end of the week, they would reward him by giving him a lesson of complete peace and quiet on the Friday. This was achieved and the success of the demonstration allowed the teacher to begin to use behavioural interventions with his pupils.

Reducing unwanted behaviour

So far we have considered only the positive side, that is, of increasing the incidence of desired behaviours, but many teachers are concerned about other behaviours such as tardiness, untidiness, disobedience, stealing and disruptive acts which they want to decrease. It is to these that we now turn. The reaction of most adults to behaviours like these would be to use punishment of some sort. But the use of punishment carries with it the risk of a number of unwanted side-effects and, anyway, it is not very effective in the long run. The behavioural view is that for all practical purposes, all behaviours, both good and bad, are learned and maintained through their consequences. The painful, but inevitable, concomitant of this is that most of the naughty and troublesome acts which children engage in and which are such an embarrassment to teachers and parents have been taught and are being maintained by them through the contingencies which they themselves have provided and continue to provide.

If behaviour is learned, then it can be unlearned and a new form of behaviour substituted. This behaviour change can be achieved by changing the consequences. It sounds simple and in principle it is so, but to change the consequences we have first to change our own behaviour because it is often we who are providing these consequences.

Extinction

The simplest way of decreasing the rate of incidence of a behaviour which is being maintained by attention is to ignore it. If the principle that consequences maintain behaviours is true, then it follows that to withdraw the consequences will cause the behaviour to cease. This process is called *extinction* and it has been shown empirically to be very effective. Unfortunately, there are two drawbacks. First, it may take a long time and, secondly, before it becomes extinguished the frequency of the behaviour may reach very high levels. Probably we have all had some experience of the spoiled boy (or girl) in a public place like a park or a supermarket, where he demonstrates his control over his mother through tantrum behaviour. He decides that he wants something, maybe sweets or ice-cream, which his mother does not want him to have. Accordingly, he throws a tantrum crying, yelling, kicking and throwing himself about. The real 'tantrum experts' have to use only the threat of this kind of behaviour to get what they want. The prototype was Violet Elizabeth Bott in the 'William' books by Richmal Crompton. She would lisp her threat to 'thcweam and thcweam and thcweam 'til I'm thick' so that William was forced to allow her a part in one of his nefarious schemes. Children like these have learned that mother will eventually respond but that sometimes she will hold out for quite a long while. They always get what they want in the end and this inconsistent schedule of rewarding teaches them to be very persistent. If the mother decides that from now on the child is never going to get his way by screaming, and so on, she will have to endure a number of really long, all-out sessions of protest before he learns that *no* amount of tantrum behaviour is going to pay off. This is going to be very hard for the mother.

Before leaving this point it is important to emphasize that attempts at extinction by ignoring will only work if the behaviour really is being maintained by adult attention. Many irritating classroom behaviours are maintained by peer attention and hence no amount of ignoring by the teacher will cause such behaviours to extinguish. It makes sense to attempt to harness the power of the peer group and to use it in your interventions. So-called *group-contingency* methods lead to a pay-off for the whole group, contingent on desired behaviour by the group or an individual within it. A clown is no longer amusing if his antics prevent the whole group from gaining a promised reward.

Punishment

Another way to bring about a decrease in this sort of behaviour is to use an aversive consequence, that is, something the child does not like: a *punishment*, in fact. If the mother in the supermarket were to administer a sharp slap and march the child straight home as soon as he began his antics, the behaviour might reduce much more rapidly than if she just ignored him. Perhaps in this case, to save her the embarrassment and the inconvenience of everyone concerned, such action could be justified. Being sharp and unexpected it might prove to be very effective but, generally, when using the behavioural approach we try to avoid the use of punishment for the reasons given already.

Incompatible behaviours

If we are not going to use punishment to choke off a behaviour, how then can we reduce its rate of occurrence? The answer is to increase the rate of another behaviour which is *incompatible* with the one we are trying to control. If noisy chattering is the problem, we will do better to encourage quietness. If a child is out of his seat too often, then we can try reinforcing in-seat behaviour. He cannot be seated and wandering about at the same time. These two behaviours are incompatible with each other. If untidiness or lateness is the problem, we could work on increasing tidiness and promptness as behaviours to be encouraged. Once we have redefined the problem in this positive way we can go back to the techniques for increasing behaviour rates which have been discussed already. On the whole, the behavioural approach concentrates on ways of increasing acceptable behaviours and is optimistic and accepting rather than punishing and forbidding.

It may be that our problem is a child who is observed to be out of his seat, talking to and distracting his neighbours twenty or more times in a lesson. Some aspects of the situation are reinforcing him positively when he does this. Ideally, we should like to know what these are, so that we can change them, but practically it may be impossible. What we could do is to devise some plan which will give him a bigger 'pay-off' to stay put and get on with his own work. We may agree with him a target of, say, ten 'out of seats' only per lesson to begin with, to be followed by some chosen reward. After a day or two, this criterion having been met, we would change the conditions so that he would be allowed first eight, then six, then four 'out of seats' until he was getting out of his seat no more than the other children, say, once or twice per lesson. If a great deal of social reinforcement has been used throughout the programme, it should now be possible to phase out the intervention. This may be done by gradually changing the time scale and/or contingencies for rewarding until social reinforcement alone is maintaining the in-seat behaviour.

Time out

We have suggested that punishment is considered inappropriate by those who advocate the behavioural approach and have given reasons for this, but there are two forms of punishment that are more acceptable. The first of these is *time out*, a contraction of 'time out from positive reinforcement'. Time out involves placing a child for a short period, of perhaps two to five minutes, in an environment which is completely without stimulation. After this period is up, he is returned to the classroom environment where, once again, he can earn positive reinforcement for behaving well. The removal of the child to the time-out area must be scheduled to follow certain well-defined behaviours and must be done expeditiously, dispassionately and without argument. When he returns there is to be no recrimination or other comment. He has 'served his time' and is allowed immediately to earn the full benefits of his appropriate behaviour.

Clearly, a good time-out area is not easy to arrange in school and the method is probably going to be most effective with smaller children. However, it has been used effectively with children up to their early 'teens. It bears some resemblance to the practice, common in schools, of putting children in the corner or outside the room or even of sending them to the headteacher. There the resemblance ends, however. A child outside the door has a great opportunity for engaging in conversation with passers-by. Even being placed in the corner allows a child to show off to his friends. Both of these outcomes are potentially highly reinforcing. Sometimes children are more of a nuisance to the teacher outside than they were in the class. Sending to the head can also be counter productive. The comings and goings in the secretary's room may be infinitely more interesting than what is going on in the classroom. It is not unknown for competitions to develop within a class to see who can be sent out most often!

Response cost

The second of these more acceptable forms of punishment, *response cost*, can be applied when a child is receiving marks or other tokens for behaviour which satisfies some criterion. For example, he/she may be receiving a star every time he/she completes a ten-minute period without leaving his/her seat. Response cost would then be applied by taking away a star every time he/she calls out to the teacher without first raising his hand to get permission to speak, a behaviour controlled in an earlier programme. An essential for the use of this technique is to ensure that a sufficiently high rate of earning is established before response cost is applied. If response cost is allowed to bring about a negative balance the whole programme can be jeopardized since children will rapidly become discouraged.

INTERVENTIONS: SOME OTHER THINGS TO KEEP IN MIND

One aspect of the behavioural approach to classroom management which differentiates it from others is the need to 'think small', which has already been exemplified in many of the illustrations given so far. Very often parents and teachers are reasonably successful in identifying children's problems but in their search for a remedy they aim at a perfect solution immediately. A parent will say, 'If you stop sniffing (meaning that I never want to hear another sniff) I will allow you to stay up and watch your favourite TV programme'. Or a teacher will say 'Those who get full marks will have a house point'. Targests such as these are quite useless to a child who is sniffing five times a minute or who never completes more than three sums out of ten set. At the beginning of a programme changes are bound to be small. The rate of change will accelerate later but, to begin with, small improvements must be made readily apparent and rewarded appropriately.

One of the clearest examples of this is to be seen in the shaping process where, at first, the response rewarded may bear little relation to the final target behaviour. To be successful a programme must set targets from the outset which are attainable by the subject with a reasonable amount of effort. A child who is calling out to the teacher fifteen times in a lesson cannot reduce this rate to nil at once but, with encouragement, will perhaps be able to manage twelve to start with.

Comment has often been made that draws attention to the fact that the effects of successful interventions seem to 'snowball'. In fact, the effect of reinforcement or the lack of it does seem to carry elements of self-perpetuation. If a child makes attempts to communicate or read or to make any response at all, in fact, and these efforts never receive any positive reinforcement, whether intrinsic or extrinsic, the general effect is bound to be inhibiting. All teachers have met children whose attempts to learn to read have been so lacking in reward of any kind that they have just given up trying. They will go to almost any lengths not to have to try again because they fear failure. Once a child begins to receive positive reinforcement for responding in ways that are acceptable to those around him/her success breeds on success and the process is carried forward by its natural momentum.

Numerous studies of children labelled 'impossible to cope with' tell the same story. Practically everything that these children do seems to engender a negative response from those near to them. These responses, however unlikely it may appear, are, in fact, maintaining the unwanted behaviours. Once a breakthrough is made, in however small an area, the people around the child begin to find opportunities for reinforcing him positively and this, in itself, changes their image of the child. They begin to find something to approve of and to say that there must be some good in him. Once again there is a snowball effect which may, of course, be very slow to develop at first. In some cases of failure to learn appropriately it may be necessary to *engineer* positive reinforcement in the early stages or to arrange for it to occur in abundance for very small changes in behaviour. Sometimes, when a lack of progress is limited to one area, say, reading, it may be better to leave this completely alone for a while and to concentrate on raising self-confidence in another sphere of activity before returning to it, by using, as far as possible, a new method of approach.

On the other hand, as has been suggested earlier, success breeds confidence and further success. Once we become accustomed to the approval and praise of others, and most of our efforts at learning and doing are positively reinforced, then we can stand occasional failure. Our confidence is not broken as we begin to depend more and more on the intrinsic reinforcement provided by accomplishment.

In setting out the strategies for bringing about behaviour change we have had to deal with them in a certain order. The more difficult and troublesome methods were sometimes described first. This, however, was not meant to suggest that these are the ones that should be tried first, quite the reverse. The heavier the armament you choose to solve your problem, the more trouble it is likely to be and the more disruptive of your normal class routine. By and large we want to choose the most appropriate and least upsetting mode of change. We do not want to use a sledge-hammer to crack a peanut. It has been shown that in certain cases all that is necessary is to spell out for the child, in unequivocal terms, what is expected of him/her in certain situations. This is often a sufficient change in the setting to bring about a desirable change in the behaviour.

TOPICS FOR DISCUSSION

1. In behavioural terms, why is the formula 'rules, praise and ignoring' (p. 174) found to be so effective?
2. Discuss the pros and cons of *contracting* (p. 175) as a way of modifying behaviour.
3. What methods of punishment are recommended by the authors and on what grounds are they said to be acceptable?

SUGGESTIONS FOR FURTHER READING

1. O'Hagan, F.J. and Edmunds, G. (1982) Pupils' attitudes towards teachers' strategies for controlling disruptive behaviour, *British Journal of Educational Psychology*, Vol. 52, pp. 331–40.

This study of secondary-school pupils' assessments of teachers' control strategies when dealing with disruptive behaviour lends weight to the suggestion of Hargreaves, Hester & Mellor (1975) *Deviance in Classrooms*, Routledge & Kegan Paul, London, that it is extremely important to take note of the *particular circumstances of an act* when accounting for either pupil evaluations or reactions. The analysis shows that initiation of aggressive strategies which may appear to be effective in the controlling of misbehaviour could well have deleterious consequences in other ways. The authors conclude that in the normal secondary school it is as important to be aware of *potentially disturbing situations* as it is to be aware of potentially disruptive pupils.

2. Hargreaves, D.H. Hester, S.K. and Mellor, F.J. (1975) Rules in context, pp. 63–105, in *Deviance in Classrooms*, Routledge & Kegan Paul, London.

This is a detailed analysis of the multifarious rules that are in play in classrooms and of the ways in which those rules imply different behaviours given their *contexts of utterance*. Thus, depending on the context, 'stop talking' can mean no cheating, don't interrupt, get on with your work, don't be impolite, don't disturb

other pupils, etc. The authors focus on the variety of contexts within whic
of classroom behaviour are applied, asking questions such as: What ɛ
contexts that teachers invoke? How are these contexts brought into exiѕ₊ᵤᵤₑ
How are these contexts changed? (that is to say, how does one context come to
replace another?) What rules are in play in a given context? How do pupils know
that a given context (and its rules) are in operation at a particular time?

3. Belson, M. (1982) Psychological principles for understanding students,
   pp. 11–43, in *Understanding Classroom Behaviour*, Australian Council for
   Educational Research, Hawthorn, Victoria.

This straightforward account of pupils' classroom behaviour draws on the
humanistic psychology of Alfred Adler one central premiss of which is that the
basic motivation of humans is *to belong* and that, as social beings, our behaviour
is *purposive, unified* and *consistent*. It follows therefore that the key to the
understanding of and modification of a pupil's unwanted behaviour in the
classroom is to identify the purpose and then to act in such a way that the
behaviour does not achieve its goal. Teachers, the author argues, 'rebuke the late-
comers, praise the model child, punish the bully, admonish the talker, fight with
the rebel, moralize with the cheat, flatter the vain child, correct the deficient,
coax the shy child and threaten the lazy. With what effect? Almost none because
the intervention is the purpose of the behaviour' (editors' emphasis).

Reading 13
COPING WITH DISRUPTION AT SCHOOL
B. Wade and M. Moore

All children have individual problems which discerning and sympathetic
teachers are normally able to overcome by observation, assessment and
appropriate provision. Those children who are frequently labelled
'problem' children are those who not only have personal difficulties but
also cause difficulty for those in their immediate environment. Their
behaviour is often antisocial and is exhibited in aggression toward other
children and sometimes staff, in bullying, refusal to co-operate, disobedience, stealing, lying and tantrums. It is important to remember that
all children show some aspects of disruptive behaviour at some time
during their school life. The fluctuation of experience such as family
quarrels, birth of a new brother or sister or some other exciting family
event can produce temporary difficulty and disruption.

B. Wade and M. Moore (1984) Coping with disruption at school, originally published in
Special Education: Forward Trends, Vol. 11, No. 3, pp. 27–30; will also appear substantially,
as one of its chapters, in B. Wade and M. Moore (forthcoming 1987) *Special Children:
Special Needs*, Robert Royce, London.

Our concern is with those children for whom these aspects of class-room behaviour are relatively permanent. A child who is disruptive and poorly motivated causes serious difficulties in the organization of learning and the maintaining of discipline of an entire class. One child demanding a disproportionate amount of a teacher's time and attention can seriously affect the learning of all children as well as the relations within the classroom. Ironically it is frequently those children who do not receive the appropriate time and attention elsewhere, who are particularly demanding in the classroom. For them, any attention, even reprimand, anger or punishment, is preferable to no attention at all.

When serious disruptive behaviour does occur it is important for a teacher to seek professional help and advice from both within the school and outside it. Disruptions to teaching are not necessarily a reflection on the professional competence of the teacher concerned. Discussions with senior colleagues and the headteacher or referrals to the schools psychological services are not admissions of failure but sensible action. They will soon show that others face exactly the same problems (a useful morale booster) and frequently practical suggestions and new strategies for action which the teacher had not considered will be offered.

ELIZABETH: 'ONE-AT-A-TIME' APPROACH

Elizabeth was ten years old when her disruptive behaviour reached its peak, when she transferred to a new class. She was one of eight children and also a twin. She tended to be the 'slower' twin at school and was also moody whereas the other twin, her brother, was straightforward and easy going.

Her behaviour at home presented difficulties in so far as her mother described her as 'moody, resentful and tantrummy'. At school she was spiteful and aggressive toward other children. She would also run off from school or have tantrums and afterwards be unable to work because of tension and anger. There had been instances of her urinating in various containers around the classroom. Such disruptive behaviour was unsettling for the rest of the class, and, although she was obviously an intelligent girl, it was having a seriously detrimental effect on her learning.

Elizabeth wanted a tremendous amount of teacher attention which she received because of her poor behaviour. We decided to tackle her various disruptive behaviours one at a time rather than to try to change her entire behaviour. The 'one-at-a-time' strategy is easier to implement and has a much greater chance of succeeding. The first area of concern was to be her tantrums: shouting, swearing, kicking and so on. We decided to tackle these by ignoring them as long as there was no possibility of her hurting herself or other children, or of her damaging school property.

CARRYING OUT THE STRATEGY

The first instance we had to test was after an incident in the playground. She had somehow managed to hurt her leg in a fracas. As her hand was taken to assess the damage she seized her opportunity by shouting, swearing and biting her teacher. Fortunately, the other children were out of the classroom, so she had no public audience. Her hand was released and eventually she sat in her seat and cried. Five minutes later she had calmed down; half an hour later she came to give one of us a hug. It is important to stress that, immediately she had quietened down, she was treated normally, as if the incident had not occurred. She was spoken to and required to do learning tasks in the normal way.

She would often stay out after playtime so that a member of staff would go and get her. She could then provoke a situation. The first time one of us did this she threw a tantrum and attacked with a broom handle. After that we preferred to wait to observe her (for her own safety) but be unseen. When she arrived nothing was said about her lateness; she was welcomed and requested to get on with her work. The length of time waiting outside gradually diminished, with very rare re-occurrences at later dates. Coming back to the classroom provided an inner battle for her. We observed that initially she returned by degrees, first to the corridor, where she waited, then to the classroom door, where she stood for several minutes, then staying in the outer area for a while before joining the class. We were very pleased with her for accomplishing this on her own and told her so.

Her tendency to run out of the classroom had a detrimental effect on the other children who took a lively interest in the proceedings. Sometimes this running out happened after a severe tantrum such as throwing over chairs or her desk. We therefore attempted to forestall her running out by locking the door. This had its dangers. The method worked but obviously rankled as one day she seized her opportunity to lock one of us out while the other children were at play. As her teacher moved out into the corridor, outwardly unconcerned, Elizabeth observed her. As she did not react, there was no pleasure for Elizabeth so she unlocked the door and sheepishly went off the play.

MEETING HER HALF WAY

We tried to meet Elizabeth half way for her to 'save face' and save her dignity. Often this meant playing a kind of game. For example, on one occasion she climbed to the top of the fire escape (which was forbidden). To get her down without provoking a crisis, hands were held out to her. Great concern was shown over her safety. Instructions were given to her to be careful. She joined in the game, climbed down extremely carefully, but came down without protest. We therefore tried to give each incident the best possible interpretation to avoid any overt confrontation.

DEALING WITH PILFERING

As her tantrums were gradually bought under control and became less frequent, we turned our attention to other aspects of her disruptive behaviour. The first of these was her pilfering from other children. In fact this aspect was treated later on because it took some time to become apparent because she was so clever at it. Open accusation had two drawbacks with Elizabeth. First, there was the risk that the accusation might be wrong. Secondly, we did not wish to provoke a return to violent tantrums. In addition, we had no wish that Elizabeth should be branded a thief when we were trying to help her to adjust in her relations with others.

Even when, on one occasion, we knew she had a rubber hidden in her folded back sleeve Elizabeth was not accused openly. The successful method we devised was to say 'You haven't by chance seen Darren's rubber? I'd be very grateful if you could help him find it'. Nearly every time the lost article was recovered. We never did completely cure Elizabeth of her pilfering but certainly stopped her from taking items home. Somehow the game for Elizabeth shifted to hiding things and then receiving praise for finding them. One day she actually demonstrated how 'other children' would steal, by folding back their sleeves and putting little items in the folds.

During this time Elizabeth's spiteful and aggressive behaviour to other children had diminished gradually. Where possible, other children were encouraged to be understanding, but antisocial hurtful acts still occurred. We began now to treat these in a systematic way. Instead of dealing with Elizabeth first by removing her from the scene and reprimanding her, all the initial attention and a great deal of sympathy were given to her victim. The other children in the class also responded to the hurt child. During these proceedings, therefore, Elizabeth was totally ignored. At a later time when Elizabeth was calmer the incident was discussed and she was encouraged to apologize. This strategy proved extremely successful. Elizabeth herself, on the occasions she was bullied by older children, now began to receive sympathy from her own classmates.

While ignoring inappropriate but relatively harmless behaviour, we took pains to ensure that Elizabeth's good behaviour was thoroughly praised and sometimes publicly rewarded with a star for her star chart. At first she was praised for almost everything she did correctly. Sitting on a chair or even picking up a pencil was noted with approval if it was appropriate. This strategy seemed to give her a certain air of confidence and well-being. Certainly, she was more relaxed in the classroom.

SUCCESS OF THE POSITIVE APPROACH

As the days progressed praise was confined to specific acts of behaviour: being kind to the other children; producing more than a mediocre amount of work; voluntarily tidying up, for instance. The praise was always genuine and not merely automatic. It is pleasing to see a 'disruptive' child behaving well. It is also less wearing to be constantly on the lookout for 'good' rather than 'bad' behaviour.

The positive approach worked for Elizabeth. It even enabled her to accept reprimands without retaliation when she saw they were justified. She was once reprimanded severely for frightening a much younger child. She chose a timid five year old, hid behind the lavatory door and leapt on him, howling like a banshee. Elizabeth was coming to know the rules and she accepted the reprimand (although she sulked for some time afterwards).

Gradually further rules, but as few as possible, were introduced. Work had to be completed. She should be polite to teachers (certainly no hitting or swearing) and she was not to be aggressive toward other children. These rules were based on what we already knew about her. They obviously fitted in with general class rules, but they were specifically explained to Elizabeth and reasons for them were given. Elizabeth now reacted well to this strategy, although it would have been impossible to succeed with it earlier. Dramatic progress in academic work followed virtually immediately after her improved behaviour. She was allowed a reward, five minutes on her favourite activity, if she completed all her work. She usually chose play with plasticine, art activities or enacting various roles in the play area. Initially, when she was working mainly for reassurance, she demanded a lot of attention. She received the attention because she was doing what we wanted her to do.

She worked to a timetable which we were prepared to operate flexibly. However, Elizabeth was entirely rigid and not prepared to allow herself any latitude. She would go through her work in the same order every day. First came maths, followed by an English exercise, then a written story, handwriting, phonics exercise and reading. It was a long time before she allowed herself to vary from her self-imposed rigidity.

There were times when we thought we had made very good progress with Elizabeth, when she would suddenly revert to some aspects of her previous behaviour. Usually these were isolated incidents but were obviously still testing us. As far as humanly possible we reacted in the same way as we had done on previous occasions, even though we were taken by surprise because we had become less vigilant. Only once did she try to test us with her school work. She handed in a carelessly presented piece of work, definitely (and one suspects deliberately) not up to her usual standard. She waited for reaction. A large red cross was put at the bottom of the paper with the suggestion that perhaps she would like to try it again. We knew she was usually so proud of her work. We had called her bluff. She returned and reappeared later with her work presented correctly and neatly.

MANAGING DISRUPTIVE BEHAVIOUR

Elizabeth's case study illustrates the way that some children are unable to cope in an unstructured situation. It is important for these children to know exactly what is required of them : they need to have the 'rules of the game' explained or demonstrated. They need to know what are the acceptable limits of their behaviour: what they are allowed to do and what they are not allowed to do in and around the classroom. This does not mean a list of rules should be written on the wall but an indication of the behaviour that the teacher expects should always be given.

The classroom discipline need not be rigid and conforming. Ideally, the fewer 'rules' the better. Only those that directly influence the day-to-day running of the class need to be explained in detail, such as putting up a hand in response to questions and remaining seated during lesson time unless instructed otherwise. Individual teachers set individual rules for the well-being of their particular class. The aim is for disruptive chilren to conform eventually to those standards. A positive approach always works best.

The knowledge that the teacher has made the rules and is obviously in charge of the situation gives an added sense of security to school life. The rules applied should be reasonable and not petty nor meaningless. The stability of the pattern of expected school behaviour is strengthened by the consistency of the teacher's responses to children's behaviour. The presence of an adult whose own behaviour and response are reliable (and indeed predictable) makes more sense to a child. We are all subject to changes of mood and at times show slightly irrational behaviour. The majority of children are able to understand and cope with this as they are able to see us as other human beings.

However, for the disruptive child, great care has to be taken that, whatever the state of mood, anxiety or tiredness we happen to be in, responses to certain behaviour must be consistent. Only in this way will socially acceptable patterns and responses be learned. Often children are used to irrational treatment at home and, consequently, have never had a chance to learn what is acceptable. For example, to accept an action one day and berate the same action the next, only brings about a state of confusion and disorder. Probably, it will also encourage the desire to try the action again to see what effect it has the next time. Children need to be able to predict the behaviour and response of their teachers to feel secure.

This consistency of responses by the teacher will not provide an overnight change in the behaviour of the child as we have seen with Elizabeth. Provoking and testing of the teacher will no doubt continue for some time. This irrational illogical action on the part of the child must still be met with a consistent response. This consistency can be very difficult to maintain because disruptive behaviour (especially when it has appeared to be improving) can produce strong feelings such as anger and resentment in the teacher. We have found it helpful to anticipate our own feelings in advance and to try to work out coping strategies for ourselves. Discussion and agreement of treatment with members of staff about disruptive children is the only way to achieve a consistency of approach throughout the school, thus providing a united 'front' and an even greater sense of security for the child with this kind of need.

DAY-TO-DAY WORKING

It is expedient to give the disruptive child a chance to settle down at the beginning of the day. Mild misdemeanors can often be overlooked as the class enters the room and settles to work. This advice is perhaps at odds with the 'consistency' of response discussed above but, if a behaviour is 'not seen', it need not be commented on. Flagrant breach of rules obviously requires action. The maxim 'make it easy for the children to be good' is most easily applied if you ensure you watch them when they are being good. A day that starts quietly rather than with anger and confrontation has more probability of continuing that way.

Most potentially disruptive children find the reliability of a timetable reassuring. This consistency of lessons linked with consistency of rules and teacher behaviour again adds security to the child's environment. The child has a secure knowledge of the order of the day-to-day activities. They are predictable.

Naturally, in the course of events, teachers make changes to the timetable, particularly in primary schools whose timetables tend to be more flexible. Topics and projects can often be the reason for an all-day art session, for example. If the child is not able to adapt, there is no harm in letting him or her continue timetabled work. Without any pressure being exerted, interest may lead the child to join in the extra activities. Eventually, Elizabeth worked out her own timeable and stuck rigidly to it. She was more demanding than her teachers of her work output.

Even with all due care, anticipation and attention, some children still try to provoke a confrontation as part of their testing of the authority relationship. It can be difficult to know when to intervene to avoid a crisis developing. Problems with work may provoke a confrontation as the child will sometimes seek conflict to escape work. It is important to encourage children with special needs to ask for help when they need it. It is important too, to identify when a child is experiencing difficulty but is as yet unable or too unwilling to ask.

AVOIDING CONFRONTATION

Sometimes peer group pressure can put an end to a child's disruptive behaviour. Children often object just as strongly as the teacher, or even more, to the classroom being disturbed by whistling and calling out. It can be worthwhile ignoring the behaviour for a while to assess if the child's classmates are able to put an end to it.

If it becomes clear that this strategy is not going to succeed then *gentle* and calm handling might still prevent an outburst. No one enjoys being shouted at or publicly reprimanded: it is demeaning and humiliating. A quiet word at close proximity with even some physical contact, such as a hand placed on the child's shoulder or arm, tends to keep the whole situation low key, particularly if the tone and approach are as sympathetic as possible.

This approach also avoids any public verbal exchange and abuse between teacher and child and may prevent beginning or continuing of disruptive behaviour. Angry exchanges can be very rewarding for a disruptive child in terms of audience attention and are therefore likely to be prolonged. Trying to revert to normality after that is time consuming and any progress previously made in social behaviour will have halted for a time. O'Leary *et al.* (1970) show that the use of soft reprimands reduces the frequency of disruptive behaviour.

Sometimes the sympathetic low-key response is not enough for a child who is either determined to have a 'scene' or is insufficiently lacking in self-control. Having a tantrum or scene or creating a disturbance serves little purpose to such children if it is not witnessed. The most effective course, therefore, is to remove the audience. If it is possible the child should be removed from the scene and put where there is no one to view the proceedings. If necessary, the rest of the class can be withdrawn for perhaps an extra five minutes' play.

Either course should be undertaken with the minimum of fuss and as much matter of factness as possible. If such children are likely to cause damage or injure themselves when left alone it is expedient to ask for the help of another adult, either to observe the child or to supervise the rest of the class. Similarly, if it is decided to remove the child from the classroom, the assistance of another member of staff may be necessary. It is advisable to have contingency plans, especially arrangements with colleagues, worked out in advance so that they may be put into effect immediately and confidently.

RECORD KEEPING

Sharing a classroom with a disruptive child can be akin to living with a time bomb: and, not knowing the time, you never know when it is going to explode. By the keeping of systematic records, however, a pattern of behaviour can often be detected. Once the pattern is perceived steps can be taken to avoid any initiating events that appear to lead to disruptive behaviour.

At any time when the child has not obeyed the rules which were agreed on, it is advisable to record as soon as possible and as far as possible *all* the events leading up to the problem and also the steps taken to remedy it. To give an example, it was noted that one child's outbursts always took place at the beginning of playtime, when classroom restraints did not apply and the child was unable to cope. Finding tasks for her to do during the playtime led to the speedy cessation of her outbursts. Systematic record keeping has the additional benefit that, if a child is so disruptive in the classroom that the ordinary school feels unable to cope, the educational psychologist can be given a wealth of records to help in assessments and provision for the child's needs.

MODIFICATION OF BEHAVIOUR

We have agreed that children are troublesome mainly to acquire attention of any kind. The problem for the teacher is that paying attention to disruptive behaviour is likely to increase that particular behaviour. Attention can be given in any form: by praise, reprimand, smiles or shouts, for example. For some children unpleasant consequences are vastly preferable to being ignored.

As far as possible it is better to under-react consistently to behaviour that is inappropriate but relatively harmless. It only takes one instance of paying attention to encourage some children to repeat undesirable behaviours. The behaviourists (for this is a behaviour-modification technique) warn that the behaviour will often get worse before it gets better, so a consistency of approach is extremely important. Probably this is easier to manage if the strategy can be coupled with giving positive attention, that is *praise* for appropriate behaviour.

Laslett (1977) gives the example of a child who, every time he entered the classroom, kicked the door to close it. His teacher consistently ignored this action until the one day he did not kick the door. She immediately gave him a toffee (one assumes she told him why) and the door kicking ceased. A very broad generalization of behaviour-modification techniques is to ignore inappropriate behaviour and to praise or reward appropriate behaviour but to do the latter immediately.

The maxim we mentioned earlier, 'Make it easy for the children to be good', could be rewritten as 'Catch them when they're being good and do or say something positive for the child'. This approach needs to be extended to the whole of the class rather than applied to one disruptive child.

ADVANTAGES OF REWARDING CHILDREN SYSTEMATICALLY FOR GOOD BEHAVIOUR

Tangible rewards for being good can also be offered but must be related to how much progress the child has made. To begin with, aim for a small target so that it is almost a certainty that a child will earn the reward. Sights then have to be set higher so that progress and improvement are maintained and the child can experience satisfaction through earning rewards.

If, for example, a star system is used, disruptive children can be given a star for each lesson of the day in which they have been 'good' according to the criteria previously agreed between teacher and children. Generally, the required period of good behaviour to earn a star can be extended to a half day, then a whole day, then two days out of three and so on. Further incentive is added if stars can be used as currency and exchanged for sweets, extra minutes of play or preferred classroom activities.

Sometimes the peer group can be used to provide additional support for individual children earning rewards, especially when this reward is occasionally extended to the whole class. Children are good at understanding situations and can be encouraged to help individual children in this way. *Their* praise when the class benefits from special treats is likely to do more good than anything the teacher says.

RELATING TO DISRUPTIVE CHILDREN

Throughout this article we have stressed the need for consistency, positive expectations and development of confidence and self-image in the way that teachers relate to disruptive children. A good deal of tension and trouble comes from anticipating bad behaviour before it happens and from meeting conflicts head on. We do not minimize the stress sometimes experienced in all classrooms but we have found that cultivation of a sense of humour is an important way to cope with that stress. See also Walker and Goodson (1977); Stebbins (1980) and Woods (1983). Humour can often defuse a classroom situation that threatens to get out of control, so long as the humour is genuine and not sarcastic. Sarcasm does not calm things down; on the contrary, it engenders feelings of hostility, thus fanning the flames of the conflict. Equally, humour directed against oneself, if appropriate, can provide a release from tension.

REFERENCES

Laslett, R.B. (1977) *Educating Maladjusted Children*, Crosby Lockwood Staples, London.

O'Leary, K. D., Kaufman, K. E., Kass, R. E. and Drabman, R. S. (1970) The effects of loud and soft reprimands on the behaviour of disruptive pupils, *Exceptional Children*, Vol. 37, pp. 145–55.

Stebbins, R. (1980) The role of humour in teaching, in P. Woods (ed.) *Teacher Strategies*, Croom Helm, London.

Walker, R. and Goodson, I. (1977) Humour in the classroom, in P. Woods and M. Hammersley (eds.) *School Experience*, Croom Helm, London.

Woods, P. (1983) Coping at school through humour, *British Journal of Sociology of Education*, Vol. 4, No. 2. pp. 111–24

TOPICS FOR DISCUSSION

1. What was the importance of 'treating Elizabeth normally as if the incident had not occurred' and 'trying to meet Elizabeth half way'?
2. Examine the authors' reasons for avoiding confrontations and the specific aspects of advice they give for dealing with them.
3. Discuss the psychological principles involved in *consistency of treatment* in dealing with disruptive children such as Elizabeth.

SUGGESTIONS FOR FURTHER READING

1. Merrett, F. E. (1981) Studies in behaviour modification in British educational settings, *Educational Psychology*, Vol. 1, No. 1, pp. 13–38.

It can be seen from this useful review of British studies that, at the time of writing, more studies were reported from junior schools than from secondary with roughly equal numbers being carried out in 'ordinary' and special-school settings. All of the experimental and case studies reported took place in the natural environment rather than the laboratory. Overall, it can be concluded that: (a) the efficacy of the behavioural approach is demonstrated; (b) the more teachers know about behavioural methods the more favourably inclined they are to their use in classrooms; (c) there is a need for more research into the usefulness of behavioural methods in 'ordinary' schools; (d) more efforts are needed to discover the best ways of teaching both parents and teachers about behavioural methods and techniques of monitoring their effects. The review is particularly interesting because of the many brief cameos of behavioural-modification programmes in classrooms and child guidance clinics given.

2. Rumsey, I. and Ballard, K. D. (1985) Teaching self-management strategies for independent story writing to children with classroom behaviour difficulties, *Educational Psychology*, Vol. 5, No. 2, pp. 147–57.

An essential component of self-management involves identifying and monitoring one's own responses. Procedures in studies of self-management often employ verbal self-statements of pupils to control their unwanted behaviour. The essential training consists of: (a) description of the required behaviours; (b) teacher commenting on the correspondence between *saying* and *doing*; (c) introduction of training sessions; (d) guidance of children's verbal statements so that they contain the required behaviours and not just those already being performed; (e) feedback to the teacher so that he/she can provide accurate comment. This study is a report on the effective application of these procedures with seven disruptive primary-school children during story-writing lessons.

3. Presland, J.L. (1981) Modifying behaviour long-term and sideways, *Journal of the Association of Educational Psychologists*, Vol. 5, No. 6, pp. 27–30.

This is a useful paper about the long-term and wider effects of the use of behaviour-modification techniques in the changing of unwanted classroom behaviour. Although the changes obtained by behaviour modification often appear specific to the circumstances there is evidence of what can be termed '*generalization*', that is to say, changes that spread to different classrooms, different teachers, different times of the day and different behaviour. The evidence that generalization can occur offers the possibility that we can do something that allows the discontinuation of the full rigour of a behaviour-modification programme. The author sets out suggestions in terms of things that teachers can do by way of maintaining the beneficial effects of changed behaviour and extending such change to other areas of classroom activities.

Reading 14
INDUCTION
STRATEGIES AND LOWER SCHOOL
J. Benyon

TEACHER COPING AND SURVIVAL STRATEGIES

Three writers in particular have developed the concept of strategy, namely Woods (1979, 1980a,b, 1981b,c) in his 'survival' model, D. Hargreaves (1978, 1979, 1980) in his 'coping' model and Pollard (1980, 1982, 1984), who has built on the latter's work and examined the impact teacher and pupil coping strategies have on each other. All attempt to draw links between actions, situation and wider society, but differ in their emphases. For Woods the primary function of all teacher strategies is survival. Indeed, they do not necessarily facilitate teaching (although they can), but take its place and assume its appearance. Woods' premise is that teachers are compelled by circumstances to think of survival first, education second, turning themselves into the kind of teachers the situation demands. As a result they are forever accommodating to institutional pressures, trapped between professional demands and recalcitrant pupils. They survive best together rather than individually and this demands that each commits him/herself to the institution and expresses personality through it. Such commitment is through survival strategies as the teacher defends his/her physical, mental, personal and career interests through short- and long-term strategies. He holds that there has recently been a confusion between separate issues, namely teaching for social control (and induction into capitalism) and situational control (necessary for the teacher's accommodation), so that survival

J. Benyon (1985) Induction strategies and lower school, in *Initial Encounters in the Secondary School: Sussing, Typing and Coping*, Falmer Press, London.

strategies have not been properly identified. Teachers are trapped by the 'logic of survival' and much that passes for teaching is really a fake commodity, a protective cocoon. Survival strategies, if successful, are highly persistent and change is slow because it throws up new survival problems. Thus strategies that are aimed at teacher domination through noise control, the reduction of strain and moves to create order assume the guise of teaching. Woods goes on to identify eight modes of teacher survival and their attendant strategies:

1. *socialization* through mortifying techniques, vigilant monitoring of pupil appearance and behaviour, and rewards, drill and will-breaking contests, these being anticipatory manoeuvres to forestall trouble
2. *domination* through corporal punishment, verbal aggression and simulated and actual anger so that teachers become 'drill sergeants'
3. *negotiation*, or exchange through appeals, apologies, promises and threats
4. *fraternization*, that may involve teachers in displaying they are on the pupils' side (in dress, speech and interests, through chat and humour, and by means of a stage manner to establish rapport)
5. *absence*, when a teacher leaves the classroom, or allows pupils to take over the lesson (as in a project) or absents him/herself 'spiritually', finding satisfaction in activities other than teaching as a career
6. *ritual/routine* into which pupils are initiated strongly (a consensus is established, authority relations remain impersonal, the school's expressive order internalized and there is strict teacher control over knowledge)
7. *occupational therapy*, the making available of 'therapeutic' tasks for pupils which also aid teacher survival
8. *morale boosting*, where the emphasis is on group cohesion as pupils are given the chance to organize their own lessons while remaining answerable to a paternalistic, supportive teacher (furthermore in difficult situations teachers are more likely to band together to strengthen solidarity and boost morale).

In D. Hargreaves' (1978, 1979, 1980) more overtly political model, coping strategies are techniques of persuasion, manipulation and domination in a system in which working-class pupils are targets for order and stability. They exhibit the state's control of knowledge acquisition through pedagogical moves which reproduce capitalism and reflect taken-for-granted ideological assumptions about, for example, the needs of working-class children. Ethnographers are reminded that they must take social and political factors, as mediated by both institutions and individuals, into account if they are to understand classroom processes.

Material constraints at the institutional level are held to be expressions of 'hidden' structural forces expressed in ways which render their origins obscure. Pedagogies are viewed as responses to these mediated constraints, which require continual resolution through teacher decision-making and coping strategies. These are constructive solutions to institutionally mediated constraints (experienced as classroom dilemmas), but they become routinized, institutionalized and taken for granted as accepted, legitimate pedagogical practices. D. Hargreaves claims that a circular movement is thus set in motion; teachers' commonsense perceptions and strategies, essentially conservative, persist because of their power to enable them to cope, but in delineating thoughts and actions they guarantee their own existence. Coping strategies enable teachers to meet often contradictory demands, the origins of which are obscured from them. As far as the position of teachers is concerned this is redolent of the Sharp and Green (1975) thesis, where the strategy of keeping pupils 'busy' is presented as an aspect of false consciousness resulting in social stratification being produced within the classroom: Mapledene's 'progressive' teachers, they argue, were compelled by circumstances to spend their time attending to the brightest children whilst others were left to undertake useful, often 'therapeutic', activities. Furthermore the responsibility for this state of affairs was attributed to the children as teachers typed them and justified their pedagogy by recourse to a 'theology' of child centredness.

The current interest accorded to the concept of 'coping strategy', stems from the fact that it holds out to the ethnographer the real prospect of relating his/her micro-level analysis to the macro-theorist's concern with social reproduction through schooling. Pollard's work is particularly notable in this respect: he argues that the working consensus of the classroom, whilst it clearly reflects the teacher's greater formal power, results from teachers and pupils accommodating to the coping necessities of the other. Their respective strategies are held to develop in response to the others' demands and depend on biography and culture, as well as institutional and specific classroom contexts. Pupils' coping strategies reinforce teachers' by 'meshing' with them, so strengthening their mutual perpetuation. Classroom differentiation is a by-product of this meshing together of teacher and pupil coping strategies, and he thus adds to the work on teacher labelling and the self-fulfilling prophecy, a social, structural dimension beyond these individualized factors. By close reference to two infant-school classrooms he illustrates how this meshing was actually reflected in particular forms of social differentiation. Mrs Rothwell saw it her role to compensate her 'deprived' pupils whereas the

other (Mr Harman) adopted a progressive stance as he encouraged pupils
to think for themselves. Mrs Rothwell's teaching strategies (for example,
seating pupils in groups determined by reading level and a star system of
incentive rewards) produced, Pollard argues, a distinct social hierarchy in
her class and delimited pupils' friendship choices. Pupils developed their
own collaborative coping strategies around those of the teacher and were
recorded negotiating among themselves the answer in mathematics while
she helped others in their reading, happy to sanction a tolerable level of
pupil chatter. The bottom group sat apart, was physically cut off and
shunned by the other children, and had poor access to the hidden means
of accomplishing lessons and winning stars. Pupils' collaborative strategies were their way of coping with Mrs Rothwell's work demands
whilst allowing her to hear readers. Social differentiation is, therefore,
traced as the direct outcome of the meshing of the two sets of strategies:
if the teacher's coping strategies created the conditions for primary
differentiation, the reactive pupil strategies led to its secondary reinforcement. In the case of Mr Harman, Pollard shows how his coping strategies
let him to implement both his personal beliefs about education (his
'subterranean value system') and the more conventional demands of the
school. A close relationship existed between his and the pupils' coping
strategies as, at the primary level, he favoured divergent, creative,
'jokers' and, at the secondary level, they took advantage of the scope he
accorded them. Although many of the children derived their strategies
from the institutionalized pupil role, Pollard concludes that 'a significant
group of boys developed alternative strategies which Mr Harman's values
and coping strategies also made possible and this was reflected in the
structure of friendship groups within the class'.

Each of these writers casts doubt on whether teachers are aware of the
true origins and outcomes of the strategies they employ, or are forced
into using. They 'survive', they 'cope', they 'mesh' with what pupils
throw at them, but they are either unable to appreciate what is, as a
consequence, taking place under their noses in terms of pupil differentiation or, if they do, then in 'hegemonic fashion', they explain and accept
it as inevitable by recourse to intelligence, home background, 'right' or
'wrong' pupil attitudes and so on. It is left to the free-floating outsider to
have the insight to chart the connection between the unseen forces
operating on teachers; their institutionally mediated forms and appearances; teachers' answering pedagogic actions; their outcomes; the terms
in which these outcomes are explained and justified by participants. Is
this the case with all teachers or are some conscious of their 'dirty work',
what they have to do and why, and blame 'the system' rather than their

pupils or themselves? Reading the literature on coping and surviving one could be forgiven for thinking that teachers have very few choices open to them, so much are they compelled by circumstances to follow, willy nilly, certain narrowly prescribed courses of action. This is reductionist in the sense that it overlooks the expertise, skill and ingenuity that teachers have to display to 'cope', 'survive' and 'mesh'; the means by which these are achieved have to be implemented and, in the case of initial encounters, often announced and clarified. Indeed, the view that teachers, whether wholly or partly, are in a state of false consciousness, falling back on a limited number of well-worn formularized strategies to deal with institutionally mediated demands (the source of which is denied them) has to be set against one which highlights their strategical acumen as, moment by moment, they resolve dilemmas. Only D. Hargreaves, perhaps, by emphasizing the creative nature of coping strategies has satisfactorily acknowledged this and only ethnography can provide the necessary detail and show how both teachers and pupils bring this off. Indeed, the relationship between teacher and pupil strategies and teacher and pupil thinking is poorly documented and demands the attention of classroom workers for some time to come. Some hold that strategies result from individuals carefully weighing up the complex situation confronting them, along with the resources available, before deciding how best they might pursue their objectives. Researchers, it is implied, have yet to capture and acknowledge the strategical sophistication and range of teacher–pupil tactics. Both teacher and pupil strategies are shaped by colleagues and peers, parents and significant others, as well as the immediate material environment; it must be stressed that behind these lie not only the mediated influences of class, economy and current political demands, but also personal and biographical factors. Teachers clearly espouse some strategies rather than others because of age, gender and past, as well as present, career experiences.

It is clear that the relationship between beliefs and strategies is a complex one. Teachers' ideologies as 'educationalists' need not be reflected in their classroom actions as 'teachers'. Neither are ideologies static but are composed of both 'recipes', which emerge when confronted with recurring problems, as well as ideas held at a higher level of generalization. Others raise a similar issue and talk of two dichotomous ideals informing teacher decision making, namely 'the moral' (where rules and values are judged as right and proper) and 'the pragmatic' (where they are held to work). Moralists sacrifice pragmatism for morality, whereas the converse is true of pragmatists; it is possible therefore to think in terms of discrete sets of moralistic and pragmatic strategies. The teacher as strategist has to decide on the spot whether the act perceived as deviant is likely to develop into a serious challenge, or whether his/her interruption will be even more disruptive than the deviant conduct itself. This helps to explain why some teachers adopt strategies of 'conflict avoidance' toward 'difficult' pupils. In similar vein Woods (1981a) uses a case study of two teachers to develop a theory of strategies as a paradigmatic–pragmatic continuum. Other crucial factors behind teacher strategies are how the teacher types pupils; what motives he/she attributes to them; his/her prediction of their future course of action; their possible reaction to correction. Indeed, whether a teacher decides to terminate or ignore a deviant act rests on his/her knowledge of act, action and situation, and whether it is likely to peter out, persist or escalate. The pressure of classroom events forces teachers to make instinctive decisions, based on experience, and suggests that the process of deliberation which underpins most teaching is one of routinized subconscious reasoning, with options limited and the criteria on which they are selected simplified. Viewed in this light teacher strategies are routinized adaptations to the circumstances in which teachers work and in which there is little time for deliberation before a decision has to be taken. In this coping model D. Hargreaves relates teachers' actions in real time to their underlying thinking by presenting coping as operating on two interdependent levels, namely: level 1, the *negotiative*, or face-to-face dealings, and level 2, the *coping*, consisting of decisions taken prior to lessons and which emphasize the behavioural and moral over the cognitive and academic. He illustrates the interplay between levels by showing how a difficult pupil was handled in a drama lesson. The class was managed through attention-maintaining devices; the close monitoring of talk and movement; the articulation of rules. In her dealings with Charlie the teacher called on the strategies of 'confrontation avoidance' and 'policing', both of which are more concerned with the moral than the cognitive. These enabled her to name Charlie but not the nature of his deviance so that he succeeded in having his identity satisfactorily recognized whilst open confrontation was avoided.

PUPIL STRATEGIES

Pupils, too, have their own specific strategies to meet the numerous demands made on them by teachers, peers and parents and which are handled in line with their own interests, goals and personalities. These need not be reactive primarily, but can be used to take the initiative. Whereas some are the product of specific orientation, others have different intentions underlying them (for example, 'doing work' can denote either instrumentalism, indifference or teacher support). As I have already made clear, some attention has been paid to pupils as 'attention seekers', 'intermittent workers', 'solitary workers' and 'quiet collaborators', but we need to know more about the defining strategies utilized by each. We know little about pupil strategies based on talk, perhaps overlooked because individuals contribute little and infrequently given the dictates of classroom discourse. What little is said by pupils can, nevertheless, serve important strategic ends in the public arena of the classroom. Meanwhile, Woods talks of threefold pupil strategies ('supportive', 'oppositional' and 'detached') in line with Hargreaves' schema of 'pleasing teacher/supportive', indifferent/detached' and 'delinquescent/oppositional'. Research interest has focused on the latter and how pupils cope with the academic demands made on them is a much neglected area. As far as pupils in school are concerned, teacher-pleasing strategies have been noted, with conformist pupils observed searching for clues in teachers' and peers' responses, gestures and actions, and then adopting strategies of reciprocity to meet demands. How pupils accomplish conformity may be less evident and dramatic than the means whereby they accomplish deviance, but considerable strategic, interpretational and diplomatic skills must be exercised by them if they are to be academically successful and/or play the part of 'good' pupils, given differences in teacher demands across the curriculum. Research is needed into strategies employed by successful pro-school pupils. So, too, research on those pupil strategies concerned with the presentation of self to peers.

'Mucking' must be the most common pupil-pleasing strategy in schools and has been commented on extensively in its different forms. For rejecting pupils school offers a challenge to search for meaning through fun, to alleviate boredom and win identity. 'Doing nothing' can be a highly successful strategy toward achieving this. Neither is it the case that opposition (either in behavioural or academic terms) is manifested solely by non-academic pupils. Even highly academic pupils sometimes challenge the teacher's definition of, and control over, knowledge. Further pupil strategies that have been commented on at various times are those aimed at 'getting by' and escaping teacher censure (for example, through guesses, whispered answers or arranging for others to do the work), 'bargaining' strategies for better marks and 'self-help' strategies. Some pupils use the dominant-teacher strategy of coercion to spawn a whole new range of macho counter-strategies to express their rejection and cocky resilience, testifying to the necessity of 'helping out your mates' (whether by allowing copying or joining in with 'lip'). There are certain rules that pupils expect of teachers and, if these are not forthcoming, retributive strategies may result, namely 'reciprocity' (insult for insult) and 'equibration' (tactics like switching off, to neutralize loss of dignity). Pupils may use similar strategies to attack teachers for awarding what they feel to be unfair grades and doing so by arriving late, leaving early and generally behaving 'cool' to obstruct their teachers.

It can be claimed, in conclusion, that whereas some strategies 'belong' uniquely to teachers (for example, the imposition of authority talk), others typically 'belong' to pupils (for example, noise raising and covert disruption). Yet others are more flexible and are used (albeit in different ways for different purposes) by both (for example, humour). Most teacher strategies are expressly aimed, not surprisingly, at imposing order and routine, failure to do so raising fears about loss of control and resulting in a reputation for incompetence. Alternatively, the above-mentioned strategy of noise raising is the most obvious and effective means of disrupting lessons and undermining teacher reputations in a traditional pedagogy. Strategies are highly situational and new strategies of control and instruction are required in different circumstances. More 'open' discovery-based settings demand a whole range of new teacher strategies to mount convincing 'mock-ups' of real-life 'hot' situations and to superintend them. Hence the importance to teachers of strategies based on group work and learning resources. Strategies available to pupils are affected similarly and Denscombe (1980) records that the high tolerance of noise in the integrated humanities lessons he observed rendered less effective strategies based solely on it. Noise is still a major problem, however, if an open classroom is located in a traditional school. The value of such research is that it shows how open classrooms call for innovative and subtle teacher-control strategies which, in turn, call forth new pupil counter-strategies. However, not all the repertoire of teacher or pupil strategic behaviour is necessarily directed toward each other. Indeed, individuals or groups of teachers may adopt strategies toward colleagues to gain or retain influence, to further career, to safeguard identity, to win departmental resources or for purely personal or historical reasons. Alternatively, in the face of a common threat teachers are likely to develop 'collective' strategies to strengthen unity and fellow feeling.

The literature on initial encounters between teachers and pupils is both slight and uneven in quality, although there are notable exceptions. I now bring together what is of relevance before examining the establishment of the moral order of Lower School life. 'Induction strategies' are defined as the means whereby teachers accomplish 'starting the year', both individually and collectively, and I show how a rule system was articulated and enforced, hierarchical relations established and pupil talk and movement curtailed. All institutions subject newcomers to admission procedures so that they can be ordered, rendered compliant and become part of the bureaucratic machinery. They are informed of their obligations and may be subjected to obedience tests or experience will-breaking contests. Indeed, those who are openly rebellious risk public humiliation in that they are held up as examples to others as part of a concerted staff-initiation programme ('the welcome') to impose regularity, uniformity and co-operation. In 'total institutions' like asylums, rigorous attempts may be made during this status passage to change new members' identities through techniques of degradation and violence (or 'contaminative exposure'). In the case of school some pupils may come with what is regarded as an inappropriate presenting culture and this may result in initial encounters being a period of retraining, a jettisoning and taking on of new values and habits. The primary function of initial encounters is sense-making and information-gathering in that when an individual enters the presence of others for the first time they make inferences and seek new information about him/her, as well as bringing into play information already possessed. Each party sets out to define the situation, a process which is particularly interesting in classrooms where one customarily has a far lower formal status than the other, but are present in greater numbers. Teachers can be seen as having three groups of predefined objectives at the start of the year, namely:

1. *political*, or sanctions and participation demands referring to what he/she wants done, what he/she is prepared to do to get it done, and what he/she will do if it is not done (persuasion, exchange, manipulation, threat, punishment, coercion, or a shifting mixture can be mobilized to this end)
2. *structural*, or social relations and status divisions
3. *cultural*, or moral values, customs, knowledge and decorum. [All teachers make moral demands on pupils when they oblige them to treat staff in a manner they consider they have the right to expect. This is established through house rules (prescriptions laying down the main requirements of inmate conduct), clearly defined rewards for obedience and punishments for rule transgressions.]

A teacher's opening presentation is more likely to express tasks rather than dwell on the performer's self, although individuals may, of course, hold very different ideas concerning sound levels, the nature of interruptions and diversions and overall behavioural requirements, but the deviation between them needs to be small if staff teamface and cohesion is to be safeguarded. The claims made by a teacher's performance can be refuted by disruptive tactics; these may function to separate a teacher's 'giving' and 'giving off' (Goffman, 1971), that is, use the ungovernable aspects of a presentation as a validity check on, or an implied criticism of, the governable. Viewed in this light initial encounters are a complex information game of concealment, discovery, revelation, corrective practices to overcome discrediting features and reassessment leading to the 'negotiation' of a working consensus between teacher, class and individuals. In pursuance of this we can expect teachers to control information, not allow pupils to receive possibly destructive evidence, and conceal aspects incompatible with the image being projected so as to safeguard the performance's validity. Furthermore, to read each other's actions and reactions during initial encounters, both teachers and pupils must formulate what Goffman terms 'predictive devices' to aid interpretive and sense-making work; these will be based on both information he/she already 'knows' and can gather as the respective parties make claims about themselves, given that crucial pieces of information often lie beyond the expression actors seek to give.

One of the few educational ethnographers to have written on initial encounters between teachers and pupils is Stephen Ball (1980). The accomplishing of social order is best observed, he maintains, during what he terms the 'process of establishment' because then the sense of community, normally part and parcel of classroom life, is unavailable to teachers and pupils and much is unformulated and problematic. Initial encounters are best viewed as 'situations of performance' in which the ethnographer can observe the development of the necessary 'sense of consociality' as teachers and pupils seek to define the, as yet, undefined situation. Ball isolates two crucial stages through which he proposes initial encounters pass: first, an observatory period in which pupils are quiet, passive and unsure where they stand. This is the honeymoon period. Secondly, there is a testing and information-exchange stage in which the teacher may have determinedly to defend his/her authority and the expectations he/she hopes to establish. This affords members of the class the opportunity to observe how trouble makers are dealt with and deduce just what is, in fact, allowable. In the negotiative process that ensues definitions are accepted, modified or rejected, and what happens in the classroom arena is the outcome of the capacity of different actors to establish and maintain their respective definitions of the situation. Furthermore, pupils and teachers obtain their knowledge of each other from a combination of sources from previous experience of classrooms, by means of generalized information about each other and, significantly, data which can only be gleaned in face-to-face contact (and, I would add, face-to-face contact of a particular, often combatory, kind). This second stage (which, incidentally, Ball claims is recognized by both parties) is a battle between official rule systems and often seemingly anarchic alternatives and during which some pupils, who base their identities on disruption, seek status by clashing purposely with teachers. The latter at this time really have to respond and show themselves to be in charge by displaying tactical superiority rather than merely talking about rules and voicing demands. Teacher rules are best created and clarified in relation to concrete 'flashpoints'.

Initial encounters can be mapped in terms of a number of negotiative phases (which are again more applicable to pupil than to teacher conduct):

1. *reconnoitering*, when parties gather data to identify each other
2. *playing-safe*, when organizational demands are met
3. *experimenting*, when strategical work to secure interests is undertaken.

My evidence suggests that in Lower School such phases were not discrete but scrambled and taken up at varying speeds by individuals and groups in different classrooms. Some boys were observed experimenting from the first day and were, thereby, aiding others' reconnaissance. I argue, therefore, for a more fluid and dynamic start to the term and that the researcher would be mistaken to regard such phases as being necessarily chronological; 'experimenting' could, for example, feed back to renewed 'reconnaissance' and/or 'playing safe'. What is clear is that initial encounters are far from being a matter of teachers stating rules; rather, at this stage, pupils demand empirical evidence of each one's managerial expertise and a clear definition and demonstration of the parameters of the control he/she seeks to establish. In spite of the heavily institutionalized authority of the teacher, in practice the laying down of rules has to be reaffirmed anew by each individual. Out of this exploratory interactional process there eventually emerges through repetition routinized patterns of relationships and interactions. Obviously, teacher–pupil relationships continue to evolve and the precarious nature of the classroom's social order can never be said to be finally settled. This, in turn, raises the wider issue of why and how some pupils at this time question and obstruct teachers' efforts at rule making and implementation. Much depends on the attitudes pupils carry into the classroom, but a major point is that all pupils quickly need to obtain information to interpret and conform to teachers' conventions and, thereby, to predict and routinize patterns of classroom interaction. Teachers can have considerably different rules of behaviour and performance and pupils need to be able to distinguish and make sense of these; they require, in other words, a comprehensive grasp of the social knowledge of all the classrooms through which their curriculum takes them and which helps them surmise a particular teacher's likely reactions as well as the extent of his/her definition and tolerance of deviant acts. Such information about the individual helps define the situation, enabling others to predict in advance what he/she will expect of them and what they may expect of him/her. Although they may not be liked, pupils are often most comfortable with stricter teachers because they provide a highly structured, constant, predictable situational definition. To date it is still the case that relatively little is known about just what features are considered most important by groups of teachers and pupils in their classroom relationships, what indications are seen as relevant and how these are actually displayed and interpreted.

Early classroom encounters are remarkable for the degree of rule inculcation that takes place. To be adjudged a competent teacher certain rules (whether institutional, relational or lesson phase) must be issued and upheld, just as a competent pupil must first identify and then follow them. Whereas school rules are usually codified and made public in handbooks or through assembly, house and tutor-group announcements, most of the rules that operate in classrooms are rarely, if ever, explicitly defined. They talk of institutional rules (referring, for example, to property and punctuality and which are generalizable across most areas of school life), situational rules tied to a specific setting and personal rules belonging to individual teachers, although many may be applicable elsewhere. They group composite classroom rules into five broad themes (talk, movement, time, teacher–pupil and pupil–pupil relations). The point is that teachers not only interpret rules differently, but an individual can be inconsistent in his/her implementation, a fact which poses great prediction problems for pupils. Context guides the myriad of fine distinctions that have to be made constantly by interactants, given that some rules are multiphasic, others phase specific. Pupils acquire interpretive skills which enable them to distinguish between, for example, a deviance imputation and an instruction, become accustomed to lesson subphases, recognize the switch signals that introduce, suspend and terminate them and distinguish which rules are multiphasic and which are of short-term duration. Order, compliance and deviance do not just occur, but are accomplished, with teachers displaying normative and technical implemental skills and pupils employing their own technical implemental skills to meet teacher demands. Teachers draw on evidential rules to interpret classroom events and these are connected intimately with the labels applied to pupils; their judgments, based on common sense and professional knowledge, lead to ways of seeing and making sense of pupils. Provisional typings emerge, although lack of information at this stage can lead to rapid de-, even re-, typing. Pupils, meanwhile, become adept at distinguishing between teachers and according to their ability to enforce the rules they proclaim, using this knowledge to type them. Indeed, typing is central to teachers' and pupils' commonsense knowledge of classrooms: it is the means by which both make sense of new people, demands and events and formulate an explanatory system that renders classrooms orderly and relatively predictable.

The fullest study of rule inculcation during initial encounters is by Smith and Geoffrey (1968), who talk of pupils being 'grooved' into roles and activity structures, a process by which the teacher as ringmaster moves them from how things are presently done toward how they ought to be done. The gradual deepening of the grooves provides the essential procedural knowledge, allows pupils to interpret what is said and increases teachers' control. This thesis has been supported more recently by some of the findings of the Oracle researchers (Galton and Willcocks, 1982), who corroborate teachers' strong emphasis on 'grooving' pupils into classroom and subject procedures. Indeed, after the publication of Smith and Geoffrey in the late 1960s there has been a sustained interest in how teachers establish themselves at the start of term. One study of classroom language was based on data collected during initial encounters in year one humanities. Three central teacher concerns at this time were earmarked, namely, the creation of:

1. *teacher authority*, given that the ownership of classroom talk is the principal means of control and survival available to teachers
2. a *procedural map*, to enforce instructural, administrative and disciplinary competence as pupils make sense of new surroundings by grafting new instructions on to an already acquired general pattern of expectations
3. *shared meanings*, essential for meeting academic, organizational and behavioural demands.

One would expect studies of transfer from junior, middle or secondary school to say something about initial encounters and teacher–pupil settling-in strategies. Many of these, however, exclude the processual through an over-reliance on a limited psychometric view of education. Youngman and Lunzer's (1977) is, perhaps, the most detailed. The authors argue for increased continuity between the junior and secondary sectors in terms of courses, staff and pedagogy, and advocate an interim year by housing pupils in a separate building (which was the case in Lower School). They point to, but do not detail, the significance of key incidents, influences and adjustments during the early period of second-ary schooling for the individual's progress. Furthermore, they say little about the activities of teachers and pupils during the time of transfer except that the former seek to control the school environment and enforce disciplinary norms, whereas pupils have to settle in and impress, explore the site and come to terms with changed organizational and curricular demands. A number of more qualitative-style studies of transfer over the past decade point to the existence of both acknowledged and hidden disjunctures between the junior, middle and senior sectors of schooling. Nash (1973) argues that as children move through junior school classes become increasingly traditional and they are prepared for a stereotypical secondary-school ethos, which in many cases no longer exists. He claims that his junior and secondary staff operated outdated misconceptions of each other, the former viewing secondary schooling as necessarily being highly formal and strict, the latter dismissing the junior sector out-of-hand as 'wet' and progressive.

An important contribution to the transfer literature is by Measor and Woods (1983), who detail how pupils' move from a middle to senior secondary school occasioned a series of guiding myths (for example, stories of initiation rites, gory science experiments and horrendously tough teachers and peers). These myths are interpreted as serving the important functions of providing information (even if grossly distorted and inaccurate) and issuing a warning concerning, for example, the toughness expected in the male peer subcultures or the amount of make-up permissible among girls. In spite of such pupil-centred work the fact remains that as yet far more is known about how teachers rather than pupils typically 'manage' initial encounters. It might even be assumed that most pupils are too overawed by new surroundings and novel demands to 'play up' at the outset of secondary schooling. Nash (1973), however, interviewed boys during their first term in a Scottish secondary school and reported that 'trying on' teachers was held to be necessary to ascertain which teachers knew the appropriate rules and whether he/she was willing, or able, to implement them. It appears, then, that the aspects of teacher behaviour which are of particular importance to pupils during initial encounters and about which they need to have reliable early information are, for example, which of their new teachers are able to maintain control and how, individual levels of leniency and toler-ance toward potentially disruptive activities and which areas of class-room life are negotiable. These are issues that can only, from a pupil standpoint, be settled effectively in the course of interaction: for a teacher to announce that he/she is a strict disciplinarian, or that his/her lessons are rivetingly interesting, is meaningless unless borne out in practice.

INDUCTION STRATEGIES IN LOWER SCHOOL

Lower School teachers operated a wide variety of strategies to accomplish the perilous business of 'starting term' and these can be ordered under three headings, namely: presentation of school subjects; teachers as disciplinarians and enforcers; hidden curriculum of classroom discourse. From the outset 1Y was lectured that successful teaching demanded co-operative and compliant pupils who had to operate the appropriate technical implemental rules of 'being sensible' and 'behaving responsibly'. These were presented as being concomitant with growing up and leaving behind the 'irresponsible' antics of the junior school and becoming members of the more 'adult' community of Lower School. The best way to display this was by showing respect and good manners, acknowledging that teacher time and expertise were valuable and not to be wasted. Staff constantly accompanied their numerous instructions with arguments and justifications supporting the 'sense' of them (for example, the virtues of neatness were extolled *ad nauseam*). Indeed, pupils had to learn to discriminate between general rules, which had validity for a number of classrooms, and local teacher-specific ones which could well be inappropriate elswhere (for example, working together as a pair or group was encouraged in some subjects, frowned on in others).

Presentation of school subjects

Teachers announced definite subject procedures as well as their personal *modus operandi* on first meeting 1Y, including their ways of opening and closing lessons (for example, standing at the start, packing away and sitting quietly at the end, cleaning paintbrushes or swabbing benches before leaving the room, etc.). Mr Bunsen, for instance, laid down numerous safety demands governing behaviour in the laboratory and Miss Floral introduced pupils to the various phase rules and mechanisms governing improvisatory drama. She adopted what she termed 'easing-in ploys' to establish a 'non-threatening, non-critical, supportive classroom environment' and presented herself less as a teacher than as a 'facilitator'. Certain obligations were emphasized from the outset (for example, 'freezing' as a device allowing her to regain and maintain overall directorial control, critical observation, showing social awareness, collaborating and working harmoniously in groups). Pupils were told about the phases into which drama sessions would be divided (opening 'static' phase, 'action' phase, 'production' phase and a 'showing' phase in which each group's production was watched and evaluated). Miss Floral disregarded many of the formalizing strategies of her colleagues: her ground rules were less concerned with terms of address, hands up, even noise, but more with a series of introductory exercises or 'try-outs' to establish the necessary working, 'studio' skills.

The announcing of subject procedures and individual demands was accompanied invariably by an 'investment theory' of educational success: the more that boys invested in Lower School subjects, then the greater the profits that would in time be reaped. Allied to this was the prospect of 'glittering prizes' for successful investors, along with the possibility of acquiring power and status in later life, the lure of 'being somebody'. If they treated Lower School as a bank, invested in its subjects, shouldered responsibility for their actions, then they would eventually pocket the benefit. Alternatively, cautionary tales were told to illustrate what happened to boys who ignored teacher advice and behaved in an irresponsible and a short-sighted way. Finally, a conspicuous feature at the outset of term was the efforts made by all Lower School staff to convince pupils of the absolute need for, and value of, their respective subjects ('subject selling'). At the same time they attempted to boost pupils' confidence that they could succeed. These were dominating activities and themes during initial encounters (both observed and acknowledged during interviews) as teachers presented themselves not in personal terms, but as representatives of discrete bodies of knowledge and rule systems. They championed the importance of their subject over and above the others and pupils were thus confronted by a succession of adults each claiming special merits and superior status for his/her subject. Although they 'tested' pupils (both openly and indirectly) to aid speculative typing, boys were simultaneously built up, urged on and eased in through a conscious process of 'sugaring' to increase pupil confidence and belittle any difficulty they might encounter. The main means of this subject 'sales drive' was to link them, if possible, with vocational outlets (for example, mathematics, science and English as 'essential' subjects), to personal development and aesthetic gains (for example, art, drama, religious education, etc.), or to general usefulness in contemporary life (for example, French, physical education, history and geography).

Teachers as disciplinarians and enforcers

Not all school or teacher rules were spelt out in any detail, but were often referred to obliquely so that pupils had to deduce their nature and import. All Lower School teachers exhibited close topic and pace control and supported (with the exception of Miss Floral) a highly didactic mode of teaching, but they differed in their objectives and how they set about controlling and organizing pupils. Some adopted an abrasive confrontational stance (that is, the 'rigid disciplinarians' were deviance provocative), whereas others employed more subtle forms of persuasion based on appeals ('light disciplinarians'). The former were prepared to use physical coercion, were observed doing so and firmly accepted the folk dictum of 'starting off hard' and 'easing up later'. They saw themselves as authoritarian and uncompromising for the good of their 'unsocialized' pupils, whereas light disciplinarians were opposed in principle to the use of any kind of physical violence. Some of the latter regarded themselves as entertainers able, through theatrical conviviality, to win pupils over on the strength of their personalities. Rules considered essential for the management of classes were brought into play or kept in play through such strategies as statings and restatings, warnings and threats, orders, dramas like 'throwing a fit', exampling and 'showing up' of individuals, acts of physical and/or verbal violence and the use of morning assembly to disseminate and justify a catalogue of rules and move pupils into belief systems.

Hidden curriculum of classroom discourse

As I have indicated, a considerable literature now exists on classroom discourse and the way it enables teachers simultaneously to control both the regulative and the instructional aspects of teaching. Lessons as practical activities do not just happen but are achieved through identifiable practices. Teachers can be seen exerting control over classrooms largely through the verbal strategies of explaining, correcting, evaluating, editing and summarizing pupils' responses, as well as specifying and placing limits on the form and relevance of what may be said. The form in which most teachers and pupils interact thus becomes the most powerful means of control available to teachers, social relations and identities being thereby announced and re-affirmed. What pupils can mean is located firmly within the teachers' frame of reference and pupils have to display a situational competence which has to be approved by a teacher who restricts the range of semantic options available to them. Teachers' questions become means of socializing pupils into learner roles and retaining teacher initiative, defining the content of interaction and of controlling participant structures. Teacher talk is typically permeated by organizational and disciplinary moves for both the controlled transmission of knowledge (content frames) and the ordering of interaction frames and contains a range of linguistic tactics: they talk most of the time; they question, check and reaffirm; they produce and take over pupils' contributions and cue them into the overall discourse framework; they strictly control content, knowledge, disciplinary and management moves; they control speaker rights and define appropriateness.

In some 'open' classrooms such a discourse structure may not be so evident, but it was clearly so during teacher–pupil initial encounters in Lower School. I want to distinguish, first, between the actual establishment of authority talk at the start of term and, secondly, what was announced and done through it. During initial encounters the 'one-speaker-at-a-time' and 'hands-up' rules, along with rules restricting movement and noise, were strongly enforced across classrooms. There was strong vertical transmission of knowledge, with pupils allocated only temporary speakership rights and with marked constraints on what was 'sayable' in answer to teachers' mostly 'closed' questions. Lower School staff cast themselves as 'tellers of news' (that is, controlled the channel, amount, content, language forms and degree of understanding), their pupils as 'receivers of news'. Locked into classroom discourse was a strong division of roles and a signalling of social distance and power differences. Teachers' control of curriculum was especially evident when pupils were instructed to accept information on trust, or taught tricks and short cuts (for example, in mathematics and science) which demanded they gave up all attempts at understanding until some later teacher-determined date.

SUMMARY AND DISCUSSION

I have highlighted the 'coping/survival' strategy (as developed in the work of Hargreaves, Woods and Pollard) as being the most useful concept to explicate Lower School's initial encounters. However, whereas in Hargreaves' strategies are taken-for-granted ideological components of schooling to reproduce capitalism, Woods presents them as primarily situational, mediating between beliefs and practices. An important aspect of the coping model is that it questions whether interactionism has overcelebrated the power of teachers to define their classroom worlds, whereas Woods' survival model is less deterministic, attributing greater autonomy to the individual. Strategies, as Pollard makes clear, do not fossilize and remain constant: rather, interaction is dialectically evolved, continuously creating events that demand new and modified strategies. My principal concern in this reading has not been with the nature or scope of teacher and pupil interactional rules *per se*, but rather with the way in which they were introduced at the start of the year. Clusters of rules were invoked simultaneously without being specifically detailed (for example, by reference to 'being sensible/responsible') and thereafter, through frequent brief reminders, the whole fabric of institutional, situational and personal rules was maintained. I have shown that from the outset some Lower School teachers employed sets of strategies to do with 'starting off hard', were verbally and even physically coercive and sought to make examples of some pupils, whereas others attempted to keep proceedings quiet and decorous, adopting an appealing and justificatory stance. All used cajolery and tried at first to win pupil co-operation by placing the responsibility for learning and behaving well with the pupil and stressing the need for qualifications for career and future well-being. Key features of their induction strategies were the:

1. tight organization of content and action frames; the imposition of key rituals and routines (for example, authority talk)
2. call for attitudes of loyalty and deference and the immediate placing, thereby, of pupils under obligations; the emergence of both personal and institutional punishment and reward structures
3. presentation of Lower School as superior to junior schools; claims for subject superiority through hard 'marketing' based variously on appeals to relevance, excitement and topicality; essential preparation for everyday living, material and professional success, vocationalism and aesthetic qualities resulting in personal development
4. myth of invested effort leading directly and inevitably to 'glittering prizes'.

To summarize, induction strategies revealed Lower School staff defining both the kind of interaction permissible and what counted as worthwhile knowledge. Furthermore Lower School teachers were observed to be engaged in calculated impression management as they established participatory demands, social relations and cultural objectives as part of their admission procedures. They set up both an activity system (what should be done, when and how) and an underlying justificatory belief system. A notable feature of the Lower School 'welcome' was a sustained attack on junior schools, which were adversely compared with the more 'adult' atmosphere of their new school. This was all part of the rejection of the boys' 'presenting culture' as a form of what Goffman terms 'disculturation' and 'untraining', with initial encounters constituting a 'reculturation' into behavioural patterns presented as being superior and in pupils' best long-term interests. Furthermore Goffman points out that admission procedures into institutions are likely to detail services rather than personalities and be impersonal; during initial encounters in Lower School teachers and pupils interacted primarily in terms of roles rather than persons and it is significant that 'sussing' was described by one boy as 'revealing the person inside the teacher'. Meanwhile teachers lacked a technical language to describe what they were doing, using instead general terms such as 'starting off hard', 'easing-up later' and 'selling' subjects.

It is a gross simplification to think of teaching in terms of a progressive-traditional dichotomy: seldom do teachers take over one or other paradigm completely (although the Lower School data suggest this is more likely to be the case at the start of the year). Woods (1980a), too, maintains that teachers hold aspects of both poles in varying strengths and that these can change over time or even vary across classes. The majority of Lower School teachers started off in a 'traditional' manner, organized their classrooms as 'little bureaucracies', were 'incorporators' and 'meaning makers', concentrating on rendering pupils dependent through transmission teaching. Only Miss Floral promised a more pupil-centred open mode of operating. They established routines based on 'seeing the sense of it', but backed up by threats and, in some cases, by coercion (both verbal and physical) itself. It has been pointed out that teachers must demonstrate early on their 'right to command' or are liable to be perceived by pupils as defaulting on an obligation; as pupils test teachers, the latter have to respond by making them believe in the myth of the shool's unlimited coercive power so that they voluntarily conform because they regard the price of disobedience as being too high. At the start of the year Lower School staff could easily be arranged along a continuum from 'rigid disciplinarians' (for example, Messrs Changeable and Megaphone), who actively sought out opportunities to be coercive, through to 'light disciplinarians', who talked in terms of inducing control rather than imposing it (for example, Miss Floral and Mrs Paint). Lower School subjects were kept apart, social control was explicit and most teachers were in full control of the pace and direction of the work. Only in drama was the pupil accorded a greater degree of autonomy and Miss Floral employed, as a result, a different range of control and survival strategies (for example, 'freezing', 'showing' the results of group planning, etc.). The Lower School curriculum was a compartmentalized collection one and the majority of teachers imposed a closed role system and dealt in particularistic meanings. The mode of control was predominantly imperative and positional, although there was some use of appeals (the 'sense of it') to spell out the dire consequences of rule infractions. There was a highly visible pedagogy and an explicit manner of transmission, with learners placed in a meaning-receiving, passive and ascribed role. Subjects were strongly differentiated and there were boundary-maintaining procedures evident as pupils were socialized into the required codes of behaviour. Teachers' personal identities were locked into subject ones as they assumed the role of ringmasters, closely controlling discourse, pace, content and movement in both the regulative and instructional contexts.

Initial encounters were taken very seriously by Lower School staff as the seedbed out of which would emerge an equitable classroom climate that would last the year. I have shown how deliberately and tightly organized was the regime into which pupils were fitted.

REFERENCES

Ball, S. J. (1980) Initial encounters in the classroom and the process of establishment, in P. Woods (ed.) *Pupil Strategies* Croom Helm, London.

Denscombe, M. (1980) Pupil strategies and the open classroom, in P. Woods (ed.) *Pupil Strategies* Croom Helm, London.

Galton, M. and Willcocks, J. (1982) *Moving from the Primary Classroom* Routledge & Kegan Paul, London.

Goffman, E. (1971) *Presentation of Self in Everyday Life* Penguin, Harmondsworth.

Hargreaves, A. (1978) Towards a theory of classroom coping strategies, in L. Barton & R. Meighan (eds.) *Sociological Interpretations of Schooling and Classrooms* Nafferton, Driffield.

Hargreaves, A. (1980) Synthesis and the study of strategies: a project for the sociological imagination, in P. Woods (ed.) *Pupil Strategies* Croom Helm, London.

Hargreaves, D. (1978) Whatever happened to symbolic interactionism?, in L. Barton & R. Meighan (eds.) *Sociological Interpretations of Schooling and Classrooms* Nafferton, Driffield.

Hargreaves, D. (1979) A phenomenological approach to classroom decision-making, in J. Eggleston (ed.) *Teacher Decision Making in the Classroom* Routledge & Kegan Paul, London.

Hargreaves, D. (1980) The occupational culture of teachers, in P. Woods (ed.) *Teacher Strategies* Croom Helm, London.

Measor, L. and Woods, P. (1983) The interpretation of pupil myths, in M. Hammersley (ed.) *The Ethnography of Schooling* Nafferton, Driffield.

Nash, R. (1973) *Classrooms Observed* Routledge & Kegan Paul, London.

Pollard, A. (1980) Teacher interests and changing situations of survival threat, in P. Woods (ed.) *Teacher Strategies* Croom Helm, London.

Pollard, A. (1982) A model of coping strategies, *British Journal of Sociology of Education*, March.

Pollard, A. (1984) Coping strategies and the multiplication of differentiation in infant classrooms, *British Educational Research Journal*, Vol. 10, No. 1, pp. 33–48.

Sharp, R. and Green, A. (1975) *Education and Social Control* Routledge & Kegan Paul, London.

Smith, L. and Geoffrey, W. (1968) *The Complexities of an Urban Classroom* Holt, Rinehart & Winston, New York.

Woods, P. (1979) *The Divided School* Routledge & Kegan Paul, London.

Woods, P. (ed.) (1980a) *Teacher Strategies* Croom Helm, London.

Woods, P. (ed.) (1980b) *Pupil Strategies* Croom Helm, London.

Woods, P. (1981a) *Schools and Deviance*, Unit 17 of E 200, Contemporary Issues in Education, Open University Press, Milton Keynes.

Woods, P. (1981b) Strategies, commitment and identity, in L. Barton & S. Walker (eds.) *Schools, Teachers and Teaching* Falmer Press, Lewes.

Woods, P. (1981c) Making and breaking the teacher role, in L. Barton & S. Walker (eds.) *Schools, Teachers and Teaching* Falmer Press, Lewes.

Youngman, M.B. and Lunzer, E.A. (1977) *Adjustment to Secondary Schooling*, Occasional Paper, Nottingham University School of Education.

TOPICS FOR DISCUSSION

1. Discuss the assertion (p. 198) that teachers are generally unaware of the 'true' origins of their 'dirty work' (i.e. what they have to do to survive in their daily transactions with disaffected pupils).

2. How true is it that 'teachers espouse some (coping) strategies rather than others because of age, gender and past, as well as present, career experiences?

3. What *subject procedures* (p. 209) operate in your own area of teaching? How many of these appear to be unique to your particular subject specialism and how many are common to all school subjects?

SUGGESTIONS FOR FURTHER READING

1. Lawrence, J. Steed, D. and Young, P. (1983) Coping with disruptive behaviour, *Special Education: Forward Trends*, Vol. 10, No. 1, pp. 9–12.

A programme of self-help for schools facing problems of disruptive behaviour is reported on. Examples of checklists and matrices for identifying and measuring the disruptive behaviour of individuals and/or classes are included. Patterns of difficulty such as wide scattering or close concentration of disruptive acts are revealed. That individual pupils who, though viewed negatively by most teachers, are seen positively by one or two, is pin-pointed. The authors demonstrate the usefulness of these monitoring methods in their own research in two comprehensive schools.

2. MacPherson, J. (1983) Mucking around, pp. 49–64, and Stirrers and clowns, pp. 91–105, in *The Feral Classroom*, Routledge & Kegan Paul, London.

MacPherson's criticism of Corrigan's (1979) and Willis' (1977) overemphasis on working-class pupils' ideologically motivated resistance to schooling and the restricted size of their samples leads him to research a complete cohort of girls ($n = 164$) and boys ($n = 202$) at Goldtown High School. His theoretical model stresses the independent origins of students' culture in the structure of schooling and focuses on the role of dominant pupils and their power to determine classmates' behaviour. MacPherson describes two sets of classroom behaviour which teachers see as misdemeanour: 'mucking around' and 'stirring'. Whereas mucking around includes most activities that prevent devotion to work, stirring is the systematic annoyance of teachers and (thus) the entertainment of fellow pupils.

3. Measor, L. and Woods, P. (1983) Deviance, conformity and knife-edging, pp. 127–55, in *Changing Schools: Pupil Perspectives on Transfer to a Comprehensive*, Open University Press, Milton Keynes.

In this part of the Measor and Woods study of boys and girls at 'Hayes' and 'Old Town' schools pupil adaptations during the third term of the first year of their secondary schooling are dealt with. The authors propose a different model of adaptation to that of Willis (1977). Whereas Willis suggested two broad stereotyped groups of deviant 'lads' and conformist 'ear' oles', the present authors argue that the majority of their first-year boys appear to react to two polarities: 'too conformist' and 'too deviant'. They introduce the concept of knife-edging to illustrate how pupils 'balance' on the thin dividing line between these two undesirable options. Thus, deviant boys do not wish to appear clever but they also shun being considered 'thick', particularly in subjects that matter such as mathematics; pp. 137–9 contain some interesting insights into knife-edging strategies employed in lessons taken by temporary teachers or by teachers who are not the regular person in charge of the class and thus not responsible for pupils' grades or their identities.

REFERENCES

Corrigan, P. (1979) *Schooling the Smash Street Kids*, Macmillan, London.

Willis, P. (1977) *Learning to Labour*, Saxon House, Farnborough.

CONFRONTATION IN THE CLASSROOM: CHILDREN WITH PROBLEMS *and* CONFRONTATION IN THE CLASSROOM: TEACHER STRATEGIES
R. Laslett and C. Smith

CONFRONTATION IN THE CLASSROOM: CHILDREN WITH PROBLEMS

On the whole, it is wise for teachers to avoid confrontations with children when these can be avoided, but there are those occasions when a confrontation cannot be avoided and those occasions when it can be beneficial. A teacher cannot avoid a confrontation if he/she is summoned by a colleague to help in some crisis which was nothing to do with him/her. The angry child may turn on the summoned teacher and continue with him/her what he/she began with the teacher's colleague. There are some circumstances when a teacher may decide that he/she is not going to put up with some child's provocative or stupid behaviour any longer, or that he/she is going to demonstrate to a child who continually bullies or teases other children that the child has met his/her match. A confrontation with such a child would be beneficial to the child concerned, to the other children who witnessed it, and to the teacher's management. But there are certain considerations that should guide the teacher in making this decision. If he/she is convinced that the confrontation would be beneficial, he/she has next to be sure that he/she can manage it, if, once it has started, the child continues in his defiance or provocation, and, if the worst comes to the worst, that he/she can manage the child, should he/she attempt to present the teacher with a physical challenge. Once started, confrontations sometimes develop very quickly and it would be foolish to bring on a confrontation with a child and then have to seek help from a stronger colleague. When confrontations are considered to be necessary, they should be deliberate and properly managed so that they do not deteriorate into undignified examples of child hostility and teacher counter-hostility.

Some teachers, either through their anxiety or inexperience, blunder into confrontations which they cannot manage and which are of no value

R. Laslett and C. Smith (1984) Confrontation in the classroom: children with problems, Confrontation in the classroom: teacher strategies, in *Effective Classroom Management: a Teacher's Guide*, Croom Helm, London.

to the child concerned, to them, or to the class. Others seek them without proper occasion. These confrontations have nothing to commend them.

Avoiding confrontations

When thinking about ways in which teachers might avoid unhelpful confrontations, it may be helpful to think about classes with reference to their stability or instability. When observing effective teachers with a class, one of the noticeable features of well-conducted lessons is the way in which the teachers do not allow the stability of the class to be threatened or upset by one or two children in it. Neither do they upset this stability themselves, as very anxious teachers tend to and as provocative teachers do.

In any school there are likely to be events, over which teachers have no control and which they cannot prevent, that upset the stability of classes. There are staff absences, which mean that a teacher is called on to cover for an absent colleague. They do not know the children whom they are suddenly called on to teach and they may not be familiar with the lesson material the children expect. An unfortunate aspect of this situation is that the very children who are likely to be difficult to manage are those who tend to be poor at adapting to unexpected changes in routine or variations in deployment of staff. There are times when building contractors and decorators are present in schools, interrupting classes with the noise they make and disturbing timetable arrangements. It is in circumstances like these that the stability of groups are threatened and confrontations are more likely to arise, unless teachers are particularly wary in their interactions with children who cannot cope with distraction nor adapt to unexpected change. Nor is it only the children whose functioning is impaired by such events. They may cause exasperation and frustration in teachers, so that they are less able to bear with any signs of unacceptable behaviour. Such negative situations are very frequently sources of confrontations. The ways in which very anxious teachers behave are also likely to upset the stability of a class; they do not mean to do this and they have little chance of managing successfully when they do. Their behaviour may bring on confrontation by accident: they unwittingly provoke a child or fall into a trap which a child prepares for them.

It is not only outside events, or very anxious teachers or those who provoke children deliberately that threaten the stability of a class (and, frequently, do destabilize it) so that confrontations are more likely to arise. Certain children have strong tendencies to do this: they either do it themselves or are the cause of it in others. Among these, the most noticeable are children with marked difficulties of adjustment, those who are seriously underachieving, and who are frustrated by their failures and very sensitive about them, the unpopular child, who may also be a 'victim child', the child whose behaviour may not be acceptable to teachers, but who is the licensed wag or buffoon, and the saboteur. The probabilities of confrontation are increased, if teachers are not aware of the presence of such children in a class, nor aware of ways of managing them.

Child with difficulties of adjustment

Behavioural psychologists have helped teachers to realize that many incidents of disruptive or inappropriate behaviour are specific to particular situations, to particular individuals and to particular environments. They emphasize that features in the environment act as stimuli, making disruptive behaviour more probable, and that contingent reinforcing events will either establish this behaviour or reduce it and extinguish it. This explanation has helped teachers to recognize that much inappropriate behaviour is not endogenous, and that they can arrange classroom environments that will significantly reduce the behaviours preventing children's learning and social progress. Application of the principles of applied behaviour analysis and the use of behaviour-modification techniques have, undoubtedly, helped teachers to find ways of establishing effective methods of classroom control.

Excellent as these techniques are, however, it is important for teachers to recognize that many children whose disruptive behaviour is a persistent problem have had experiences of other people and of themselves which go a long way to account for the difficulties they cause. This is not to deny that the actual classroom environment may or may not increase their tendency to misbehave, but rather to emphasize that there are factors outside the control of teachers which make these children more likely than others to become the cause of instability in the classroom. Their need for counselling and support, for assessment of their problems at home, help for their parents and the involvement of supportive personnel from outside the school show that their problems are not of management alone.

Among disruptive children are those whose experiences of parent figures have led them to regard themselves as unworthy and undeserving. Because they were neither wanted nor loved they have not been esteemed by those whom they might legitimately expect to esteem them. Consequently, they do not esteem themselves. We know that a negative self-concept interferes seriously with children's functioning. The experiences of alienation and of failure, not only in school-based learning tasks, but in their relationships and in many social situations, are just the negative experiences many disruptive children have had. Among the older ones especially, it is little use for teachers who find themselves in conflict with them to appeal to their self-respect, for they have very little, and what they do have needs careful nurturing before any meaningful reference can be made to it. At the same time, they are not much influenced by punishment, because overfamiliarity with it has made them indifferent. Although some children who have had long experience of neglect and deprivation seek punishment, because it is at least one way of gaining attention, the punishment does nothing to alter their behaviour for the better. Indeed, it is more likely to increase the probability of unwanted behaviour, because it brings about some reward to the child, unpleasant though that may appear to be.

The experiences of such children have affected them in other ways, which show in their behaviour in school. Not only do they perceive themselves as unworthy and undeserving, they also tend to perceive adults in authority as potentially uncaring and hostile. This perception has developed because of their experiences of the behaviour of hostile and uncaring adults in their own environments, it has led them to displace the hostility they feel toward these adults on to teachers, who have to frustrate them, as they do when they control them. Whereas most children, however much they protest, usually accept criticism or punishment as fair, and they are able to make the necessary connections between the punishment and their responsibility for it, this is not the case for those disruptive children who do not perceive themselves and others as more fortunate children do. Because they have not been able to trust others, and because their relationships with others have been impaired by the destructive influences of rejection and hostility, they are much more likely to regard punishment as evidence of vindictiveness or spite. There are illuminating accounts of the attitudes that overpunished and under-esteemed children have toward teachers to whom they present difficult problems of management.

Mention has been made already of discipline as an interpersonal matter. Teachers agree that they have little chance of managing classes successfully unless they establish positive relations with some of the children in them, and hopefully with all of them. The children who are so often in the worst kind of trouble in schools are those with whom the staff complain that they are unable to make any meaningful contact. It is a feature of children with problems of adjustment that they find the making and the sustaining of good relationships with others difficult, and some of them never succeed in doing this. They are either too demanding and too impetuous, or too passive and dependent. They give way to temper and to anger, which other children find distasteful or frightening. They are selfish and inconsiderate, or ingratiating and clinging. They are wary of making relationships with adults, as their relationship with some of them have caused them a great deal of pain or unhappiness in the past, when they were let down or rejected by others on whom they relied for affection and support. When they have some evidence to believe that some adult, perhaps a teacher who shows concern for them and who teaches them in a subject where their motiviation is high, cares about them, many of these children behave in ways that seem paradoxical and self-destructive. They exhibit toward this adult their most unattractive and demanding characteristics. This does not always happen when such children perceive in a friendly teacher the understanding patience or concern which they most seek and need. They react positively to this teacher and show unusual co-operation. But when the opposite happens, due to the degree and persistence of their deprivation, and they put the relationship to severe tests, this is perplexing and wounding to the teacher concerned. At the conscious level, it seems that such children are declaring that they have heard expressions of goodwill many times before, but, as this goodwill was withdrawn rapidly when they made demands on it, they will see how the teacher can stand up to such demands. They then proceed to make these demands, some of which are aimed at those particular vulnerabilities in the teacher that their suspicious and active interest has discovered. It is when this happens that teachers are heard to remark that, as they tried kindness and the child took advantage of it, this is evidence that their approach will not succeed. When this happens, it is not only sad for the teacher concerned, but it is sad for the child, because it strengthens the belief that he/she is unlikeable and others are hostile. It strengthens the child's reliance on which has been described as the deprived-child's delusional system, in which his/her perception of him/herself and of other people is distorted by his/her previous experiences. Such children have succeeded in dragging into their contemporary relationships just those features which destroyed previous ones, and they have manipulated benevolent people into behaving toward them as they did not mean to behave. If this process continues, their reactions toward others harden into fixed patterns of behaviour which are not changed quickly or easily.

Sometimes such hostile behaviour is motivated by feelings of revenge. Deprived, alienated children are likely to feel revengeful because of the treatment they have received in the past from those who failed them in their relationships and acted with hostility toward them. Here the process of displacement shows itself. The hostility they feel toward significant figures in their own environment alights on those who stand in for the rejecting or uncaring person, usually a parent who is too formidable for them to risk declaring their true feeling of hostility. Many children with problems of adjustment have a limited repertoire of behavioural responses anyway, and in this repertoire, displacement and projection (the ascribing to others of their own shortcomings and weaknesses) are too ready at hand. Their fixity of response limits their adaptability. They behave in inappropriate and unsatisfying ways, in circumstances that better-adjusted children perceive as requiring the adaptive responses they are capable of, and they seem particularly inept at differentiating between people and circumstances.

There is another explanation of such inappropriate, hostile and unacceptable behaviour. Some children have learned to behave in the ways that they do. In the face of disappointment, frustration or denial they copy or imitate the ways in which their parents or other significant figures behave. Not only do they witness this behaviour in models in their environment, they are aware that such behaviour brings its rewards. The father who vents his frustrations at home relies on this to bring about the attention or solace he needs. Siblings who make demands because of their jealousy or envy of other family members are given attention to pacify them. They themselves are indulged or gratified, according to the frequency and intensity of their demanding behaviour. In the true sense of the term, these children have never learned to behave properly.

Fortunately, there are not many such children in the ordinary school system, but there are some and teachers meet with them. Although it is not true that all maladjusted children present their teachers with problems of management, many do. They are disruptive and unstable members of classes. For many of them, the excitement and inevitable attention that goes with challenging a teacher is an irresistible temptation. They delight in drawing teachers into confrontations and they are skilled at bringing about their defeat in them.

Underachieving child

Other children who may threaten the stability of a class group are those who are seriously behind in their acquisition of basic educational skills and who are sensitive about their failures. Although it is convenient to discuss these children separately from the children who show marked problems of adjustment, educational difficulties are common to both. In their surveys of nine- to eleven-year-olds in the Isle of Wight, Rutter and co-authors found that a large proportion of the children with behaviour disorders were twenty-eight months retarded in their reading (Rutter, Tizard and Whitmore, 1970), and evidence from the Schools Council project on the education of disturbed children supports these findings. In many children, their difficulties in reading lead them into compensatory behaviour, which, as it is so frequently attention seeking, is not acceptable. In others, their anxieties and frustrations prevent them from acquiring skills in reading. These connections between reading failure and behaviour disorder are reasonably straightforward, but the authors of the Isle of Wight studies also suggest that there may be a factor in some children's personality that is responsible for both their academic and social difficulties.

Of all failures in acquiring basic educational skills, children are most sensitive about their failures in reading. It is this which is such a blow to their self-esteem, even among those who make out that they do not care whether they can read or not. This is borne out in the remarks that adults make about their schooldays. Of the many who may declare publicly that they never understood maths and most of the maths instruction went over their heads, there are very few who admit to not being able to read. This is certainly true of children, and many of them go to great lengths to hide their reading difficulties, unless they are confident that they can rely on the sympathy of those to whom they disclose them.

It is because reading failure is such an embarrassment to a child that an unwary teacher might stumble into a confrontation with the child, because of his/her ignorance of the child's predicament, if she asks him/her to read aloud. The last thing the child wants is to have his/her failure made public. If it is, it is unlikely that the child, especially one in the secondary school, will say quietly to the teacher 'Please miss, I can't read.' What is more probable is that he/she will either make a stumbling start on the passage that he/she is asked to read and hope to be rescued by the teacher's awareness of his predicament, or reply to the request that he/she reads aloud with some comment that the teacher considers to be impertinent. If the child does make a start and the teacher realizes his/her predicament, then there is a simple way for them both out of the situation. But if his/her fluster and anxiety leads him/her to respond with a provocative comment, as fluster and anxiety frequently do, and if the unsuspecting teacher reacts to that with indignation or criticism, then a path leading into a confrontation opens up quickly. This exchange may be the first step up the 'escalation-detonation staircase'.

It is in the child's response to the teacher's request to read that the non-reader may be seen to threaten the stability of the class. This would be aggravated if he/she is, at the same time, a child who has difficulties in his/her relation with other children. Another child may make some slighting comment on the non-reader, who flares up at the comment, so that the teacher is suddenly faced with a quarrel. The compensatory behaviour of the non-reader who, if he/she cannot shine in acceptable ways, is determined to seek recognition, even if this brings about some unpleasant consequences, is another threat to class stability. However this threat arises, the best way of prevent it is for the teacher to be aware, as soon as possible, of which children in a class are sensitive to their failure in reading or in other basic subjects of the curriculum. In his/her own class, this presents no problems. Difficulties arise when he/she has to cover for an absent colleague or never does have an opportunity to find out as much as he/she would like about a class that he/she teaches.

Victim child

The victim child also is likely to threaten the stability of a class of children. He/she is unlikely to draw a teacher into a confrontation, but may well be the source of one involving another child. He is the boy (or girl) who is continually teased, or bullied, or taken advantage of by other children, and who, according to his perception of these events, is the innocent victim. It is true that bullies will attack those who are weaker than they are, however the victim of the attack behaves, but with the victim child, there are aspects of his behaviour which elicit aggressive behaviour in others. He is usually unaware that this is so. He knows that he is unpopular, but he cannot account for his unpopularity. Hostile reactions to his behaviour may arise from his irritating ways: he is forever interfering or giving unwanted advice. He may make undue demands on the friendship of other children, wanting to have another member of the class as a friend to the exclusion of other children, showing jealousy of any other friend his companion has. He may be a chatterbox and a sneak. He may be fussy, over-dependent and so poor in his personal organization that friendship with him is a burden. Whatever it is about him, he makes undue demands on the tolerance and goodwill of other children, so that his companionship is insufficiently rewarding for them to overlook his short-comings. Other children will not tolerate from him what they meet with equanimity in others. It is this intolerence of others of him, rather than what he does himself, that makes him a threat to group stability. He is likely to do or say something that is too much for the self-control of an-other child and to become the centre of angry exchanges in the classroom.

A teacher may best help such a child, and therefore his control over the class, by pointing out to him that he cannot continue forever to blame other children for his misfortunes and that he should begin to look at his own behaviour. It is probable at the start of such a discussion, the boy will stoutly deny that the fault is in him, and it is not unlikely that long periods of denial will have convinced him that this is so. In denying his own responsibility for his unpopularity and his misfortunes, he is not telling untruths: he is bolstering himself against what he suspects is the truth, which is not easy to face. Sometimes victim children can be helped if a teacher calls on whatever friends they have to add an opinion to the teacher's, and children will frequently listen to their peers with more belief than to teachers. Such a child can be helped by teacher intervention, when he/she observes the child saying things or doing things that will inevitably bring trouble on his head: the teacher's part in this would not be to prevent the other children's hostile reaction to him, but rather to draw the boy's attention to the fact that he is provoking them again.

A behaviour-modification programme would fit in very appropriately for this kind of behaviour, as a teacher easily can devise one in which the boy (or girl) is regularly rewarded for his successes in not being made a victim. If the teacher adopts another approach and is concerned about the possibility of the masochistic qualities of his behaviour, then he might refer the boy (or girl) to somebody who could counsel him at the level appropriate for him to explore this behaviour and bring it under control.

The situation of the child with physical, mental or sensory handicap is not quite the same as the victim child who elicits hostility or rejection in other children. There is the possibility that such children will be teased or shunned by other children, but studies of integration programmes show that this does not happen very frequently.

Trapped-in-role child

In many classes there is one child who is the class buffoon or wit or one who dares to try the teacher's patience beyond reasonable bounds. The girl (or boy) is not a teacher baiter in the usual meaning of this term, and is not usually set on a confrontation, although one may develop from her behaviour. What is at work here is more subtle and less sinister. It has more to do with her relations with the group of children and theirs with her, than her relationship with the teacher. She is uncertain of her status in the group and believes she can enhance this by drawing children's attention to her boldness. She is uncertain of her status with teachers, unless she brings herself to their attention. She is, in fact, uncertain of herself. She discovers that her ready wit or her intrepid behaviour wins group approval and ensures popularity with her peers. Her behaviour is less welcome to teaching staff and has a certain price which is sometimes exacted, but, on the whole, the status she acquires is worth the cost. It brings attention, it gives some recognition which she may not be able to achieve in more acceptable ways, and it is exciting. Sooner or later she is the licensed wit and the description is an interesting one. The other children give her this licence, because her behaviour is not without some value to them. If she oversteps the mark, they lose patience with her, and they withdraw the licence, but she manages well enough within the rules as they are understood in the class. By various messages, sometimes overt and sometimes covert, the group of children sustain her in her role.

After a time, the girl (or boy) would like to give up her role. It is inconvenient and, as she develops better ways of functioning and gaining staff attention, it is no longer necessary. But she cannot do this alone: her wish to change is not enough. The group has to change in their relationships with her and allow her to leave the role she no longer wants nor needs. Her attempts to change are not sufficient to overcome group expectations. They do not easily surrender the satisfaction that her behaviour gives them. Now the girl (or boy) is in a dilemma. She has to rework her relations with the group and put them on a sounder basis and repair her relations with staff. She needs help to do this. The help that she needs will be more easily given if teachers are aware of the group dynamics that produce this situation. It is not uncommon for a teacher to become involved in a confrontation with such a girl (or boy) whose humourous sallies or impertinence goads them into an angry response. As with the non-reader who reacts negatively to what seems to be a reasonable request, the angry response may be the first step up the escalation-detonation staircase. Such a confrontation can be avoided if the teacher, aware of what the girl (or boy) is doing in response to group pressure, and what the class is doing for its own satisfaction, shows that he/she is aware of these processes and discusses them with all the parties involved. This will be much more effective than continual expressions of irritation or anger with the girl (or boy).

Saboteur

There is another child who threatens to upset the balance of a class and for whom a teacher is well advised to be prepared. He (or she) is the saboteur, a boy (or girl) who enjoys the drama of a teacher in conflict with another child or other children, even if he does not escape from such conflicts unscathed. He is not as noticeable as the child with more obvious signs of adjustment difficulties and does not give way to openly disruptive behaviour, but he has developed strategies for irritating other children and egging them on toward confrontation. He will defeat a teacher's intention to ignore the provocative behaviour of other children by drawing attention to it. He knows just what to say or do when he observes a classroom crisis on the wane so that it may start up again. If a child subsides from a temper outburst, he manages to provoke the former into another. If a quarrel subsides, he knows what comments will rekindle it. If he observes a teacher struggling with his/her irritation, because of the behaviour of some child in the class, he will succeed in ensuring that he/she fails in the attempt. A good deal of his subversive and devious behaviour goes on in playgrounds or corridors, when no teacher is at hand to intervene. He is dextrous in avoiding the consequences of his own behaviour and successful in drawing teachers into confrontations. In some ways, he is like a ferret who works underground, as he whispers to one child about another or makes provocative comments about a teacher from behind the raised lid of his desk.

In managing a saboteur, it is better if a teacher avoids questioning him about what he does or has done, because he enjoys the opportunity this presents to make whatever capital he can from the occasion. If the teacher makes any error in his accusations, then he siezes the opportunity to deny that he did what the teacher knows he did, but did not recount it accurately. One exasperated teacher related the dialogue which followed the late arrival in his class of a child he had seen a few minutes earlier combing her hair before a mirror in the domestic science room. When she did arrive, and the teacher asked why she had stopped 'to comb her hair in the mirror', the girl replied that she had not been combing her hair in the mirror. This flat denial and untruth which the girl repeated during the exchange made the teacher increasingly angry. The naughty girl at last announced that she had not been combing her hair in the mirror because that was impossible! It is this kind of cool and exasperating exchange that demonstrates the dangers of involving such children in questioning and it is best avoided. The mounting irritation in the dispute is just what the saboteurs enjoy. It is better to tell them what they have done and to make sure that there are no possibilities for ingenious word play. It is also reassuring to other children, many of whom have reasons to regret the saboteur's activities, to perceive that the teacher is ahead of the game and has kept the initiative. Such anticipatory observations prevent the saboteur from drawing a teacher into a confrontation which, at its close, was probably not worth the time spent on it. If the behaviour is worth a confrontation, then a teacher would be well advised to make it when he/she is not flustered by the approach to it which the child has prepared.

A knowledge of the behaviour patterns of children who threaten the stability of a class prevents those confrontations which impair, rather than improve, a teacher's management. In their own classes, teachers have time to know the children well enough to avoid useless and ill-considered confrontations. When this time is limited, for whatever reasons, it is advisable for teachers to pause and to reflect on the possible motives for a disruptive-child's behaviour, so that the poorly adjusted child, the frustrated and sensitive non-reader, or the licensed wag, the victim child and the saboteur do not trap them into a situation which moves, often very swiftly, into the opening stages of an ill-advised confrontation.

CONFRONTATION IN THE CLASSROOM: TEACHER STRATEGIES

When we consider the variety of factors that affect the interactions between teachers and classes, it becomes plain that it is not possible to suggest ways in which teachers can always manage to avoid unnecessary and unhelpful confrontations. The most that anyone at a distance from the classroom can do is to suggest guidelines which might help teachers to avoid those confrontations that serve no useful purpose and, at worst, result in consequences which they did not forsee and which they regret. In some circumstances, usually when there is tension in a classroom, it only needs a teacher to say the wrong thing, or do the wrong thing, for him to find that he has a confrontation on his hands for which he is not prepared and which he did not want. The guidelines, if followed, should reduce this possibility.

Guidelines for avoiding confrontations

Avoiding public denigration of a child

Although criticism of some children cannot be avoided, it is a mistake for a teacher to denigrate a child loudly and publicly. This stirs up resentment and hostility and, even if the child darc not express this openly, it sours his/her relations with the teacher. It is a poor example of adult behaviour. If the child is addressed in unmeasured tones, he/she loses face with his/her peers and he/she then has the problem of putting this right. If he/she redresses the balance by some verbal attack on the teacher, then this may be the starting point of a confrontation. Children, especially older children, resent being 'bawled out' as much as adults do and, like adults, they resent particularly any sarcasm that accompanies such comments. For a teacher to use his/her superior wit and readiness with words is really a form of bullying and it is as unpleasant and as likely to stir up hostility as physical bullying does.

Children are surprisingly unanimous in their comments about teachers' behaviour. They do not mind strict teachers, so long as they are not nasty as well, and they do not mind being made to work and to behave. It is the overbearing and sarcastic teacher who is unpopular. Some teachers, of course, are given to sarcasm, but many sarcastic teachers speak in the way that they do because of their anxiety and lack of self-confidence. For these teachers, letting slip a sarcastic comment is particularly unfortunate, if it sets off a crisis they do not want and cannot manage.

Ignoring behaviour

It is worthwhile to emphasize that planned ignoring is not the same as overlooking behaviour because the teacher cannot do anything else. Only the teacher in the classroom knows whether he/she can ignore behaviour or not. It would not have been appropriate for the history teacher to ignore Martin's comment that began the confrontation described later in this reading, although he could have responded to it more wisely than he did. Ignoring provocative behaviour need not be complete ignoring: a teacher may ignore a provocative comment when it is made and return to it when the child is deflated by the teacher's lack of response. Nor need the ignoring be complete. One of the disconcerting reactions of the maths teacher described earlier, disconcerting to the child, that is, was his way of looking at someone who said the wrong thing or did the wrong thing and making no comment. While he looked, he may have been thinking about Euclid or he may have been deciding whether or not to have recourse to his well-known notebook. The child could not be certain. Although this ignoring is not quite what behavioural psychologists usually mean by ignoring unwanted behaviour, it was very effective. However, it went with his whole battery of management strategies. It is unlikely that a teacher will establish his/her authority by ignoring all the behaviour he/she finds unacceptable. He/she must have, and have demonstrated, other strategies for managing unwanted behaviour.

Awareness of the effects on non-verbal communication

It is very easy for a teacher, especially if he/she is angry, to forget the effects of non-verbal communications. For some children, these communicate a challenge which they take up. For others, they show that the teacher is flustered and they take advantage of this. Many confrontations begin, or are maintained, not only by what a teacher says but by the way he/she walks or strides toward a child, glares at him/her or points at him/her. Once a confrontation starts, it is the angry presence of the teacher close to a child that acts as a powerful irritant in the situation and prolongs or sharpens the crisis. In the confrontation described later in this reading, the history teacher would have saved much of the trouble, if he had stepped back from the boy who saw his presence as a challenge, as indeed it was.

Avoiding physical intervention

A very common feature of some crises in the classroom, which makes a confrontation much more probable, is a teacher's attempting to grab hold of some object a child has that is causing a disturbance. In these circumstances, especially if the teacher is bigger and stronger than the child, it is tempting for him/her to make a grab at the transistor radio, or whatever it is that the child has and that he/she has refused to surrender when asked. The teacher may be successful, but grabbing at the radio, or pushing the child to get hold of it, moves the crisis into a much more unpredictable dimension. It may very quickly become the first step in the confrontation with little chance of escaping from it.

The child with the radio may begin the tantalizing game of moving it out of the teacher's reach. There is no end to this catch-as-catch-can manoeuvre. Each move in it increases the teacher's discomfort, increases the child's satisfaction and adds to the tension. For the spectators in the class, it is hard to beat as a diverting spectacle. For the teacher, it is hard to beat as an exasperating and undignified display of impotence. He/she may succeed in loosening the child's grip on the radio, but it then falls and is damaged. The situation has now taken a turn for the worse. Although the child was in the wrong, the damaged radio has complicated the situation and lessened the distinction between the rights and wrongs of it. The teacher will be accused of damaging the radio, and although this is not fair and it is certainly not what he/she intended, he/she has given a hostage to fortune. If the radio was a treasured possession, the boy (or girl) who owned it may be so incensed by the damage to it that he will turn on the teacher and his language or his behaviour then makes a confrontation probable. In the ensuing mêlée, with its unpredictable consequences, the original offence is lost sight of. At the end of it all, the trigger that began the swift march of events was the teacher's impatient grab at the radio. This did not cause the crisis: the child did that by having the radio and not giving it up when asked to. But the grabbing and pushing moved the crisis toward the confrontation.

The Open University film *It All Depends upon Your Point of View*
demonstrates the dangers of a teacher making a physical intervention. A
teacher goes to take a fountain pen from a girl, who raises her hand with
the pen in it. This action releases ink from the pen so that it sprays out
across the girl's blouse. Shouting 'It's all your fault!' she either hits the
teacher or the teacher hits her, or the teacher's face hits her hand, or it
doesn't, or whatever. In the moment of confrontation, brought on by the
teacher grabbing at the pen, no one knows what happened: who struck
whom, who struck first, whose hand got in the way, whose face was in the
way. This confusion and panic, which so often go with attempted physical
interventions, emphasize that they are best avoided.

Apologizing

It is not uncommon to see a teacher make a blunder in classroom
management, perhaps by accusing a child unjustly, or snapping at a child
who is not the real culprit, to be patently in the wrong and then to
compound the error by persisting, when an apology would have avoided a
confrontation.

It is not demeaning to make an apology. Teachers are not super
people. They are human beings and human beings make mistakes,
especially when they are under stress. If a teacher is really in the wrong,
then it is courteous, as it shows respect for children, if he/she apologizes
to them. It is what teachers teach children to do and what they expect
them to do. If they do not apologize when they are in the wrong, it is not
because they are like that as people, but because they have the strange
notion that they weaken their authority if they admit to fallibility.

It is better to be open about an apology. To hum and haw, and then
say 'Well, perhaps I owe you an apology' is easier than saying 'I am sorry;
I was mistaken,' but it is less fair and it is less likely to disarm an offended
and potentially disruptive child.

Escalation and detonation in confrontations

We have seen already that there are usually some children in classes
whose behaviour makes a confrontation more probable. When teachers
know who such children are, they can adapt their approaches to them to
avoid conflict, or use whatever methods they find appropriate to temper
the wind to the shorn lamb. It sometimes happens, however, that a
teacher will stir up a confrontation because he/she does not know of the
antecedent events that affect a child's reactions to reproof or criticism.
When this does happen, and when the matter is discussed afterwards,
then one hears such phrases as 'If only I had known she was worried

about her sister' or 'I wish I had known he had just had a flare up with . . .'

The confrontation described below is an ugly and serious one, but it is not one unknown in many classrooms. The teacher concerned made a reasonable request to a boy, but he has, unknowingly, stumbled against a boy whose mood at the time, arising from events over which the teacher had no control, made it important for the teacher to avoid any provocative comments or hasty actions. The teacher's manner unfortunately aggravated the situation that arose in the classroom and this swiftly moved into a confrontation that went out of control. The serious consequences were not altogether due to mood or antecedent events. The teacher made mistakes and the boy contributed his measure of unpleasant behaviours. One of the sad features of the confrontation was that both the teacher and the boy regretted what they had done, but it was too late. In his comments on conflicts between teachers and children, Pik (1981) (see Reading II) has drawn attention to the sadness that teachers feel when the consequences of some upset in a classroom are more serious than they intended them to be, and these feelings are very real. In some ways ugly confrontations with serious consequences are like accidents. They happen very quickly and the situations of those concerned after they have happened are dramatically different from their situations before they began. They also illustrate the maxim that great things arise from little ones, but not because of them.

The boy concerned was reasonable enough in school. He was a third-year boy and there was no evidence that he had problems of adjustment. He had the usual uncertainties of mood associated with adolescence, but on the whole he was pleasant and co-operative. However, on the morning of the confrontation, matters had not gone well for him and the history lesson was at a climax of unfortunate events. He did not wake in time to go on his paper round, which meant that he had an unpleasant interview to manage when he next saw his employer. He was also late for school and that meant that he would be in detention later in the week. He accepted this, but he found the events of the physical education (PE) lesson, which preceded the history lesson, harder to bear. He had come to school without his PE kit. This was particularly unfortunate, because that had meant he was not allowed to join in the PE lesson, to which he had been looking forward as a bright spot in a rather dreary day. He had had words with the PE teacher about this and had come off the worse. His difficulties were largely owing to the rather disorganized home in which he lived, but in this he was no different from many youngsters. He had put out his kit, he had cleaned his PE shoes and all this preparation and anticipation had gone for nothing.

He had chosen history as an option in the third year, but more because of the exigencies of the school timetable than his interest in the subject. He was present at the lessons, rather than a participant in them. The lesson which marked the end of his attendance at school for the next fortnight was one in which the teacher talked to the class, and asked them to read passages from their history books. It was a rather lifeless lesson, until Martin leaned across his neighbour's desk and remarked, loudly enough for the teacher to hear, but not loudly enough for those not near them to hear, 'Who cares about the flipping Renaissance anyway?'. In leaning across the desk, he knocked his history book on to the floor, but this was accidental.

The teacher, who was explaining some fact about Brunelleschi's dome, was aware that he had only a tenuous hold on the children's attention. He recognized that the lesson had not gone well and that there were other ways of presenting his material. He was really just holding on till the bell went and was glad to notice that this would be in ten minutes' time. When Martin made his interruption, he stopped his discourse and asked 'What did you say?'. Now he had heard what Martin had said only too well, which accounted for the challenging tone which he put into the question. He intended to convey that he was annoyed at the interruption, that he had heard what the boy had said and did not like it much. He did not intend that Martin should repeat the remark. Indeed, he meant the opposite. His question was meant to be a warning. Martin would realize that he had heard something unpleasant and, as many children do in such circumstances, he would shuffle out of the difficulty, mumbling 'Oh, nothing, sir. I just asked Fred if he liked the Renaissance'. Unfortunately, this did not happen. Martin was sore already at the morning's events, he did not particularly like history or the history teacher. The challenge in the teacher's tone further piqued him and he was ready to take him on. He was a less impressive figure than the PE teacher, whose actions in the previous lesson still smouldered in his mind. He repeated his remark, loud and clear. It produced a silence that had not hitherto been a feature of the lesson.

Whatever the teacher might have done about the first interruption, when he asked the boy what he had said, he made a mistake. He then made another. Angry at this impertinence, and conscious that he had asked for what he did not want to have, he advanced toward Martin in a series of strides and, looking angry and flustered, pointing his finger at him, he snapped 'Pick that book up!'. The confrontation was now set.

Events then followed at surprising speed. The teacher's looks, his gait and his movements further increased the challenge in the confrontation.

He did not overawe Martin, but the challenge incited him to further defiance. Both he and Martin were now on the 'escalation-detonation staircase' and their subsequent challenges and responses drove each other further up it. Martin's response to the command was a surly refusal (he went another step of the staircase). The teacher, growing increasingly angry, shouted 'Pick it up at once!' (he went several steps higher up the stairs). By this time, the whole class was aware that dire events were about to happen. The silence had given way to noisy interchanges that encouraged the boy and further discomforted the teacher. He was aware that the affair was slipping out of his control and he was also conscious of the fact that the noise could be heard in the next classroom. The teacher was now standing over Martin, looking extremely angry and maintaining the tension in the confrontation by his angry presence so close to the boy.

When Martin met the command 'Pick it up at once!' with the rejoinder 'Pick it up yourself' another feature of the confrontation appeared: both he and the teacher began to give way to panic. Martin, for all his apparent coolness, had now defied the teacher to the point of no return and he could not back off and disappoint the audience. At the same time, he was not sure that he could manage what he had started. He was not a hardened rebel. What was happening now was outside his experience. The teacher, conscious of the corner into which he had been manoeuvred, also gave way to panic. He made a last and unsuccessful attempt to overawe Martin, despite the evidence that this was not going to succeed. His panic prevented him from realizing this and, in fact, it was his last few steps up the staircase from which the confrontation escalated. He made a verbal assault, shouting in passionate tones what he would not usually contemplate saying 'Pick it up! Pick it up! How dare you speak to me like that? You lout! You look like a lout, you act like one! Pick that book up or I will ... '. No one knew what the end of the sentence might have been, what threat or ultimatum was to follow. When he called Martin a lout, this so stung the boy that he got to his feet in a reflex action in the face of the assault. What then happened was confused and illustrated exactly the way in which panic leads to the misperception of intentions and actions.

Martin stood up. The teacher reached out his hand. What he meant to do, as he said afterwards, was to push the boy back into his seat. For a split second Martin saw this hand coming toward his face. He raised his hand to push it aside. In the next split second the teacher saw Martin's hand and he thought the boy was going to strike him. He struck him with his other hand. It was not a heavy blow, but Martin returned it with a more directed punch, which knocked the teacher off balance and cut his lip. In the awful silence that followed he ran out of the classroom. The whole confrontation, from the moment when Martin said 'Who cares about the flipping Renaissance anyway' to his exit from the classroom, had taken just under a minute.

His flight from the classroom, the slamming of the door, after the noise of the confrontation, had brought the teacher from the next room on to the scene. He did what he could to restore order, the history teacher withdrew to the staffroom and the lesson fizzled out. In the subsequent inquiry, Martin was suspended from school for ten days. Both he and the history teacher regretted the incident, although neither would believe the other's description of what had happened when they both raised their hands.

On analysis of the origin and development of this unpleasant incident, its antecedent events are worth considering. Although the history teacher's control of the class was not calamitous, the diminishing interest in the lesson and his lack-lustre presentation of the material had a direct bearing on the interruption which led to so much trouble. The teacher did not pick up the warning signs from the class, showing that he had almost lost the initiative. When unmotivated children do not pay attention to a teacher, they very soon find something else to interest them. The teacher could have done something to renew interest in his topic. The boredom in the class was the gestation period for the crisis. Crises do not usually erupt without some warning and we may draw an analogy from railway practice. When a fast-moving train is moving toward danger, the driver is not suddenly confronted with a red signal. The danger is indicated to him first by a double yellow signal, then a single yellow and, finally, the red one. In a class where there is trouble ahead, it is the yellow signals that alert the teacher, before the danger is on him. In this lesson, the history teacher did not notice the yellow signals: he continued at speed to overshoot the red!

It was Martin's comment that began the series of events that led to the confrontation. The book falling on to the floor, which assumed major importance in the confrontation, was fortuitous and accidental. As it was simultaneous with the comment the boy made, it strongly influenced the teacher's reaction. But had he had more success in dealing with what the boy said, he might have managed to keep the matter of the book in perspective.

As to the comment itself, he could hardly have ignored it. Although Martin should not have said what he did, it was not an outrageous comment. How different the outcome would have been if the teacher had said something which showed his displeasure at the interruption in more reasonable terms. Supposing he had said 'That will do Martin. You keep your comments to yourself. Just pick up the book like a good lad and give me your attention for a few more minutes'. Or suppose he had managed a little pleasantry, saying 'Well, Martin, Bruneschelli's dome might not be quite your cup of tea, but you wait until you see it. Now come on, it will soon be dinner time'. Or, even better, 'Martin, please stop talking to Fred. What's the matter with you anyway; you have been sitting like a bear with a sore head all morning'. This would have given the boy an opportunity to say something about his frustrating morning. He may not have taken the opportunity, but if the teacher's question was not put in a way that slighted him and if 'What's the matter with you anyway?' was said with concern and not with challenge, it is quite likely he would. Whatever the teacher said, what was needed was something which would have given him room for manoeuvre and not something which decreased this. Unless, of course, his comment was sharp enough to wrap the whole incident up at once. The fact that he said 'What did you say?' suggests that he was not able to do this: he was playing for time. He *had* heard what Martin said, Asking him 'What did you say?' was a mistake. The question might have worked out to his advantage with another child, who had not had the frustrations and disappointments that Martin had had. The teacher did not know of these, but Martin's loud repetition of what he had said took the teacher past the point when he might have given him a chance to say something, which, if it did not excuse his offence, could have been accepted as a plea in mitigation. His repetition of his comment increased the heat in the exchange, which already was beginning to show in the teacher's challenging tone. It gave the teacher less elbow room. There was now no chance of keeping the interchange after it reasonably private. Those in the class who had not heard what Martin said originally now had their attention focused on his interruption. He now had an audience.

In the situation in the history lesson, there were two active protagonists who, between them, maintained the momentum of the confrontation, but the presence of the other children added to the momentum. Their presence and their attention, which the history teacher had aroused, influenced both him and Martin. Their involvement added to the tension and it also made it more difficult for either Martin or the teacher to back down. Thus, the unfortunate question 'What did you say?' not only affected any following interchange between the two principals, it brought another element into the situation. It exposed it to the pressure of twenty-four children. More than that, the imminent drama, the tension that was now manifest, brought these twenty-four individuals into a more cohesive group. This reduced their chances of acting as individuals. It did not altogether prevent them, because some member of the class might have said something to Martin that would have extinguished his increasing belligerence, but it reduced the chances of this happening.

In fact, the verbal and non-verbal messages that reached both the teacher and Martin from the rest of the children illustrated some aspects of group behaviour. A bold child, or a hostile child, will act out the feelings of a class: will gather these up, so to speak, and represent them. Most of the children were bored with the lesson and the last ten minutes of it particularly. When Martin said 'Who cares about the flipping Renaissance anyway?', he said what most of them felt and would like to have said. He said it because he did not much care for the history teacher and because his frustrations overcame his usual restraints. These were not of a very high order anyway, and certainly not strong enough to keep back his increasing belligerence, when challenged in the ways that he was.

Before leaving this point, it is worthwhile to link it with one made earlier: that in some circumstances a confrontation is justifiable and may be beneficial. Before a teacher brings on a confrontation deliberately, it is important for him or her to reflect on the role of the child in the class where it comes about. If the child to be confronted is representing group feelings of resentment or even hostility to the teacher who brings the confrontation on, their sympathies, which might take the form of open support, will be behind the child. In the short term, when a confrontation is actually taking place, their support for a belligerent child may have important consequences. In the long term, demonstrations of support for the child, even if muted, would suggest that the teacher could look with advantage on his relationships with the class, who find their spokeschild important. This is not to suggest that a teacher should ignore a wrong because of support for the wrongdoer, but rather to emphasize the value of awareness of group behaviour. The chances of a class of children making use of one child to defy or oppose a teacher are likely to be greater, if the teacher falls into the 'deviance-provocative' category.

Returning to the confrontation in the history lesson, it can be seen that after Martin had repeated the remark about the Renaissance, the teacher had lost the initiative. He tried to regain it, but his attempt not only failed, it made matters worse. There was clear evidence that Martin was not going to be overawed. If he had, he would not have repeated his comment with such sang-froid. Anyone not as wound up as the teacher was could see that the boy was intent on a power struggle and that he would match whatever the teacher would contribute to it. Thus the angry advance, the strides and the pointed finger emphasized the teacher's challenge and prompted Martin to increase his. The situation probably could have been saved if, instead of switching attention to the fallen book, the teacher had concentrated on Martin's comment. It would have been better *had he stood where he was* and done his best to recover from the error he made in asking for the repetition. It was when he advanced so challengingly that both he and Martin began to ascend the escalation-detonation staircase.

Angry teachers sometimes forget how much of a challenge they present to children when they advance toward them. If this overawes a child, then further difficulties do not follow. But if it serves only to provoke a counter-challenge and exacerbate the situation, it is plainly counter-productive. Whereas teachers recognize that what they say can bring on hostile reactions, they tend to be less aware of the effects of their facial expressions, their gait and gestures as these demonstrate their anger or impatience. Non-verbal communications can be very explicit; body language can be very strong language. Certainly, the history teacher was unware of what his gait, his raised arm and outraged expression were doing to Martin. At the same time, he was unaware of the effect on him of his increasing proximity.

It was when the teacher shouted 'Pick it up at once!' that the panic began to influence the confrontation. Neither of them could now back down easily, but one of them could have done something, or said something, which would have interrupted the swift ascent up the staircase. Unless one of them did this, it was almost certain that they would reach the point of detonation: the top of the staircase. As Martin showed it was not going to be him, it was up to the senior partner to back off. He was, after all, the more mature of the two. The situation was deplorable, but as it had reached the stage it had, all that was left was for the teacher to save what he could. He could have saved his dignity at least.

Backing off is not a pleasant prospect for a teacher, but it has to be weighed against the alternative. As he and Martin were now eyeball to eyeball, any further provocation was bound to lead to some physical encounter, as the children in the class realized: they were waiting for it to happen. In such a physical struggle, especially as there was no clear physical advantage on either side, the outcome was unpredictable. It is better for a teacher, in such circumstance, to avoid this than to attempt it and come off worse in it. Even if it is successful, it is undignified and demeaning. Whatever else an audience of children may say about a teacher's behaviour, if he backs off before the physical encounter begins, they will at least recognize that he has preserved some of his adult status by refusing to be drawn into physical combat. Unhappily, the history teacher's anger and the panic in the situation so clouded his judgement that he did not even wait for a response to his command. He followed it immediately by the verbal assault that marked the detonation at the top of the staircase. From that moment on, the situation was lost.

It began with a provocative and uncalled for comment and an accident. Within sixty seconds, it ended in a disaster which neither of the principals forsaw and neither wished. The outcome was out of all proportion to the original offence. Martin should not have said what he did or have done what he did. But at no time did the teacher allow an opportunity for the momentum of the confrontation to subside. He was caught up in the tension that he, as well as the boy, maintained in the confrontation. There were opportunities on each step of the staircase for one of them to call a halt. As the older, more responsible partner, the teacher should have pocketed his pride and taken that initiative. It was not a pleasant thing to have to do, but what happened was worse. It was true that, as Martin was suspended, he did not 'get away with it'. But no one gave the teacher credit for the affair: it was not as if he had made an example of a hardened and persistent offender. The history teacher himself regretted what happened.

The description of the confrontation between Martin and the history teacher shows how rapidly such a situation may deteriorate once a teacher makes an initial error in the management of an unexpected disruptive incident. Initial errors often are compounded when confused thinking, anxiety, anger and panic combine to accelerate the decline toward unpredictable and regrettable outcomes. There are many classroom situations where teachers have much to bear. They are vulnerable, as all individuals are, but because they have to meet stresses and challenges that are peculiar to their profession, their vulnerabilities are likely to be exposed. In some situations, although such exposure is unpleasant, this does not lead to serious consequences. In others it plainly does. In this book, we have shown how teachers can avoid the errors that the history teacher made. The effects on the class of his unsuccessful confrontation, its effects on his subsequent management of his classes and the consequences for Martin could have been avoided had he been more aware of appropriate techniques of classroom management.

REFERENCES

Pik, R. (1981) Confrontation situations and teacher support systems, in B. Gillham (ed.) *Problem Behaviour in the Secondary School*, Croom Helm, London.

Rutter, M., Tizard, J. and Whitmore, K. (1970) *Education, Health and Behaviour*, Longman, London.

TOPICS FOR DISCUSSION

1. What specific recommendations are made in respect of the so-called 'victim child' (p. 225) in the classroom?
2. In what way does the recommendation about *ignoring behaviour* (p. 230) differ from the behavioural psychologist's rule of *ignoring unwanted behaviour?*
3. In what circumstances is a confrontation held to be justifiable and, possibly, beneficial?

SUGGESTIONS FOR FURTHER READING

1. Cohen, L. and Manion, L. (1983) Management and control in the classroom, pp. 177–218, in *A Guide to Teaching Practice*, Methuen, London.

This is a comprehensive review of the extensive literature on classroom management and control that is aimed specifically at the beginning teacher though the treatment of the topics is suitable for teachers generally. It opens with a brief outline of various schools of thought on classroom management before asking the question 'What makes pupils misbehave?'. There is a section on rules in the classroom that leads on to a discussion of three levels of disruptive behaviour (minor misbehaviour problems, repeated minor misbehaviour and persistent disruptive misbehaviour) and suggestions for their amelioration. The final sixteen pages of the extract deal with the ripple effect, issuing orders and instructions, rewards and punishments, behaviour modification and behavioural problems with some ethnic-minority pupils.

2. Denscombe, M. (1984) Keeping 'em quiet: the significance of noise for the practical activity of teaching, pp. 134–59, in S. Delamont (ed.) *Readings on Interaction in the Classroom*, Methuen, London.

The author contends that the implications of noise for teacher competence mean that noise is a feature of classroom life to which teachers are particularly sensitive. It identifies certain kinds of pupil activity that warrant urgent attention and provides the 'cue' for teacher intervention. Noisy pupils are 'disruptive', Denscombe asserts because, not only do they interfere with the establishment of a climate for learning, but also because they pose immediate threats to the *appearance of control in the classroom*. Noise therefore provides a means for socialization of new teachers and exerts a pressure on teachers, generally, to operate in ways which they may not regard as appropriate under ideal circumstances.

3. Wilson, P. and Bottomley, V. (1980) The emotional climate in the classroom: the interaction between adult teacher and early adolescent students, pp. 13–23, in G. Upton and A. Gobell (eds.) *Behaviour Problems in the Comprehensive School*, Faculty of Education, University College, Cardiff.

This short paper provides a jargon-free account of the developmental experience of early adolescence. It deals with physiological and psychological aspects of development and focuses specifically on the phenomenon of transference in explaining the tensions that can be generated in teacher–student interactions in the classroom Teachers' responses to the variety of emotional demands that are made of them are discussed in some detail. The authors concede that readers may regard the account as an overstatement of the emotional forces generated in classroom settings. Their concern, they argue, is that these emotional factors should not be so minimized that they are excluded entirely from consideration.

Reading 16
THE EFFECTS AND EFFECTIVENESS OF PUNISHMENT IN SCHOOLS
J. W. Docking
PUNISHMENT IN SCHOOL

Punishment as a means of social control

The view of most teachers is that some punishment is necessary for deterrent purposes; in this they are supported in law. Teachers are said to stand *in loco parentis* while children are in their care. This implies that, in the interests of an orderly community, a member of school staff would be justified in using the same amount of restraint as a reasonable parent would honestly consider necessary. Because punishment necessarily involves the infliction of pain or unpleasantness, many people would agree with the philosopher Jeremy Bentham that the only justification of punishment is in terms of its social expediency and unique deterrent powers:

> But all punishment is a mischief: all punishment is in itself evil ... It ought only to be admitted in as far as it promises to exclude some greater evil. (*Principles of Morals and Legislation.*)

Bentham's position was a utilitarian one. This means to say that punishment is justified only in so far as it can be demonstrated to be in the interests of a law-abiding society. It would therefore be wrong to inflict punishment if it was unlikely to bring about greater social order, or if it produced problems worse than those it was designed to prevent, or if the wrong doing could be prevented by some other means. Essentially, it is a means to an end, and has no value in itself.

Docking, J. W. (1986) The effects and the effectiveness of punishment in schools, in *Control and Discipline in Schools: Perspectives and Approaches* (2nd edn, 1987), Harper and Row, London.

Applying this argument to the schools situation, Peters (1966) acknowledges the force of the utilitarian claim in so far as the existence of punishment in the background may be a necessary condition for the maintenance of classroom order, the upholding of rules which are morally important or are enshrined in law and the general smooth running of the school. At the same time he recognizes that punishment 'is one of the most potent devices for bringing about estrangement' and is 'at best a necessary nuisance'.

However, although punishment in school may be intended to deter children from behaving unacceptably, whether it actually does so is a different matter. That punishment can sometimes have an immediate impact in the control of a child is not in dispute, as common experience will testify. What is more problematic is the long term influence on the individual and the general pervasive influence of punishment inside and outside school. Certainly, the evidence suggests that there are good reasons for doubting the efficacy of punishment as a general means of social control. This is partly because, for punishment to be optimally effective, certain conditions must be satisfied. A second reason concerns the personality of the child who receives punishment. Thirdly, punishment may produce certain undesirable side-effects. Each of these issues will now be considered in turn.

Optimal conditions for effectiveness of punishment

From their studies in clinical settings, learning theorists have maintained that punishment is more likely to be effective if it is administered consistently and at the onset of misbehaviour. Both these conditions, however, are rarely satisfied in normal school settings.

In an experiment that manipulated the consistency of punishment, Parke and Deur (1972) invited ninety eight-to-ten year olds to put on boxing gloves and punch a large doll. The researchers demonstrated that the children who were deterred most effectively from their aggressive behaviour were those who were punished by being consistently subjected to the noise of a loud buzzer on punching the doll, rather than those who either received the same treatment half the time and a reward of marbles the other half, or who were neither punished nor rewarded. The researchers went on to argue that punishment is often less effective in real-life situations because of the erratic manner in which it is characteristically employed.

There are problems, however, in drawing conclusions for everyday behaviour from studies involving highly contrived situations. For one thing, the term punishment, as used in laboratory-type experiments, does not have the same connotations as in real-life situations because the experiments are not concerned with misbehaviour as such, still less with actions which are morally wrong. In the above experiment the aggression was artificially produced and the children had not done anything for which they should have felt guilty. Another problem is that the form of punishment in such experiments is hardly typical of normal school practice. Furthermore, success is measured purely in terms of the suppressive effects of an aversive stimulus, and does not involve any consideration of changes in children's understanding of their behaviour.

Of course, children who are subjected to erratic and arbitrary responses, whereby an action is condoned one day but attracts punishment the next, will obviously be confused about what is acceptable and unacceptable behaviour. The oft-quoted remark that 'children need to know where they are' therefore contains a good deal of sense. However, the consistency argument often fails to make the important distinction between an erratic and a flexible use of punishment. Although punishment will not be effective if applied unpredictably or arbitrarily, it is unlikely to be effective in the long term if applied inexorably on a particular offence being committed. This is because, as Paul Nash (1966) has pointed out, consistent punishment without regard to the child's perception of the circumstances may serve only to suppress unwanted behaviour when its threat is present, thus encouraging a dependence on external restraint. On the other hand, if administered discriminatively, though not erratically, punishment may successfully prompt the culprit to raise questions about his conduct and ultimately stand in self-judgement. Reynolds (1976) argues that inflexible punishment styles simply serve to alienate pupils, especially in those areas of behaviour in which adolescents believe they should have autonomy. Teachers in secondary schools who experienced the least behaviour problems with low-aspiring working-class pupils were those who seemed to adopt an unofficial 'truce' with pupils in their stance toward regulations about eating chewing gum and smoking. In one of the schools with the least conformist behaviour, staff on break or lunchtime duty would patrol the premises looking for children who chewed gum or smoked. When found, the culprits were invariably reprimanded and usually hit round the head and arms being told to put the gum in the bin or surrender the cigarettes, and they were sometimes caned as well. In contrast, teachers in the schools with the more conforming behaviour refused to make an issue out of these rules and were more discriminating in their use of punishment. In contrast to teachers in schools which did not adopt a 'truce' regime, they found that high rates of punishment were unnecessary, and that a simple telling off or mild punishment was usually sufficient to secure conformity.

It is important, of course, not to confuse the 'truce', which Reynolds identifies with the more successful schools, with permissiveness. The findings from this study do not imply that rules should never be enforced or that punishment should not be used; rather it is that the school authority should not seem perverse and insensitive to what the pupil perceives as just and reasonable. Teachers who regard their relations with pupils as involving a power struggle between 'us' who know what's right and 'them' who don't will invite hostility; the more inexorably and severely teachers punish, the less effective will be verbal reprimand and mild forms of punishment.

Apart from the consistency factor, the timing of punishment is also held to affect success in extinguishing unacceptable behaviour. From the results of another laboratory-type experiment, in which young children were conditioned to refrain from playing with certain toys, Aronfreed (1976) argued that a child who is punished as he begins to act in an unwanted way will subsequently invoke the feelings associated with the punishment when he is next tempted to behave similarly: that is, the punishment will have helped the child to develop an inhibitory conscience. But if administered after the offence, when the child may already be feeling guilty, the punishment will result in anxiety being associated with that guilt; rather than have a deterrent effect, it will increase guilt feelings and build up resentment. If this hypothesis has application to normal situations, the timing of punishment could be a significant factor in reducing the childs' temptation to misbehave another time. In classrooms, of course, teachers cannot be so consistently observant as in experimental situations and, even if they were, they might well think it unwise to resort to punishment before more positive measures have been tried. However, if punishment does seem in order, it may be more efficacious, circumstances permitting, to wait until the child begins to repeat the act, and then punish him at that point. Another possibility, suggested by Burton (1976), is to verbally reinstate the stimulus conditions under which misbehaviour occurred and then administer punishment at the appropriate point in the recreated account.

Personality of the child

Children vary in the degree to which they appear to respond positively to punishment. Thus personality differences may be a factor which affects the success of punishment as a means of training children to behave acceptably. Eysenck (1970) has proposed that introverts are more susceptible to conditioning and therefore more likely to respond both to positive and negative stimuli. Punishment is thus more likely to 'work' with children who are extremely introverted than with those who are extremely extraverted.

Undesirable side-effects of punishment

It is probably the unintended consequences of punishment which, most of all, should warn teachers against resorting to punishment lightly. Put shortly, it appears that, however effective punishment may appear in the short term, adults who engage in a punitive style of child management may unwittingly be instrumental in producing undesirable behaviour, feelings and dispositions in children.

First of all, because punishment represents a confrontation between the culprit and the punisher, it teaches children not what they ought to do but what to refrain from doing, and in whose presence. For these reasons punishment simply may teach children avoidance tactics and encourage them to behave acceptably only when the adult concerned is present.

Secondly, in cases where children misbehave because they feel impelled to seek attention, punishment can reinforce the very behaviour it is meant to extinguish. This is because the pupil's attention-seeking behaviour has paid off in successfully eliciting a response from the teacher and sometimes the other pupils too. Seeing the teacher upset can also be rewarding for some children. Teachers therefore are sometimes tempted to ignore misbehaviour rather than punish the offender. Yet pretending the behaviour has not occurred will not make it go away. For, as Foss (1965, p.8) has pointed out, 'a teacher may be fairly successful in ignoring attention-seeking behaviour, but the rest of the class will not be, and will provide reinforcement — probably irregularly, and therefore (as animal studies have shown) more potently'. It is for this reason that behaviourists recommend strategies which involve rewarding children for their good behaviour as well as ignoring them for their bad behaviour.

A teacher's loud voice in reprimanding children can also help to maintain attention-seeking behaviour since the offender becomes the focus of attention of the whole class. Loud reprimands also disrupt the work of the class and a constant loud nagging may create tension which leads to verbal abuse and confrontation. In an experiment by O'Leary *et al.* (1970), based in a natural setting, teachers of children whose behaviour was disruptive were asked primarily to use soft reprimands, audible only to the offender. The frequency to misbehaviour was then found to decline. When the teachers were asked to return to their customary loud reprimands, the disruption increased. The researchers suggest that the ideal combination would be frequent praise, soft reprimands and only very occasion loud reprimands.

Thirdly, punishment can fuel disaffection with school life. This may be so not only in relation to physical punishment but also when children are 'shown up' through devices such as sarcasm or public embarrassment. From his observations, Woods (1975) concluded that when children are denigrated in front of the class, they experience an assault on their identity and feel confused. The teacher's action may have a dramatic shockwave impact, but in the end it breeds scepticism and bitterness, leading to a destruction of the self.

Fourthly, punishment in some circumstances exposes children to an inappropriate model of adult behaviour, which they may copy. As Wright (1971) has pointed out, while pupils can be vicariously conditioned by seeing an offender punished, the effect will be dependent on the degree to which the pupils regard the punishment as just or unjust. Wright goes on to warn that teachers can, without realizing it, set an inappropriate model if they 'imperceptibly slide into the habit of more or less continually setting an example of bad manners, injustice, bullying, or even mild sadism'. According to social-learning theory (Bandura, 1977), children are prompted to behave aggressively through imitating the aggressive behaviour of adults who are perceived as powerful. It is important here to remember that aggression can be fostered unwittingly not only directly through the experience of receiving aggressive punishment, but also vicariously through witnessing or knowing about others who are being punished. Fortunately, observational learning in punishment situations can be turned to advantage. If the teacher is seen to hold back her natural impulses to act aggressively when under stress, an appropriate model of adult behaviour is being provided for the pupils to imitate.

Finally, children who are subjected to regular punishment may be prevented from developing the virtues of kindness and sensitivity to the needs of others. To understand this, it is necessary to say something about the growth of conscience. Within the framework of psychoanalytic psychology, children in the nursery years take on aspects of the personality of those adults with whom they have close dealings, especially parents. When a child is punished or rebuked by an adult, he builds up aggression toward that adult as a result of his frustration. If he expresses this aggression outwardly, he finds he receives more punishment. The child therefore has to learn how to restrain his natural aggressive impulses. This he does by turning his aggression in on himself, identifying with the parent and so reducing anxiety over potential punishment. According to this view, then, punishment would help the child to develop an intropunitive conscience.

However, if punishment is frequent or severe, it may influence the degree to which children develop a conscience which is based more on a sympathetic concern for others than on fear of detection or a wish to conform. Hoffman (1970) found that twelve-year-old children who were compassionate, who showed a concern for the consequences of their behaviour on others and who recognized extenuating circumstances, were more likely to have parents who varied their means of control, who suggested means of reparation wherever possible, who expressed affection frequently and who were less punitive. Comparable findings emerged in Paul Light's (1979) work with four-year-olds. Pre-school children who were beginning to recognize and adjust to other people's points of view tended to be those whose mothers refrained from adopting a generally punitive style of management, preferring to treat the child on a personal level. It would seem therefore that the development of a strong altruistic conscience depends on the child's perception of his parents as warm and loving. Pupils who are frequently punished at home and who also perceive the teacher as someone who resorts easily to punishment to ensure implicit obedience will have their attention focused on the personal power of adults in authority. When punished, they may then sense a feeling of rejection, which in turn may impede the development of a conscience based on compassion and concern. In short, frequent punishment may induce the child to feel self-regarding rather than other-regarding.

Practical implications

From the evidence presented in this section, it would seem that punishment is an unreliable means of social control, at least in the long term. It does not necessarily deter and it can have a number of undesirable side-effects. However, this in itself does not mean that it should never be used. Rawls (1954) has pointed out how justifying a practice as a system of rules is one thing and justifying a particular action falling under those rules is another. There is therefore nothing logically contradictory in being wary about punishing a particular child for a particular offence committed in particular circumstances for particular reasons, whilst also justifying the institution of punishment for its potentiality to deter and control. Further although children will not respect punishment which is administered by a hostile and rejecting adult, evidence suggests that they will respect punishment which is used judiciously by a responsible and concerned person. In a recent investigation of comprehensive pupils' attitudes and reactions to different kinds of control strategy, O'Hagan and Edmunds (1982) showed that the teacher who never punishes, even when the class is not behaving properly, generally is not respected. On the other hand, teachers who use punishment fairly but not too severely are usually held in high regard.

Punishment probably stands a greater chance of 'working' and without unfortunate side-effects if certain conditions are observed. In particular, the focus of punishment should be on the inherent reasonableness of the rule and not on the power of the punisher, while the manner of punishing should convey to the culprit that it is the behaviour which is unacceptable, not the child as a person. To prevent children becoming unduly dependent on external constraint, and to provide opportunity for them to learn what is acceptable and unacceptable behaviour, punishment should not be erratic or irrational or frequent or unnecessarily severe. Rather it should be flexible in so far as it takes account of the circumstances and the child's perception of the situation, for punishment is more likely to 'work' if the culprit perceives it to be fair. 'Showing up', or punishing for offences which the pupil cannot accept as serious, should be avoided since such acts generate feelings of alienation. Reprimands are best given quietly whenever possible since nagging in a loud voice may not only reward attention-seeking behaviour but disrupt the work of the whole class and create a general atmosphere of tension. Aggressive punishment should be avoided lest the culprit learns to imitate the aggressiveness of the punisher rather than respond to the intended 'message'.

No form of punishment is without its problems, which is why many teachers prefer to rely on more positive approaches to social control, as discussed in the previous chapters on management skills, praise and rewards. Given the need for some punishment, however, it is important to choose forms which enhance rather than damage the quality of teacher–pupil relationships. Isolating the offender from the group (sometimes called 'time out') may serve to provide a cooling-off period and an opportunity to reflect on the misbehaviour. On the other hand, the experience must not be effectively rewarding, which it can be if the offender spends the time talking to his friends in the corridor or distracting everyone by looking through the window in the classroom door! The use of withdrawal classes is potentially a positive approach. Measures that involve the loss (or winning) of house points are often employed in secondary schools. Francis (1975, p. 137) has commented that this practice is 'hallowed by tradition, highly respectable, and quite useless'! No doubt its effectiveness depends on how well the offender relates to the house group. The widely adopted institution of detention in secondary schools is of dubious deterrent value. Although it can be an occasion for seeing that work gets done, it creates problems with parents who are anxious about children coming home late, and with teachers who are resentful at having to give up time in this way, especially for their less resourceful colleagues.

Less problematic, perhaps, are restrictions on freedom about where to sit or the withdrawal of special benefits. These may serve to remind pupils that privileges cannot be taken for granted but have to be earned through good behaviour. Placing on report, a system which involves the pupil carrying a card which teachers sign at the end of each lesson, can be used as a basis for the monitoring of behaviour and for discussion with the child about his behaviour in different situations. Enlisting the support of parents can be very helpful, provided that the bad behaviour does not stem from a rejecting mother or father who may be inclined to 'take it out' on the child. For this reason, parents need to be discouraged from adopting a punitive approach and encouraged to regulate the child's privileges in accordance with his behaviour.

Whatever form the punishment takes, the reasons for it should be explicit, and it should be presented by the teacher and perceived by the pupil as a last resort after reminders and reprimands have failed to 'get through'. The alternative behaviours that are desired and by which the pupil can redeem himself also must be made clear.

Corporal punishment

Although, according to a poll in 1984, over half the teachers in Britain still believe in the value of corporal punishment as a last resort (*Times Educational Supplement*, 21 September 1984), an alternative view is that the practice in schools is both physically and emotionally damaging and, as such, is a form of institutionalized child abuse. It was observed in 1984 that children in school were the only sector of our society who lacked adequate legal protection from violence. There is strong circumstantial evidence which suggests that corporal punishment is associated with worse rather than better behaviour, even when pupils' social background and behaviour at entry to the school are taken into account. Clegg (1962), investigating the position in thirty schools in the West Riding of Yorkshire, found that schools using corporal punishment 'positively engender rebelliousness and do little to inhibit bad behaviour'. Similar conclusions were reached by Reynolds and Murgatroyd (1977) as a result of their survey in Wales, while others found that behaviour in a group of twelve London schools was worse where there were high levels of corporal punishment.

The arguments presented in the previous section help to explain why corporal punishment is often counterproductive, at least in the long term.

In particular, the practice exposes pupils to a model of adult behaviour which legitimizes aggression in the face of unwanted behaviour. Additionally, corporal punishment may serve the interests of its recipients by helping to confirm a reputation of 'being tough'.

One argument often heard in support of corporal punishment is that it is the only 'language' which some children understand. The children in question tend to be those from working-class backgrounds who are more accustomed to physical punishment at home. It is true, according to a survey by the Newsons (1968, 1976), that physical punishment among mothers of four- and seven-year-olds is more prevalent in homes where the father is unskilled. However, the use of such facts to support the use of corporal punishment in schools is simply to advocate the continuation of the vicious circle in which violence begets violence. Further, corporal punishment may actually reinforce attention-seeking behaviour. Writing about the punishment of maladjusted children, Evans (1967) remarks 'Many deprived children are so hungry for contact with an adult who has become a meaningful person to them that they would rather be hit by that person than ignored by him . . . and if corporal punishment is the rule, the more outrageous one's behaviour the most contact one will achieve'.

Corporal punishment is therefore unsuitable precisely in those circumstances where its use may seem most justified. The practice may also have adverse effects on sensitive pupils who, though not receiving the punishment or even witnessing it, nevertheless feel its impact by being in an environment in which it is used. There is also evidence to suggest an association between flagellation and sado-masochistic tendencies. Much pornographic literature thrives on allusions to school beatings. Some children may deal with their fear of the cane by fantasy, where the introduction of a sexual element can make the experience more acceptable; even for those not affected directly, a caning environment can create a climate in which flagellant fantasies are allowed to develop.

Another kind of argument, based primarily on ethical principles, is that corporal punishment is wrong because it is humiliating and degrading for both teachers and pupils. This point of view is then countered by evidence to suggest that children 'do not view punishments as being "humiliating" or "degrading" but as fair or unfair, merited or unmerited' (McCann, 1978). However, in so far as the boys in Corrigan's (1979) interviews described teachers who hit them in such terms as 'bastard', 'twat' or 'puff', it is plain that they saw their treatment as unjustified and vindictive.

An understandable fear among some teachers is that the abolition of corporal punishment will lead to an increase in disruptive behaviour. For instance, one teachers' union used this argument to explain a dramatic rise in the number of suspensions from London schools in the early 1980s (*Times Educational Supplement*, 18 March 1983). However, this increase could, in part at least, have reflected the more stringent procedures for recording suspensions which London introduced in 1981. Moreover, in two British studies of schools which had abolished corporal punishment (British Psychological Society, 1980; Cumming *et al.*, 1981), no noticeable decline in school discipline was detected, and acceptable alternative sanctions had been found.

Can punishment be educative?

So far, we have seen that punishment in schools might be justified as an instrument for the control of behaviour, though it can often be ineffective and even counterproductive. Now, if punishment is simply seen as an unpleasant means to a desirable end, and especially if it is known to have adverse side-effects, teachers need not feel obliged to punish. Alternative means might achieve the same ends more surely and more humanely. Punishment could then disappear from schools along with slates and learning by catechism, and schools would be all the better for it. However, some writers have argued that punishment can serve an educative function, helping children to develop moral feelings and constructive ways of thinking about social behaviour. If this is so, then the notion that all punishment could be substituted by alternative practices is misplaced, and the ideal of a school which eschews punishment regardless of the circumstances is ill conceived.

There are three main strands to the argument that punishment can serve an educative function. One is based on the idea that punishment provides a logically necessary condition for children to acquire the concept of a social rule; a second is based on the place of punishment in the development of moral growth; a third is based on the notion that punishment in certain circumstances is the appropriate moral response to wrong doing. We shall deal with each of these in turn.

Punishment and concept of a social rule

John Wilson (1977,1984), sees punishment as logically bound up in the idea of rule following. This conclusion is reached in the following way. The existence of society, or social groups such as schools, depends on the members subscribing to rules, written or unwritten. Rules entail enforcement, which in turn entails placing some disadvantage on the rule breaker. If people generally do not see themselves as advantaged in obeying rules and disadvantaged in breaking them, the notion of rules would be unintelligible. Authorities such as teachers must therefore enforce social rules and this is particularly important with children who may be too young or inexperienced to appreciate the reason for rules.

Place of punishment in moral growth

Whether or not rules logically require enforcement by punishing, all children, according to cognitive-developmental theory, seem to go through a stage in which the idea of punishment plays a significant role. Children in infancy are in a stage when beliefs of what is right and wrong are determined by experiences of rewards and punishment and the commands of adults. Moreover, young children do not distinguish between their own and other people's point of view. They have no reason to reflect on their judgement since the notion of deliberation between alternative courses of action is quite foreign to them. However, from the age of seven years or so, as described by Piaget's (1932) theory, children develop feelings of co-operation and mutual respect as they interact more with each other and become less dependent on adult authority. Gradually, they lose their egocentrism, and learn to take the point of view of others when this conflicts with their own. The impulsive intuitive action of earlier years gives way to reflective deliberate action. Punishments which are 'fair' are no longer those which hurt most (expiatory punishments) but those which relate to the offence (punishment by reciprocity). Piaget thus sees the typical junior child thinking of punishment as simple retribution where the offender must put right the damage he has caused or return what he has taken. In short, the child has come to see himself as a moral agent, and so morally responsible, deserving of blame and praise. Around eleven or twelve years of age, feelings of justice are refined as the child appreciates that applying the same punishment for the same offence may not be fair since circumstances must be taken into account.

What are the practical implications of Piaget's ideas on punishment? Although the young child seems to develop his moral understanding partly through his experiences of external constraint, it is also likely that the more adults use punishment to encourage an authority–subject relation the longer the children take to develop feelings of reciprocity and of justice. Development toward autonomous ways of thinking does not just occur naturally. Rather, it is dependent on the quality of social environment experienced by the child. Indeed, the way in which children's beliefs about punishment are affected by their teachers' beliefs has been demonstrated in an American study by Jeannette Haviland (1979). She found that punishment which is based on the power of the adult enforces unilateral respect in young children. As early as possible, then, punishment should be based more on reciprocity and the legitimacy of authority, so that the child is gradually encouraged to see punishment as arising from his disregard of the rights and feelings of others rather than from his disobedience.

Recent work concerned with children's judgements of others in relation to cause, blame and punishment (Fincham, 1983; Docking, 1986) suggests that, provided that the situation is within their experiences and is presented simply, children of six-to-eight years are more able than Piaget supposed to take the point of view of others and to discriminate between accidental, malicious and altruistic action. Punishment is also more likely to be effective in changing a pupil's behaviour if it is accompanied by comments which help the offender to reason about his actions. Children need practice in reasoning about their behaviour to help them acquire general rules which operate across a range of comparable situations. In this connection, Wright (1972) points out how important it is for adults to give the deviant act a label, such as 'stealing' or 'lying', and to explain why acts subsumed under the label are wrong. The label helps the child to 'instruct himself' when next confronted by a similar temptation.

Punishment as a moral response to wrong doing

The assumption behind the retributionist argument is that people can choose to behave in a prosocial or antisocial way. The American behaviourist, Skinner, however, unequivocally maintains that to blame individuals on the grounds that they are autonomous and the cause of their own behaviour is misleading and unhelpful. Rather, 'it is the environment which is "responsible" for objectionable behaviour, and it is the environment, not some attribute in the individual which must be changed' (Skinner, 1972).In contrast, Kant (1887) saw man as a purposeful being, who can plan his actions. As such, individuals should be made to feel accountable for what they do. When they do not act responsibly, it is the duty of others to inflict punishment to uphold the sanctity of the moral law. If this argument is applied to children, the assumption must be that, to some extent at least, children can be regarded as responsible for their behaviour and thus deserving of praise and blame.

It is the role of punishment in treating children as responsible moral agents which is the concern of P.S. Wilson (1971). Wilson carefully distinguishes between 'penalties', which are given simply to control children's behaviour, and 'punishment', which is given to confirm for children the existence of a moral order. 'Penalties' are for breaking school rules and regulations, whereas 'punishment' is for deliberate moral negligence.

It is in this sense that Wilson sees punishment as educative. 'A rule-breaker is liable for a penalty whether or not he can see good reason for the rule, but a wrong-doer is liable for punishment because he can see good reason for the rules (and has nevertheless broken them) ... The force of what we say or do in punishing hurts, while its meaning educates'. 'Punishment', in Wilson's sense is not to extract obedience but to communicate the moral significance of behaviour. The argument is that pupils ought to feel the pain of a teacher's displeasure when they are guilty of moral failings. This is not coercion, Wilson insists, since it is not intended to extract obedience: rather it is treating children as moral agents who have views about appropriate behaviour and some control over their own actions. P. S. Wilson is not saying that the control of children through penalties is wrong: he recognizes the social justification in stopping undesirable acts such as crossing a road carelessly or disturbing other children who are trying to concentrate in class. What he is pointing out is that the act of inflicting pain when the culprit is technically culpable of breaching a rule but unaware that such actions is wrong, as distinct from disallowed, will not aid moral learning, whereas to make a child feel uncomfortable for moral culpability, i.e. when the child himself recognizes the wrongness of his action and not just that it is forbidden, is to make a contribution to the child's moral growth. Certainly, we might suppose that a child who, on his own account, believes his behaviour to be wrong will perceive the punishment as more justified than if he sees his breaching of the teacher's rule as a mere technicality.

Critics ask how the act of punishing can be educative if the child knows his action to be wrong already. However, this argument does not seem to take account of the gap between the child knowing something is wrong and caring sufficiently to modify his behaviour accordingly. Although, as we saw previously in this reading, punishment can estrange relations and be counterproductive, it may, if handled sensitively in cases of moral failings, help the child to care about what he accepts intellectually as right and wrong already.

Practical implications

It is not easy to accept the view that punishment can educate when so much evidence suggests that it can more easily alienate. One obvious problem here concerns the form which punishment takes if it is to have educative potential. Punishments in schools vary from frowns, looks of displeasure and mild 'tellings off', at one end of the continuum, to sarcasm, smacks and beatings at the other. Given the research findings reviewed in previous sections, those who argue that punishment can

contribute to a child's moral growth must, clearly, be excluding physical
and psychological punishment which is vindictive, relentless or humiliating. The anxiety brought about by punishment of this kind will interfere
with the cognitive tasks of discrimination between acceptable and unacceptable behaviour and between conceptually related acts such as stealing
and borrowing. That said, three main points seem to emerge from the
discussion in this section.

1. A society depends on rules and their enforcement. Although rules can
   often be enforced by means other than punishment, it may be that a
   background of punishment in some form is needed to ensure that rules
   in general are taken seriously and that children acquire the concept of
   rule following.
2. In infancy children seem to depend on external constraints to develop
   an understanding of rules. At the same time, a punitive style of
   upbringing will not only alienate and estrange relationships but impede
   the development of empathy and independent thinking.
3. If children are to be regarded as developing moral agents, they should
   be increasingly treated as responsible for their actions and therefore
   liable to blame and punishment. This is easier to justify with older
   children who are more able to take account of others' points of view
   and to deliberate about their actions. But even in the infant school
   children are able to reason about appropriate behaviour in a limited
   way. Moreover, in so far as children can increasingly discriminate
   between what they accept as wrong and what they perceive as disallowed or unconventional, then the occasion of punishment may have a
   significant moral function in prompting children to care about what
   they themselves regard as appropriate behaviour.

Finally, if the rightness of punishment arises from the rightness of basic
moral principles, then it is vital for punishments in school to bear a clear
relation to the moral seriousness of the offences. If the infringement of
basic moral principles, such as truth telling or treating others as equals or
not hurting people unnecessarily, is not handled as rigorously as breaches
of local regulations, such as those concerning hair style or uniform,
punishment can be miseducative in conveying to children a confused
picture in which infringements of moral rules and arbitrary conventions
are undifferentiated and seen as equally reprehensible.

Thus for any system of punishment in schools to be educative, rather
than simply a crude form of training, it must help to convey to the child
what matters morally rather than what others expect. Clearly, therefore,
the reasons for which punishment is given, the form which it takes, and
the manner in which it is delivered, together with the degree to which the
pupils perceive it as just, are all important.

REFERENCES

Aronfreed, J. (1976) Moral development from the standpoint of a general psychological theory, in T. Lickona (ed.) *Moral Development and Behaviour: Theory, Research and Social Issues*, Holt, Rinehart and Winston, New York.

Bandura, A. (1977) *Social Learning Theory*, Prentice-Hall, Englewood Cliffs, New York.

British Psychological Society (1980) *The Report of a Working Party on Corporal Punishment in Schools*.

Burton, R. V. (1976) Honesty and dishonesty, in T. Lickona (ed.) *Moral Development and Behaviour: Theory, Research and Social Issues*, Holt, Rinehart and Winston, New York.

Clegg, A. B. (1962) *Delinquency and Discipline*, Council & Education Press.

Corrigan, P. (1979) *Schooling the Smash Street Kids*, Macmillan, London.

Cumming, C. E., Lowe, T., Tulips, J. and Wakeling, C. (1981) *Making the Change: a Study of the Process of the Abolition of Corporal Punishment*, Hodder & Stoughton, London/Scottish Council for Research in Education.

Docking, J. W. (1986) The attribution of personal responsibility: a development study. Ph.D. thesis, University of Surrey.

Evans, M. (1967) Punishment in a day school for maladjusted children, *Therapeutic Education*, June, pp. 32–5.

Eysenck, H. J. (1970) *The Structure of Human Personality* (3rd edn), Methuen, London.

Fincham, F. D. (1983) Developmental dimensions in attribution theory, in J. Jaspars, F. D. Fincham and M. Hewstone (eds.) *Attribution Theory and Research: Conceptual, Developmental and Social Dimensions*, Academic Press, London.

Foss, B. (1965) Punishment, rewards and the child, *New Society*, Vol. 6, No. 154, pp. 8–10.

Francis, P. (1975) *Beyond Control? A Study of Discipline in the Comprehensive School*, Allen & Unwin, London.

Haviland, J. M. (1979) Teachers' and students' beliefs about punishment, *Journal of Educational Psychology*, Vol. 71, No. 4, pp. 563–70.

Hoffman, M. L. (1970) Conscience, personality and socialization techniques, *Human Development*, Vol. 13, No. 2, pp. 90–126.

Kant , I. (1887) *The Philosophy of Law* (translation, E. Hastie), T & T. Clark, Edinburgh.

Light, P. (1979) *The Development of Social Sensitivity*, Cambridge University Press.

McCann, E. (1978) Children's perceptions of corporal punishment, *Educational Studies*, Vol. 4, No. 2, pp. 167–72.

Nash, P. (1966) *Authority and Freedom in Education*, Wiley, New York.

Newson, J. and Newson, E. (1968) *Four Years Old in an Urban Community*, Allen & Unwin, London.

Newson, J. and Newson, E. (1976) *Seven Years Old in the Home Environment*, Allen & Unwin, London.

O'Hagan, F. J. and Edmunds, S. G. (1982) Pupils' attitudes towards teachers' strategies for controlling disruptive behaviour, *British Journal of Educational Psychology*, Vol. 5, pp. 331–40.

O'Leary, K. D., Kaufman, K. F., Kass, R. E. and Drabman, R. S. (1970) The effects of loud and soft reprimands on the behaviour of disruptive students, *Exceptional Children*, Vol. 37, pp. 144–5.

Parke, R. D. and Deur, J. L. (1972) Schedule of punishment and inhibition of aggression in children, *Developmental Psychology*, Vol. 7, No. 3, pp. 231–4.

Peters, R. S. (1966) *Ethics and Education*, Allen & Unwin, London.

Piaget, J. (1932) *The Moral Judgement of the Child*, Routledge & Kegan Paul, London.

Rawls, J. (1954) Two concepts of rules, in H.B. Acton (ed.) *The Philosophy of Punishment*, Macmillan, London.

Reynolds, D. (1976) The delinquent school, in M. Hammersley and P. Woods (eds.) *The Process of Schooling*, Routledge & Kegan Paul, London/Open University, Milton Keynes.

Reynolds, D. and Murgatroyd, D. S. (1977) The sociology of schooling and the absent pupil: the school as a factor in the generation of truancy, in H.C.M. Carroll (ed.) *Absenteeism in South Wales: Studies of Pupils, their Homes and their Secondary Schools*, Faculty of Education, University of Swansea.

Skinner, B. F. (1972) *Beyond Freedom and Dignity*, Penguin, Harmondsworth.

Wilson, J. (1977) *Philosophy and Practical Education*, Routledge & Kegan Paul, London.

Wilson, J. (1984) A reply to James Marshall, *Journal of Philosophy of Education*, Vol. 18, No. 1. pp. 105–70.

Wilson, P. S. (1971) *Interest and Discipline in Education*, Routledge & Kegan Paul, London.

Woods, P. (1975) Showing them up in secondary school, in G. Chanan and S. Delamont (eds.) *Frontiers of Classroom Research*, National Foundation for Educational Research, Slough.

Wright, D. (1971) *The Psychology of Moral Behaviour*, Penguin, Harmondsworth.

Wright, D. (1972) The punishment for children: a review of experimental studies, *Journal of Moral Education*, Vol. 7, No. 3, pp. 199–205.

TOPICS FOR DISCUSSION

1. Of the several criticisms that the author makes of experiments on the effects of punishment, which, in your view, has the most important application to the classroom teacher?

2. Discuss the suggestion that to be effective punishment has to be 'reasonably predictable and certainly non-arbitrary'.

3. Given the evidence, can any support be found for the retention of corporal punishment in schools?

SUGGESTIONS FOR FURTHER READING

1. Piaget, J. (1932) *The Moral Judgement of the Child*, Routledge & Kegan Paul, London.

Piaget develops a theory of cognitive development which identifies the ways in which children consciously interpret their social experiences. Infant moral thinking, he contends, is characterized by moral realism, the nature of which has significance for the punishment of the young child. From about the age of seven years onwards, Piaget shows how children develop feelings of co-operation and mutual respect. Punishment at this stage should reflect reciprocity rather than expiation. From twelve years of age onwards, Piaget argues, feelings of equity emerge as the growing child develops a more rational sense of justice. Thus the same punishment for the same offence may no longer be fair in light of the particular circumstances governing the misdemeanour.

2. Haviland, J. M. (1979) Teachers' and students' beliefs about punishment, *Journal of Educational Psychology*, Vol.71, No. 4, pp. 563–70.

Haviland's research is particularly relevant in that it shows how teachers can unwittingly inhibit or promote pupils' beliefs about punishment; schools themselves may be distinguished in terms of their 'punishment ethos' so that 'messages' that pupils receive from their own class teacher are likely to be reinforced by the values of the teaching staff as a whole. The study involved some three hundred and sixty pupils aged between five and eleven years from three different American elementary schools together with their sixteen teachers. One of the most interesting findings was that at each age-level pupils whose teachers believed more in punishment were themselves more punitively orientated in their thinking.

3. Topping, K. J. (1983) Routine sanctions, pp. 129–40, in *Educational Systems for Disruptive Adolescents*, Croom Helm, London.

This is a broadly-based discussion of sanctions in school that draws on recent research both in Britain and North America. *Inter alia*, it deals with (a) verbal reprimands, (b) detention, (c) corporal punishment, (d) deprivation of privileges, (e) rewards, (f) school reports and (g) pupils' perceptions of teachers' responses to disruptive behaviour. The chapter ends with a useful summary of the effectiveness of various forms of punishment.

AUTHOR INDEX

Page numbers in italics refer to bibliographic details.

SUBJECT INDEX